Being Better Better

Living with Systems Intelligence

Contents

Preface

This book is about improvement as an innate capability in us humans.

The aim is to help the reader to become more aware of our astonishing skills of systems intelligence – our in-built drive to live with more or less but always with some intelligence in the situations and contexts that we encounter as we live our life.

Systems intelligence is about us as active agents. It is about the betterment of life. It deals with intelligent behavior in the context and environments involving interaction, co-creation, feedback and multifaceted back-and-forth influence. A person acting with systems intelligence engages with the multifarious systemic aspects of her life successfully and productively. Experiencing herself as part of a whole, she connects with that whole. Influencing the whole while being influenced by it, she adjusts to the contexts seeking for an appropriate fit, works her way toward survival, growth and success. She fosters her life in the midst of a complex set of circumstances, much of the time with considerable productivity and intelligence.

In many ways, systems intelligence celebrates the miracle of life. It takes seriously the ancient promise of philosophy to promote better living through better thinking. While aware of the deficits in our systemic abilities, the chief message is one of reassurance: since early infancy each of us has displayed astonishing abilities to connect with our environment, to grow and to make things better through the dynamic resources at hand. We cannot but live in the midst of wholes, i.e., systems, and to make the most of it.

Without potent abilities to connect and co-create, none of us would be here or read these lines. Our early endowment for reaching out and attuning to our environment has been the foundation of our developmental processes since early infancy. It is remarkable that leading researchers in infant studies use the concept of a system to describe what may be the single most warmly attuned domain of human life, the infant-mother relationship. For us this is paradigmatic: while almost totally ignorant of the objective functioning of her environment, the infant enters a system that supports her development and makes possible her growth. Facial mirroring, vocal rhythm, spatial orientation, touching and self-touching are among the non-conceptual means that the baby utilizes as part of her own active participation in that dance. Very much a participant and not only an object for influence from without, the baby's systems intelligence facilitates her growth.

The key words here are growth, betterment, change, intelligence, and systems. "System" is a key word because the contexts of our life come in different disguises, but it is good to have one word to refer to the various forms of holistic dynamisms in the midst of which our life unfolds. Systemic everyday contexts, such as the care of a baby, family, work, personal relationships, friends, an encounter on the street with a stranger, hobby, sport, nutrition, economy, various forms of spiritual life, our physical body, home, the functioning of a benefit organization, musical performance, country, the internet, United Nations, army, the natural environment, to name a few, share crucial features with one another. It is useful to approach them as "systems".

Understood as a system, a whole is somehow more than its parts, and parts are different within the whole than when considered separately; relations count more than individual parts; with time, something small can grow to something big and make the entire system reach a qualitatively higher level. A chief idea of this book is that human orientation towards success in wholes is structurally the same irrespective of the specific nature of the whole. Irrespective of the system, systems intelligence involves a positive attitude, willingness to engage, abilities to perceive the system, eagerness to take action and also to have an eye for the longer term, sensibilities to attune to the system and its dynamism, an open mind to try things out, as well as the meta-level ability for reflection.

Your systems intelligence is your quintessentially human capability that makes use of such core capabilities, and thus builds your creative action-thought repertoires for the benefit of succeeding in the systems of your life. Systems intelligence is an operative skillset through which you thrive to make your life work out and succeed better.

The aim of the present volume is to help you to reach out to that dimension of your betterment.

The human race has developed tremendously powerful system structures that have enormous leverage both positively and negatively. What is called for is increased systems awareness, sensibility and intelligence with the man-made environments, constructs, institutions, practices and technologies and the natural life. With the creation of powerful man-made systems environments, new forms of systems skills are taking high priority in terms of success and even survival. The systems intelligence perspective tries to activate the imperatives of our personal intelligence in that vital setting.

We are academic intellectuals deeply concerned with what happens in the actual life of people. Ultimately it is only actions that count. Systems intelligence is a theory and a conceptual perspective, but it is offered here as catch phrase and an intuitive conceptual tool that we hope would benefit the reader's everyday life and orientation to the future.

No matter how brilliantly adaptive someone is in the confines of a given life system, say at work or at a hobby, there are always domains where our systems skills are less impressive than we would like them to be. There is always room to improve – and not only in a particular domain, but more generally in the dimension of improvement itself, in the way our life is lived as an integration of thought, action and specific systems skills. The more there is complexity to the unfolding environment and to us as human beings, the more there is space for growth for our systems intelligence.

We hope you will find this book illuminating and stimulating. Our hope is that you would find it humorous, surprising, delightful and empowering. And, above all, we hope you will find something of yourself from the following pages – as an astonishing complex system capable of being better, better.

Helsinki, Finland, November 2014

Raimo P. Hämäläinen, Rachel Jones and Esa Saarinen

Introduction

A baby is born. Within hours, she is already tracking movement in her environment, attending to its rhythms, anticipating and sending signals and even reading her caregivers' intentions. Connected to her immediate surroundings and her parents without any effort, the baby is an active participant in her own growth. She is already engaged with, shaped by, and an essential part of a *system*.

The family she has joined now differs from the family that existed just one week before. The woman is now a mother. The man is now a father. The lover is now a parent. The couple is now a family. The natural act of birth has given them new identities, individually and collectively. They see themselves and each other differently. They think and feel about each other in new ways. They do things differently. Even though fundamentally nothing about them has changed, in some ways everything about them has changed. A new system has replaced the old system.

The parents perceive and interact in fresh ways with what once seemed ordinary aspects of their immediate environment. The elevator they used to think was an unnecessary luxury is now a welcome necessity. The big vase on the coffee table poses a risk. The once-annoying cries of the toddler across the hall represent a future playmate. The visually striking designer coffee table becomes conspicuous because of its sharp edges. Is the inner city the place to live with an infant? The upbeat road they live on, with its busy nightlife, doesn't seem like such a great location anymore. They see the familiar with new eyes. Their *systems perception* has transformed.

Even more remarkably, there is the child that reaches out and calls for immediate interaction. Baby talk is heard from the father, perhaps feared at work for his curt no-nonsense style. But as he *attunes* himself to their infant, entering a shared field of experience and exchange of oral sounds, the man is transformed. What other way is there to be rhythmically in sync with your daughter in infancy? The infant, unable to control her movements, still manages to engage the parents in a mutual dance of gestures and eye-to-eye connectedness of considerable subtlety. Her eyes follow keenly the actions of her mother, taking delight in what she expects to be the mother's tender movement forward. She gurgles as her mother comes in sight, playfully participating in the joint game of movement, sound and connectivity.

The baby, with astonishing capabilities of "systemicity," as one leading researcher put it, responds to and connects with her environment and the people near her. Without any "knowledge" of the system in which she lives, she is effectively and actively an integral part of forces that shape her at the same times she is shaping them. She participates in the processes through which her growth takes place and fundamentally affects the parents who in their micro behaviors reflect the needs of their baby. All three enter a process that calls for adjustment, tuning in and constant engagement.

Suddenly functioning as nurturers involves the new parents reorienting themselves to time. Career and vacation plans, once so important and all-consuming, will become secondary to those related to the child's wellbeing. They will consider work differently, juggling competing demands with new priorities. Some hours will feel like days; some days will pass in the blink of an eye. Time alone and time for being a couple will be valued differently. There is a longer perspective when it comes to making decisions. What are the consequences of feeding her this food or that food? Which vaccinations should we administer? Are we spending enough time with our child? The parents know that every action in the present can have a consequence in their baby's future.

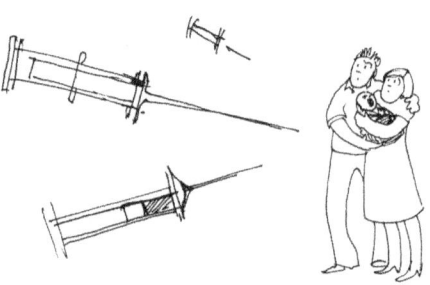

Wise action that acknowledges achieving results takes time will be called for in the system.

It won't be long before the family realizes that the system of caretaking, the system of the infant's growth, has a life of its own. Importantly, the parents cannot dictate their own will upon the infant if the process is to continue, but have to adjust themselves to a higher-level authority dictated by the mysteries of the infant's development. The daily rhythm of the family's existence will be driven by this little person's needs. Feeds and sleeps, diaper changes and cries, will shape the structure of a day. The couple will utilize *effective responsiveness* as they deal to the needs of each moment in the best way they can.

As part of this new family system, the parents will begin to think and act differently. They will need to learn patience, find humor in what once would have caused frustration, take delight in the simplest of pleasures. But baby's arrival will not only affect them. Others will have to adjust to the new family member, too. Employers, friends, relatives may have to adapt to the new demands put on the household. A *positive attitude* will help everyone navigate the ups and downs of their new life.

Tenderly, the mother and father will amuse and entertain, embrace and support, their new baby. They will shy away from harsh words and sharp tones, focusing instead on lovingly whispered utterances and soothing cadences. They will instinctively seek *positive engagement* with their child as they nurture her growth. Needing support themselves, the couple will also seek out positive engagement with others. They will likely gravitate towards other couples with children, shared experiences binding them together. Grandparents and aunts and uncles and cousins will develop roles over time as the new family makes choices about the kinds of connections they want, as the new baby responds warmly to particular individuals. Everyone involved will contribute to the new system as it unfolds.

There is no blueprint for how this family will work their new circumstances out. They will handle each situation as it emerges. They will try things out, delighting in successes, learning from failures. Their *spirited discovery* will be strengthened as they see what works and doesn't work. Together, the three of them will adjust what they do based on the consequences of their actions. The parents won't just be focused on solving problems, however. They will also want to create possibilities for their child. It won't be enough to simply feed the baby; they will want to give her the most nutritious food. It won't be enough for their child to go to daycare; they will want to ensure that she has the best experiences possible. For the parents, with their fully developed capacity for thought, *reflection* will help them to understand their experiences, their hopes, the changes in their world.

The arrival of an infant is a life-altering experience. Yet, despite being first time parents, this new family will figure it out. They will work together to raise their child well, and they will always be on the lookout for ways they could be a better family, a better system. At the same time as they shape the infant's course through life, their child will mold their own growth, fully participating in the system that emerges.

And should a sibling come along down the track, the family unit will shift again. Malleable and elastic, it and the people who create it will stretch to accommodate a new arrival. Each person will establish their place, and they will evolve together.

As they learn to act more effectively, and at the same strive to improve the ways they can be better in their family life, then they are sensing, thinking and acting with *systems intelligence*.

Systems intelligence is the capacity we have as humans to figure out what works in the emergent situations and environments of our lives. It allows us to adjust and to anticipate, to look out for and to initiate change, to enter into mutual processes and to co-create situations. It is an intangible fundamental capability in our human constitution that allows us to adapt, survive, succeed and thrive within contexts and situations even when they are largely beyond our control and cognitive reach.

Systems Intelligence

This book presents our innate systems intelligence as a powerful core of our being. Our aim is to convince you of the functioning of capabilities that are deceptively familiar and still far-reaching and nothing short of ingenious in their intertwined effects. Yet these magnificent forces often remain hidden from our conscious focus.

Living with systems intelligence is at its heart about successfully living in situations, contexts and environments, typically with other people and subject to forces that are overwhelming and unknown to us. The foremost species on earth, we do succeed much of the time and often in ways that improve our situation as well as the situation of those who matter to us. The holistic, surprisingly efficient systemic capabilities that step in place as soon as we are born connect us to our environment from the point of view of adaptation, growth and living together. But somewhere during our development our holistic, innate systems intelligence becomes obscured by a fragmented worldview. That innate systems intelligence does not disappear, though. It continues to form the basis of our existence in an unrecognized capacity that awaits revitalization.

Becoming more keenly aware of our tacit systems intelligence makes us capable of taking advantage of its tremendous leverage potential and positive change. It opens the door to improve our experiences, and to learn to sense life and its potentials more fully. Life is about adaptation, togetherness, connectivity and success. When appreciating more fully the general functioning of our innate systems intelligence we gain insight into the process of improving our lives not only in some specific context but from the point of view of the very process of improvement itself. By becoming more systems intelligent we learn to live better, better.

A human baby is born with many of the dimensions of systems intelligence. She immediately makes connections to others revealing her systems perception. She attunes to the moods of her caregivers and positively engages with them. She responds effectively to her environment and engages with her world with the open curiosity of spirited discovery even without knowing any language. Though unable to think of longer time frames, her every action is oriented towards her growth, and, over time, she will develop cognitively and become capable of both projection and reflection.

It is tempting to dismiss a baby's responsiveness to her immediate environment as something of relevance only to a helpless infant who relies on the care of others for her very survival. As adults, our ability to stand as independent individuals seems to nullify the need for these systems capabilities. They key word here is "seems" because in fact as adults we, too, participate in a systemic world. Our big mistake is to think that we are isolated from the systems we live in by our capacity for independent thought, when in reality we are connected to our environment and others as tightly as a baby is to hers. Our adult life naively takes us away from and obscures our innate systems intelligence leading us to a kind of systems idiocy.

Take the example of our workplaces. Some years ago, the concept of "emotional intelligence" led to a revolutionary breakthrough in how people saw organizations.[1] Suddenly, we started paying attention to the idea that workplaces are not just production or service facilities but are places where people go to connect, to interact, to live. Organizations are full of humans experiencing the full range of human emotions. That such an idea was so revolutionary points to how separated we have become from our fundamental human capacities. Not acknowledging the rich texture of human experience led to many organizations ignoring a holistic view of humans and their relationship to one another and their environment. It led to systems idiocy.

The systems intelligent alternative calls for organizations to encourage attunement, positive engagement and all the other dimensions of systems intelligence that nourish as human beings. For, as you will have noticed, the family with a newborn is but one instance of a human system. Couples, schools, workplaces, sports teams, social clubs, orchestras, and neighborhoods – all these groups of individuals functioning together as wholes can be described with the term *system* and we act in them with greater or lesser intelligence. The challenge is to take those capabilities, develop them and learn to do better, better.

What is Systems Intelligence?

Systems Intelligence is defined as our ability to behave intelligently in the context of complex systems involving interaction, dynamics and feedback. When we act systems intelligently we engage successfully and productively with the holistic feedback mechanisms of our environment. We perceive ourselves as part of a whole, noticing the influence of the whole upon us as well as our own influence upon the whole. Because we observe our own interdependence in the feedback intensive environment, we are able to act intelligently.

The concept was introduced by Professors Raimo P. Hämäläinen and Esa Saarinen of Aalto University in Helsinki. If you are interested in the academic papers on Systems Intelligence go to http://systemsintelligence.aalto.fi. Much research has been done on the topic, including the development of a self-evaluation instrument. If you would like to measure your own Systems Intelligence you can find the test on the website. **www.systemsintelligence.aalto.fi/test**

Understanding systems intelligence changes the way we see ourselves, allowing us to more fully appreciate the existing capabilities we have and motivate us to improve them. Perceiving the systems we live in enables us to see the world through a new lens, a lens that helps us to interact better in the world. We can, in the words of pioneering systems scholar Donella Meadows, learn to dance with systems.[2] The idea of dancing with systems is something that professionals in a number of academic fields have embraced. A well-known example is management expert Peter Senge whose groundbreaking book *The Fifth Discipline* introduced thinking about systems to organizations.[3] The systems thinking approach has since been applied extensively in management and encouraged in relation to the environment.[4]

Now, through awakening our personal systems intelligence, dancing with systems becomes possible in our daily life, too.

The systems intelligent perspective emphasizes the fundamentally contextual and relational nature of intelligence. An action that is intelligent works because it finds a fit with a host of relevant others factors supplied by the context. In another situation, perhaps only slightly different, the same action might not be successful at all. Intelligence depends on the environment, and systems intelligence refers to the human capability of making a virtue out of the inescapability of life as an embedded affair.

Our focus shows success and survival always requires something beyond the intelligence of the creature or the action itself. This something we refer to as a system. Thus "system" is an umbrella term for the family of entities customarily referred to as "context," "environment," "neighborhood," "situation," "circumstances," and the like. Clearly, the concept of a system is not new. What is new, groundbreaking even, is to draw attention to the fact that we always live in the midst of and create systems. All the time. Every day. All of us. We can all see systems in varying ways. And we all act with varying degrees of intelligence according to the system we are in.

Given that some systems are local and some are global, some are micro and some are macro, some of them are relevant now but not relevant tomorrow, systems intelligence is a super-capability of calculating options, figuring out alternatives, of framing situations and anticipating future processes. In microseconds, those imaginings allow us to live in the contexts of our life, most of the time spectacularly well. Systems intelligence is the fundamentally human capability of implementing change – of making life work and making us work with what life delivers us.

Yet, even if we think we are making life work, we often could do better. Adjusting our behavior as we move from one system to another is instinctive for us – that's our innate systems intelligence in action. Most of the time we are content with our choices, accepting the ups and downs of life in systems, but sometimes we aim to improve our capabilities. Typically, that involves celebrating a small improvement here, a slightly better outcome there. Few of us, however, push ourselves to test the limits of our capacities within systems. Yet, there is little doubt that with just minimal effort we could make much more intelligent choices with respect to the contexts we find ourselves in. We can make ourselves better at being better.

The types of change a new baby stimulates occur around transformative events in other systems, too. When new players are recruited to a sports team, when a new manager arrives at work, when we move into a new neighborhood previously predictable and comfortable patterns of existence are disrupted. If we dip into the treasure chest that is our systems intelligence we find a portfolio of skills that enable us to embrace those changes, as well as our everyday lives, positively. The challenge is to not just rely on unconsciously manifesting our systems intelligence, but to bring this portfolio of skills to the fore in our lives so we can develop it more fully.

To do that we can make ourselves more aware of the range of skills we have and how we can best use them in harmony with the systems in our life. What if we started to notice what we do really well in one system and bring that skill into a new context? What if we identified a weakness in how we handle conflict situations at work but recognized that we can import the capabilities we have at home to be more effective at work? And, because we are attending to how we do things, what if we paid attention not just to how we can be better but how we can become better at being better. With systems intelligence we open up a range of skills we can use in different domains to activate our personal growth. So systems intelligence offers a higher-level perspective, looking at not just how we can better our lives, but how we can better the bettering of our lives. It gives us a way of being intelligent about being intelligent.

When considering intelligence, most people automatically think of their intelligent quotient or IQ. IQ aims to measure people's inherent cognitive abilities, particularly their analytical, mathematical and spatial abilities. Over the last few decades, however, a more general perspective about intelligence has gained prominence.[5] In the 1980s, Harvard professor of cognition and education Howard Gardner wrote an influential book advocating multiple intelligences.[6] This book, *Frames of Mind*, opens by asking the reader to expand their ideas about what typically constitutes intelligence and think freely about the capabilities of the chess player, the violinist, and the athlete. How do we account for talents in these endeavors? IQ only measures a limited aspect of human capacity and leaves us without a way to acknowledge individuals' talents in music, language, and movement, amongst other areas. Gardner challenged his readers to see intelligence as a rich and varied capacity that can be developed, not only as a genetically determined skill that we are born with.

Undeniably, there are more possibilities and more challenges in life that can be addressed by our intellectual abilities alone. That's where systems intelligence comes in. Systems intelligence complements and extends earlier work on intelligences, sharing the idea that humans have a range of capacities, but also pointing to a higher-level ability related to living in a systemic world.[7] We are always part of systems. What's more, we can act intelligently within those systems. Systems intelligence involves understanding and improving the ways in which we act with our emotions and relate to others. But it also acknowledges the social, organizational, and physical structures that shape our behavior, and the possibilities we have for action in those. Just think how the make-up of a sports teams, the hierarchy of a workplace, or the layout of a house affect what goes on in each of those contexts. Or how the arrival of a new baby changes our world.

Systems intelligence is grounded in Gardner's premise that intelligence is something we can develop. Sure, it is a capability that is innate to us, but with practice and effort we can always extend ourselves. Our skills, orientations, and qualities are not fixed. This idea seems straightforward but consider how often we describe others and ourselves as if we were static. *He's decisive. She's an optimist. I am outgoing.* While we may have general tendencies towards these attributes, we also have the capacity to be other things, at other times, in other situations. What we are capable of is open to constant redefinition. We actually have the choice to act any way at any time. Realizing this opens up to us many more possibilities than a narrow self-definition offers.

Just as we tend to fix a version of ourselves, we are also prone to fixing a version of the systems we live in in our own minds, and then we tend to assume that our version is shared by others. We think we know how our relatives see the family systems, our friends see our friendships, our colleagues see our workplace, and so on. Life systems are not physical entities. They are not stable; they have no set boundaries. As a result we can only have our own assumptions about how things will go when we interact in those systems, and those assumptions drive our behavior, sometimes closing off the possibilities for other things to occur.

But as the birth of a baby shows, a system is not fixed. A family, or any other system, is redefined in a moment by a major event like the introduction of a child. However, it can also be shaped by the daily decisions and actions of its members. Through active engagement we sculpt and create systems. Like people, they shift and alter over time, sometimes dramatically but more often imperceptibly and incrementally. Indeed, people and systems shape one another, evolving together, each influencing the other. Often what we see as fixed is only the visible part of a system – beneath the surface lay emotions and relationships that when influenced bring about changes.

Living better in the inescapable systems of our lives is about experiencing and influencing changes, adapting our behavior to the new situation as it emerges, and finding ways to flourish in these dynamic conditions. We do that unconsciously all the time – that is our natural systems intelligence at work. But it's also possible to bring that set of skills to the conscious part of our minds. We can move to a higher level of engagement that involves us thinking about our thinking, attending more fully to our environment and bettering the ways we have available to improve our lives. When we do this, we are engaging our systems intelligence.

The Eight Dimensions of Systems Intelligence

There are eight dimensions to our systems intelligence.[8] Each chapter of this book explores a different dimension. Drawing on examples of systems intelligent behavior in real life, *Being Better, Better* illustrates the amazing possibilities for intervention that a systems lens opens. Inevitably, we are all more proficient in some dimensions than others. Just because we have preferences for behaving in certain ways, however, does not mean that we cannot learn to act differently. Improving in just one dimension that may not come naturally to us can give us enormous leverage. It helps us to strengthen ourselves. It gives us more options so we have a portfolio of actions available to us that we can select from in any given context.

Many of the skills covered within each dimension will be familiar to you. [9]

The Eight Dimensions of Systems Intelligence

Systems Perception: Our ability to see the systems around us;

Attunement: The capability we have to feel and tune into systems;

Reflection: Our capacity to reflect on our thoughts and think about our thinking;

Positive Engagement: The character of our communicative interactions;

Spirited Discovery: Passionate engagement with new ideas;

Effective Responsiveness: Our talent at taking timely, appropriate actions;

Wise Action: Our ability to behave with understanding and a long time horizon;

Positive Attitude: Our overall approach to life in systems.

What is unique about the systems intelligent perspective is that it unites these skills under the common purpose of engaging effectively with systems. The integrated dimensions extend the focus of personal growth from the more typical "getting along better with others" to the higher-level "creating better systems better with others."

The significance of this shift in focus should not be underestimated. Systems exert a powerful influence over our lives; they take on a kind of life of their own. Somehow the setting we are in seems to limit the possibilities of our actions. We may freely praise our children when they do well, for example, but hold back from praising a great taxi driver, or shop assistant, or waiter. Somehow the latter contexts usually tell us not to give compliments even though they cost us nothing and create a positive atmosphere. Similarly, we may be full of creative ideas when it comes to contributing to the community group we belong to, but somehow at work our creativity can be dulled by the bureaucratic atmosphere. Settings – systems – affect our performance.

Being alert to the influence of systems on our behavior opens up new possibilities for us. We can learn to see, think and behave differently. We can do better not just in the moment but also across systems, as we develop skills that help us to flourish in any systemic setting. Within each dimension is a cluster of specific skills that we can draw on as we orient ourselves to the systemic level of life. It is this higher-level orientation that pushes us to grow and gives us the framework in which we can do better at doing better. Systems intelligence calls for expanding the way we sense, think about and act in systems.

It may sound simple, but approaching life with this higher-level orientation (being sensitive to our environment, thinking about thinking, acting instead of reacting) will prove revolutionary. We can shake off the feeling of being unable to make a difference, of being oppressed by external forces. Instead we know we have the power to instigate change, both in ourselves and in the communities we live in. We can learn to resist negative systems. We can figure out how to positively contribute to inspiring systems. We can even create new systems to fulfill needs as they arise.

The eight dimensions are skills that overlap and feed into one another. As you read, you will see the recurrent themes of sensing, thinking and acting. You will recognize skill areas that you are strong in and those that could do with more development. You might even notice that in some systems you do well in some dimensions, while in other contexts different skills come to the fore. The challenge is to become able to deliberately carry skills from setting to setting. If you want to assess your own systems intelligence at this point, you can take the questionnaire available on the web at www.systemsintelligence.info. The quiz gives you a snapshot of your current level of systems intelligence, including your strengths and challenges.

Sensing

This involves learning to experience the world with a systems lens. Typically we regard ourselves as independent, autonomous individuals. But if we adopt a systems lens, instead of seeing ourselves as separate from everyone else we begin to perceive connections between others and ourselves. Sometimes those connections are pretty obvious – like the ties we have with our family – but others are less so – like the connections we have with fellow public transport users or shoppers. Most of us don't look for the systems around us on a daily basis. Therefore we don't always make conscious decisions about how to act based on what we know about those systems. We can learn to see systems. But perception is about more than just sight – we can also improve our ability to feel or attune to systems. We do this intuitively at times, such as when we walk into a party and figure out how to join in, but we can teach ourselves to do it more often and more insightfully. The chapters Seeing Systems and Attunement offer ways of sensing the systems we live in.

Thinking

Sensing the systems we live in helps us to think about how to act systems intelligently. It is helpful to become more aware of and articulate about our thoughts, to think about our thinking. Our ability to be reflective, to bring our attention to the way our mind operates, enhances our life in systems. With reflectiveness we can override the automatic processes of our brains that sometimes limit us. We can adopt new perspectives, understand our own thought processes and engage in self-reflection. These skills broaden our horizons and develop our cognitive powers and are explored in Reflection.

Being armed with a fresh way of experiencing and thinking about the world is the basis for acting better, better. Sensing and thinking about how the systems we engage with function gives us options about how we can do better, so our attitude changes. We begin to see opportunities to try new things and see how they go. When we understand that we live in the midst of systems we learn to purposely act in situations instead of simply react to them. We also open up new possibilities for being proactive, for being creative and adventurous. We utilize our ability to create systems. Our outlook becomes more positive. Positive Engagement, Spirited Discovery, Effective Responsiveness, Wise Action and Positive Attitude identify the actions and attitudes that work effectively together to help us make systems intelligent choices.

The Promise

When we become a parent for the first time our skills seem to expand overnight. We find more in us than we ever expected. The creation of a new family system reveals capabilities we didn't know we had and also provides a platform for us to import skills from other areas of our life. Parenthood stretches us, challenges us, improves us. We don't have to rely on such a dramatic change to bring out the best in us. By purposely engaging with the concept of systems intelligence, we can stretch, challenge ourselves and improve on a daily basis.

We already have systems skills. We live in and create systems all the time and we have the ability to work with and act in them. What this book does is make that ability more visible. In doing so, it offers ways to improve how we get along in the systems of our lives. Even if a system appears to have a life of its own, it actually responds to the actions of its members just as they adapt their behavior to the system. The eight, interrelated dimensions of our systems intelligence provide a framework through which we can enrich our possibilities for action. When we adopt the systems intelligence lens, we see the opportunities we have for bringing skills from context to context, allowing us to be better at being better.

Systems Perception

"In nature nothing exists alone." ~ Rachel Carson[10]

Imagine a world in which no birds sing. A lifeless and withered countryside. A place where blight crosses the land and the shadow of death lingers over communities. That's what scientist Rachel Carson did. Prompted by a letter from a friend describing the death of numerous birds around her neighborhood, Carson envisaged a world without birdsong. The alarming possibility that her imaginings might come true motivated her to research, write and publish one of the most influential books of the twentieth century.

Carson had long had an interest in the natural world. Beginning her career as an aquatic biologist, she soon turned her passion for science writing into her main profession. In the late 1950s, Carson began to take increasing notice of emerging environmental problems. An aerial spraying of the pesticide dichloro-diphenyl-tricloro-ethane (DDT) that poisoned the local wildlife had provoked her friend's letter. Carson knew that pesticide use in general had dramatically increased in the wake of World War Two as research on chemical weapons looked for profitable outlets in peacetime. She researched the topic extensively. She consulted with many government scientists, read the scientific literature widely and began to talk to health professionals. She quickly formed a rich overall picture of the emerging situation.

Previously, Carson's writing intended to teach people to marvel at the beauty of the natural world, but she felt compelled to change her focus and warn the public about the reckless use of synthetic pesticides like DDT. Appearing in 1962, *Silent Spring* voiced Carson's fears that the increasing and unregulated use of toxic pesticides would irrevocably change the natural world. Serialized by *The New Yorker* and chosen as a Book-of-the-Month Club must read, *Silent Spring* came to have an enormous impact at all levels of American society. In effect, it became the book that launched the modern environmental movement.

The goal of *Silent Spring* was to make the public aware that pesticides were harming not only pests, but birds, animals and humans, too. Carson reminded the ordinary reader that the natural world is a delicate ecology, a system in which all parts depend upon one another to function effectively as a whole. [11] The government, agricultural scientists, and companies involved in manufacturing and using pesticides like DDT were, in Carson's eyes, negatively affecting nature, perhaps irreversibly. She compellingly described the devastating effects of ill-considered human actions on the health of the overall system.

As a scientist, Rachel Carson was trained to see the systems around her. She knew that dropping DDT on large swathes of farmland would not only kill the pests it was targeting but would <u>also</u> have an impact on other wildlife, the soil, the water and all the other natural systems it touched. Her goal was to find out what that impact was and communicate it to the public. Unlike Carson, most of us are not scientists. For us, perceiving the systems we live within is not always second nature. Yet we have the ability to see the patterns of relationships that form systems, and that ability enhances our power to act intelligently within them.

While Carson was primarily interested in the world of ecosystems, it is not only in nature that we find systems. The social world is also organized into systems. We humans are systems creatures, connected to many others through the various social groups we participate in. Once we sense the systemic nature of our environment we can start to purposefully add systems intelligent behavior to our innate systems engagement. The first step in opening up our senses is to start looking at the world differently.

Seeing Systems

Systems perception is not complicated. It is about looking for the organizing patterns of interconnection – the systems – that have an enormous impact on how we get on in life. In the academic world, systems research is about the analysis and study of the organizational whole of relationships between interdependent components.[12] To put it more simply, it is about what happens when things interact with one another. In *Silent Spring* Rachel Carson focused on a fairly obvious system. She wanted to know what happened when synthetic pesticides were introduced in large amounts into the natural world.

When DDT was introduced it became a new input for the systems of nature. What would happen to nature's normal output as a result of this new addition, wondered Carson? She wanted to understand both the immediate impact and the long-term consequences; she wanted to grasp the big picture. So Carson looked at the health of birds, other animals and humans to see what feedback nature was providing about the pesticide use. Carson knew the effects could take time to manifest and so researched what had happened in places some years after DDT had been used. She found unintended consequences of the pesticide's use. One of these was a reduction in the product's effectiveness. Sure DDT killed the pests it was intended to, at least for the first few years, but within a decade insects had developed resistance to the chemicals. Moreover, DDT accumulated throughout the food chain. Crops dusted with DDT were eaten by chickens that laid eggs that were eaten by women who breastfed their babies who in turn began life with DDT's chemicals in their bodies – and no one knew the effect of this accumulation of toxins on human health.

For those of us who have lived in a world where environmental concerns are prominent Carson's approach may seem pretty obvious. But in the 1960s her outlook was radical. The American people had been sold a dream of progress. Science and technology was going to give humans complete mastery over the environment. It was a blinkered approach that valued immediate results, glossing over long term and possible unintended consequences. *Silent Spring* helped lead to a rethink of advances in science as the panacea to all ills. It showed the ordinary person that tinkering with natural systems had effects that hadn't been reckoned with. It made the general public want to proceed with caution, and consider the impact of human interventions on nature.

Nowadays most of us accept that human actions affect the environment, even if we disagree about the exact details. We have essentially adopted a systems view of how nature and humanity interact. We grasp that the connected, interdependent parts of a system affect each other, that actions can result in unintended consequences, that it can take time for the impact of actions to be felt and that they make take surprising routes. The challenge now is for us to extend that perspective to the wider world of systems so we can make intelligent choices about how we act in those systems, too.

Social Systems

Social systems are driven by the collective power of human minds in tandem with the physical world. Consider a school, for example. Schools consist of physical things like buildings, grounds, and equipment. But more important than these, schools have people – pupils, teachers, parents of the children, administration staff, principals, cleaners, and so on. Many interdependent relationships between these individuals make up the school. A school has inputs like the daily actions of all the people who make up the school, as well as the contributions of the parents' support at home. A school also has outputs. The most obvious intended output of a school is well-educated children, but we also hope that it produces children who work well with others and are able to interact successfully in the social world, happy teachers and a satisfied community. Taking a wider perspective, schools also have outputs in terms of maintaining culture and contributing to economic growth by educating people.

As in other types of systems, the actions of the individuals in the school system affect both each other and the school as a whole. A single disruptive child can change the dynamics of a classroom and negatively affect the experience of others in that room. By the same token, a single highly motivated teacher may have an overwhelmingly positive effect on the pupils he or she teaches. Schools also provide feedback on their performance, through report cards and test results, for example. Feedback can also be quite delayed. It might be several years after leaving a particular classroom that a child's parents realize their youngster has developed a love of reading or compassion and empathy for others.

While all schools have the same basic structure they also have some variations. No two schools will be identical, even if they have the same kind of buildings, the same funding, the same organizational rules and regulations. How could they be the same? When the participants – the people – in the systems are different, then the systems are different. Even parents, who don't physically attend so whom you might think of as peripheral, have an effect on the school, and it also affects them. The greater environment also plays a role in how the systems vary. An urban school and a rural school will be different, as will a school set in a low socio-economic neighborhood versus in a wealthy area.

Not only are any two schools different, but a single school system also looks and feels differently to the individual participants. The principal's experience of a school can be significantly different to a pupil's experience, even though they are participating in the same system. Even students in the same class are likely to have different perceptions of their school, affected by their particular experiences, their families' points of view and so on. A key aspect of our systems perception is to see that not only do instances of the same kind of system differ from one another, but that every individual's experience of the same system can also be different.

While a school is an easily recognized example of many individuals acting as a greater unit, a system, this phenomenon of people coming together through various connections surrounds us in both formal and informal ways. We can see this just by taking a few minutes to think about how society is organized. Individuals begin life born into groups called families, which come in a variety of forms and follow assorted rules and traditions depending on culture and circumstances. We not only belong to family systems, however. As we go through life we develop a range of social networks by befriending others. We attend and participate in various institutions like sports clubs, community organizations, and social groups. We take jobs and meet new groups of people we call workmates or colleagues. We identify ourselves as belonging to a particular culture and often also to a subculture. We see ourselves as members of a local community, a profession, a language group, a nation, perhaps even a group of nations.

Even our relationship with our spouse or romantic partner creates a social system. When we establish a romantic partnership we join two individuals together to create a third entity, a system – the couple. The **you** and **me** becomes an **us**. Of course, a couple still consists of two individuals, but it is also a separate unit in its own right. Think about how interactions with others change when you are partnered. People begin to treat what was previously two individuals as a single entity. The couple interacts differently with the world – sometimes they act as individuals and sometimes they act as a twosome, as parents who have worked at presenting a united front to their children know. Entering a relationship means becoming part of a system, and the dynamics of that system are different to the dynamics of singleness. Developing systems perception helps us to negotiate those changes and balance the needs of different systems.

We can marry, we have citizenship in a particular country, we enroll in schools and join sports teams. All these systems represent official, fairly long-lasting groupings. But new systems are also created fairly regularly because they are an effective means of organization for dealing with complex issues. Companies come and go, as do activist groups, bands, and social movements. These types of systems typically arise out of a particular set of circumstances, or in response to particular needs. They can come about through collective action, but they can also be created by the actions of a single individual. Environment Online (ENO) is a great example of social system that has emerged from a single teacher's desire to teach children how to care about climate change. Founded in Finland in 2002, ENO is now a virtual network of schools worldwide working for sustainable development and organizes tree planting days around the globe.[13]

Systems can also emerge out of the coming together of like-minded people. In times of crisis previously unconnected people will often band together to deal with the situation at hand. In the 1980s, a small group of Californian surfers united in an effort to maintain their local coastal environment. Now, thirty years later this small community group has become the global grassroots coastal protection organization, **Surfrider**.[14] Similarly, famous British musicians and singers formed a temporary group named Band Aid in 1984 to release a single to raise funds for Ethiopia when it was in the grip of a major famine. Even in our own neighborhoods, when people come together to work on a community garden or watch one another's houses while they are on holiday they effectively create systems.

We even create systems unintentionally. Every encounter we have with one another generates a system. When you visit the hairstylist, the person cutting your hair and you produce a temporary system. For the length of the haircut, you affect one another, interacting together to produce the desired result – a hairstyle you can live with. Similarly, attendees at a concert form a temporary system. Though connected only by their desire to listen to a particular musician, for the duration of the concert they will be members of a system. Together with the artist, the audience will share emotional and physical responses to the music, only to disperse again at the end of the show. Systems may be formal or informal, long-lasting or temporary, created by individuals or by collective action, but one thing is for sure – they are all around us.

Consciously perceiving the systems around us is not always a prerequisite for intelligent action. Every one of us intuitively and unconsciously engages with systems on a daily basis, and often we do so pretty well. However, perceiving the systems in our lives enables us to form a richer and more nuanced picture than if we don't see them. With a sense of the overall picture we are more likely to make different choices about what's going in a given context, what's essential and what matters. Rachel Carson's systems perception meant she saw the link between the failure of a robin's eggs to hatch and the presence of DDT in the parent birds, and she was able to show others that something needed to be done. When we see systems, we can bring similar insights to our own lives.

Systems Blindness

To develop our systems perception, however, we need to overcome our tendency to suffer from systems blindness. In the course of our lifetime we participate in a wide range of organized systems, some by choice, some by chance, some created by ourselves. They are inescapable. And yet, we rarely see our lives as influenced and formed by social systems, or as being part of the process of influencing and forming those systems. We simply react to stimuli without seeing the whole and the consequences of that reactive behavior. No one really teaches us about systems and their characteristics. The concept of "system" is barely on our radar. Why do we suffer from this blindness towards systems?

There are a number of reasons that the concept of system is absent from our daily lives. For one, the systems we belong to tend to be disguised under other names. We have "families", we work in "organizations" and we live in "communities." Because each of these systems has a separate name, we do not always see their common characteristics –interdependent parts, networked relationships, feedback loops and inputs and outputs. The separate names also conceal the dynamic relationships between these systems, making them appear physically distinct, unconnected to one another, and separated in time. In addition, most of us tend to focus on and react to what is in front of us on a day-to-day basis. As a result, we miss seeing the bigger picture that we are connected to.

Another reason we don't notice the presence of systems is that we already live so naturally within systems that the benefit of increasing our awareness of them is not obvious. This laissez-faire approach towards systems applies not just to individuals but also to our society as a whole. Remember your parents sitting you down to explain systems to you? Remember your teacher talking about "social systems" or "systems thinking" or "systems theory"? Probably not. Systems, and big picture thinking in general, have traditionally had a relatively low profile in school education curricula (we may not be explicitly exposed to systems concepts until we reach higher education and unless we study disciplines like engineering, computer science sociology and politics). Even if we do across systems ideas, perhaps in the study of ecology, for example, the emphasis is usually on taking a bird's eye view of the systems we study where we are external to the system and all seeing.[15]

Where we do sense and perceive systems in our lives we often see them as big and overwhelming. A system, to most of us, is a nameless, faceless, thing out there that is separate from us. We don't fully understand how it works and thus we are suspicious of it. It can even feel like something to fight or at least complain about. Insurance companies, banks, governments, the police, the military, healthcare – at times we feel as if these huge social systems work against rather than for us. We've all heard people complain about the bureaucracy of any number of large institutions. "That's the system for you," "you can't fight the system" or "it's just me against the system" are reasonably common catch cries when we find ourselves stymied by apparently unreasonable processes and excessive red tape. It is no coincidence that these phrases are heard much more regularly than their more positive counterparts like "what a wonderful system," "I was treated really well by the system," or "that system really gave me a chance to flourish." Our default is often to be antagonistic towards systems – things that we perceive as oppressing us because we usually apply the word only to large entities.

That's not altogether surprising because large social systems can exert pressure on us. We feel we have no choice but to comply with their expectations of our behavior, such as when we dutifully fill in our annual tax returns or resignedly accept the latest rise in bank fees. We become so anchored in the systems we know that we do not question why they are the way they are.

When we take systems for granted they become lost in overfamiliarity. In part that's because systems are features of our lives that mostly predate and mostly outlast us. We belong to many of them by default. They help us to create order in what could potentially be a chaotic world filled with disconnected people. We cannot imagine how a society could be organized without them. Because they are so familiar to us and we are so comfortable in them, we tend not to question how the systems around us function, and consequently we can fail to see where we could improve them or our actions within them.

It is easy to become so entrenched in systems that we *think* we see that we no longer see the actual system that is. Making an effort to perceive systems creates opportunities to make things better. One way we can do that is by experiencing a different environment that opens our ideas about how life could be organized differently. Just think of those times when you have moved towns or visited elsewhere and discovered a new way of doing things, be it a system of garbage collection, or mail delivery, or metering power. We broaden our systems perception because we can see alternatives.

It is also possible to overestimate our ability to perceive systems. Sometimes we think we correctly perceive a system and are acting well in accordance with that. But systems intelligence can be counterintuitive. Take the example of golfer Ernie Els. A successful professional golfer, he thought his systems perception when it came to the relationship between the elements of his sport (golf ball, club, bodily movements and so on) was acute. So when Dr Sherylle Calder approached him about visualization coaching, a new arm of sports science, Els initially rebuffed her. He didn't need any help.

But in the mid-2000s, Els hit a bit of a slump in his career. His putting, in particular, was frustrating him. Calder still believed she could help him, and finally Els decided to give her method a go. Calder literally trained him to see differently. She revealed to Els how he functioned, showing him where his eye focused, where and how he glanced, and what he did with his body as he lined up a putt. The eye doctor showed him intellectually what his body was doing automatically. As a result, he was able to use his conscious thinking to override the automatic processes of his mind and body. He needed an outsider, Dr. Calder, to uncover a hidden system of his own body, because he couldn't see it himself.[16]

Systems blindness can have significant consequences. One problem is that it becomes all too easy to fall into the trap of systems un-intelligence, what we might call systems idiocy. In other words, if we don't perceive and understand the systems around us then we run the risk of acting unintelligently within them. We might worry about exposing our weaknesses so we don't ask for information that would give us the bigger picture. We tell ourselves that the responsibility for change lies elsewhere and as a result our perception is narrowed. We react to what's right in front of us and forget to see the big picture. We develop a kind of tunnel vision that impedes us from seeing what's possible.

Holding Back

Another problem is that the choices we make because of systems blindness can actually generate negative systems. They might give rise, for example, to the common phenomenon of holding back. Holding back refers to our tendency to not act positively and constructively when engaging with others. Take the example of a group of people coming together for the first time perhaps at a workplace seminar. Invariably, individuals are wary; they check each other out and wait to see how others behave before deciding how to participate themselves. However, they could engage openly and warmly from the outset if they chose to – it's just that something makes them hold back.

Often we hold back either because we believe it is not our duty to act in a situation or it is someone else's responsibility to do something first. We don't smile warmly as we arrive at a workshop because we are waiting to see how others will greet us first. We don't do something extraordinarily nice for our spouse because he or she never does anything special for us. We don't praise someone because we think they should know themselves that they have done a good job. We don't fight for the environment because nobody else seems to bother.

We also sometimes hold back because we feel we can make no real difference in a situation. When our colleagues chat and text during meetings, we don't ask them to stop. It's not our responsibility. If people complain about the local school system, we don't bother to make suggestions about how it could be enhanced. Nobody would listen to us. When nobody else tries to improve road congestion by taking public transport, then we don't bother either. What difference will our one car make?

Holding back from making behavioral changes that could benefit others generates negativity that has a disproportional effect. We co-create a system, a less than optimal way of interacting where everyone is holding back, without seeing our own part in that.

Let's take the example of a friendship. Perhaps you have a friend you believe doesn't deal well with your emotional distress. In the past, when you have sought her sympathy due to some hurt, she has given you a quick pep talk and wanted to carry on as usual instead of providing the nurturing care and attention you craved. So now in times of trouble you don't call her. In your opinion, she's a friend for good times, not bad.

But consider your friend's perspective and the system of interaction that has been created. Perhaps in her family, hard times were dealt with by trying to cheer someone up rather than by offering comfort. Perhaps she feels hurt that you no longer call her when you are down. Perhaps she feels you only want to see her in happy mode, so that's what she presents to you, and because of that she doesn't call you when she needs support either. The dynamic between you has become one of "good times only" by default. Because you are both anticipating and imagining one another's intentions and desires the friendship never moves from a superficial to deep connection even though you both want it to.

This is holding back in action. When everyone is holding back instead of positively engaging, then a system of holding back emerges, and it's a system we are typically blind to. We all end up waiting for someone else to make the first move, to take responsibility, and to change the way things are done. And because most other people are thinking the same way we are, it's hardly surprising that systems stagnate. Holding back is a habit for most of us, but like all habits it can be broken. Looking for and recognizing the patterns of holding back in our lives is the first step towards changing them.

To overcome our tendency towards systems blindness, it is helpful to look at the world with new eyes, develop a fresh sense of how it is organized, and get a sense of what that organization means for our daily lives. The main idea that we need is that if we want to have a positive impact in life we need to be able to perceive what is happening in the social systems around us. Guided by that perception, we can find the best inputs and the most effective actions for creating beneficial outcomes. We can begin to make deliberately systems intelligent choices about how to be in the world.

Reflection: Systems in Your Life

What systems were you born into?

What systems do you belong to by choice?

What influence do those systems have on your behavior?

What temporary systems have you experienced?

What systems have you actively created?

How have your individual actions influenced particular systems?

What examples of *holding back* can you think of in your life?

What do these systems of holding back produce?

Multiple Systems

In the weeks leading up to the publication of *Silent Spring*, Rachel Carson found herself at the center of a storm of controversy. Forewarned thanks to the early circulation of proof copies and plenty of publicity, leading chemical companies, the manufacturers of the pesticides that Carson was criticizing, compiled reports on the book's likely impact on their business. They threatened legal action against the publishers. They prepared literature that countered Carson's arguments. They attacked both Carson and her credentials as a scientist, painting her as nothing but a hysterical woman and probably a communist to boot – the worst insults of the time her foes could direct at her.[17]

Carson had expected and prepared for the attacks. She knew that her focus on the damage caused by pesticides, though primarily an ecological issue for her, would have consequences in many other systems. The manufacturers, the users, and the advocates of pesticides would all be affected by her book. Carson made sure her research was rigorous and she gathered the support of prominent academics and others, including political figures and a supreme court judge. Carson knew that *Silent Spring* was about more than damage to the environment: it would have consequences for companies' profits, individuals' reputations, and, as it turned out, the creation of national policy.

In other words, Rachel Carson was aware of and adjusted for the presence of multiple systems. The content of her book might have focused on an ecosystem, but she knew its impact would be far reaching. It is of benefit to bring the same insight to our own life in systems. Let's return to the example of a school. A school can appear to be a stand-alone social system, but it is actually a system embedded within other systems. A school exists in a community. An educational authority governs it. It is part of the local economy. The parents, teachers and other members of the school community all belong to their own cultural systems. A huge number of people and products and systems contribute to building and running a school. Every system is connected to other systems.

Part of systems perception is not only seeing the obvious systems around us, but also being mindful of the presence of multiple, overlapping and interconnected systems. Living in and adjusting to multiple systems is what we do every day. As individuals, we all engage with numerous systems, often simultaneously. We are members of our family, we belong to sports teams, we volunteer in community organizations, we go to work. What's more, when we join a new system we often take on even more systemic connections than we realize at first. If we become part of a couple, for example, we often become part of a new family, are involved in a new network of friends, and are connected to a new workplace.

Because we belong to a variety of systems, we all have numerous, sometimes competing, responsibilities and loyalties in life and that means we can benefit from perceiving our systemic environment more fully. Take, for example, a typical workplace meeting. Let's say there's nine people at this meeting, (depicted in the diagram below). Together, the nine form a department in a larger organization. The boss plays golf most weekends with three of the other men, one of whom is a childhood friend. Meanwhile, there's a married couple in the department and another group of three guys who have lunch together every day. The three workers at the side of the table work on a particular project together and have become close colleagues. Three of the men are working on another, rival, project. Half the group has young children who attend the same school.

Most of us would quickly see the nine people in the department as a system, but very few of us would immediately, explicitly understand the impact that all the other relationships and connections in the group have on one another. The manager would have to balance, if not prioritize, his commitments to the different systems he participates in. In a time of crisis, will he value his relationship with his friend over the team as a whole or his position in the larger organization? How will the married worker manage his commitments to his wife, his lunch buddies, and his project team? Do the women feel excluded from the golfing group within the department? How do the social connections outside of work affect those in the office?

Typically, problems arise when we fail to consider that everybody can see systems differently. It's likely everyone in the department knows about the married couple, but perhaps not everyone is aware of the golfing quartet. Yet the conversations they have on the golf course could have an enormous influence on the processes and dynamics of the department. Clearly, close friendships or a romantic relationship could also have a large impact on the group, whether they start, continue or end. In addition, individuals could have false expectations and erroneous ides about the various systems in play. Perhaps the non-golfers falsely assume the manager likes them less because they don't golf, and this creates unnecessary tension between those who golf and those who don't.

If we are sensitive to the variety of systems present at any given time, including our own position and responsibilities in them, it is easier to grasp what is going on. That helps us make more informed decisions about how to act, and better understand the likely effects of our actions. It also allows us to better evaluate why others are behaving the way they are. We may take things that don't go our way much less personally. For example, we might respect our colleague's decision to prioritize her family's needs over keeping an appointment with us, or understand that our manager sometimes feels his first responsibility is to his immediate superior rather than his staff. Even if we don't agree with the way other people manage their overlapping systems relationships, sensitivity to the existence of those systems means we can at least have a richer understanding of what is happening and adjust our own behavior accordingly. We can be like Rachel Carson and prepare for the likely effects that our actions in one system will have on others.

One consequence of the presence of multiple systems is that it is possible to be highly perceptive in a specific setting and yet systems blind in another. Some people are extremely good at understanding the dynamics and relationships of their workplace. Others are more perceptive when it comes to family or their primary relationship. You can probably easily identify the system settings where you feel most sensitive to connections. The challenge is to apply this aspect of our systems intelligence when we shift from context to context – how can we learn to be more perceptive in all systems? One way is to be on the lookout for more than the obvious connections.

Systems We Do Not See

In the visible parts of social systems like families and schools, organizations and governments, it's pretty obvious how the organization of the systems works. There's a shared understanding of what to expect from these common systems. You would think, then, that life in these systems would be pretty straightforward. Yes and no. If life in systems were easy there would be fewer problems in families, workplaces and societies. The challenge we face is that the parts of the systems we typically see are not the whole story. We can understand a group of people acting together form a system and so understand something of how they work together, but there is usually more. We may not observe the hidden systems that are also acting in them. Just as Rachel Carson's probing research allowed her to form a rich picture of the ecosystems she studied, we can make an effort to form a rich picture of the systems we participate in.

When we think we have the systems around us figured out we also need to remind ourselves that what we see is usually only part of the picture. Looking for a system can sometimes be like looking through a tiny keyhole – we can see into the room but we only see a limited part of it. Economist John Kay argues that "the most complex systems come into being, and function, without anyone having knowledge of the whole."[18] While Kay is referring to systems like the financial markets, governments, and huge corporations, the same idea applies to all systems. We see glimpses of them at work but we are limited by our own perspective, and also by the very structures of the systems themselves.

Take your family, for example. If you were asked to describe your family and the various members' relationships with one another you'd probably do so with ease. After all, it is a system that is familiar to you. But what if your parent, or your spouse, or your child were asked to describe your family and its relationships? They might name the same people as you, but they would probably characterize the relationships between those people somewhat differently. Even though you are members of the same system – your family – you would see different aspects of that system. Just as a school is a different system to the principal than it is to the pupil, so is a family system different to the parent and the child. Of course, the same applies in other systems, too. We experience our workplace differently to our colleagues, our community differently to our neighbors, our country differently to our fellow citizens. Every individual in a system has their own feelings, expectations and ideas about life that have a dynamic impact on the relationships in any given system.

Understanding that our own perspective of any system can be limited to a kind of keyhole view is crucial to acting with systems intelligence. It is all too easy to react to situations based on our limited perspective rather than take the time to imagine what might be happening outside our field of vision. When we act systems intelligently, we act based on the knowledge that we can only see part of the picture, and so our behavior takes that into account. This means breaking the habit most of us have of assuming that what we see is what everyone else sees – or should be seeing.

Our view of systems is not just limited by the boundaries of our vision. It is also clouded by the things that happen below the surface. To perceive systems as fully as we can, we need to tune in to their obvious physical and organizational connections but also to the less obvious emotional and informal connections. Take a look at the diagrams. Which system is more complex, the first one or the second one?

Most people see the first system with all its interrelationships as the most complex, and the second one as simple. In fact, the second system is deceptive. Sure, there are only four people in this system, compared to seven in the other one, but we do not know the connections between them. This means it may be more complex than the first one. It is certainly harder for us to understand this system because of what we don't know. In *Silent Spring* Rachel Carson turned a second diagram where birds, and animals, and people and pesticides seemed unconnected into a first diagram that revealed relationships that most people were unaware of.

An everyday illustration of this phenomenon occurs when we join a new workplace. When we first arrive, our experience is like the second system. We know all the people in our new office are connected on a personal and organizational level, but we don't know exactly how. Because of that, we are usually pretty careful initially about what we do and say. Over time, the nature of the relationships will become clearer. After a few months in the job, our mental picture of our workplace will look more like the first system. We will have a better understanding of how people are connected, and that will affect how we behave.

But even after we have figured out the obvious connections, we shouldn't expect to understand everything. Interestingly, we may be given a first-picture like description of our workplace – a formal organizational chart, for example – when we first join. However, we may soon learn that the official relationships described may not accurately represent the everyday connections. After a while on the job we can perceive some of the informal relationships, but other dimensions will always remain hidden. There's an easy-to-see system – but there can also be a deeper, unobvious, hidden part of the system.

What goes on at the surface is visible for all to see. That might be a new sales account coming to an organization, resulting in the manager telling an employee to produce a report, and such a report being written. In parallel though, below the surface hidden aspects of the system also exist. Maybe the manager thinks this new account represents a chance for promotion so she aggressively demands the employee produce a top-quality report more quickly than usual. As a result, the employee feels pressured, and becomes wary and distrustful of the manager. The manager has not taken the emotional aspects of her actions into account. So even though the report might be produced and the inputs and outputs seem to match, this apparently innocuous interaction damages the manager and employee's future relationship. The distrust may even spread to other staff as colleagues talk with one another.

The hidden dimensions of a system interact with the visible dimensions of a system and so impact on what is ultimately produced. A systems intelligent manager would manage the emotional dimensions of the system as well as the work output. She would realize that her expectations put pressure on the employee so would adjust her interaction to acknowledge that. By doing so, she could generate trust and respect as invisible outputs in conjunction with a good quality report. Likewise, parents who desire particular behavior in their children are more likely to achieve cooperation if they attend to the emotional needs of their child as well as their actions. It is systems intelligent to be able to discern and work with the essentials of the hidden systems as well as the obvious.

When we are trying to perceive the systems around us, it often helps to look for what is not being produced as an output as much as what is being produced. Knowing that it is important to attend to the unseen is not a new idea: Irish essayist Jonathon Swift commented in the eighteenth century "vision is the art of seeing the invisible."[19] In other words, at some level, conscious or unconscious, we must learn to consider things that we cannot fully see or comprehend, or at least realize that they exist and have an impact on our lives.

One way to do that is to look for the ghost system at work in the shadow of the visible system. The ghost system is a system that nobody wants or plans but which can emerge because of the absence of systems intelligent behavior, and it

often ends up dictating people's actions. In organizations, for example, if fear, personal interest and secrecy drive behavior, a system of interaction is created that no one actually wants. Yet because organizational members believe this is how things work around here – in other words, they develop expectations and mental models of their colleagues' actions – then the system self-perpetuates. Once we see this ghost system at work, however, it is possible to notice what is missing – things like trust, teamwork, and openness – and introduce systems intelligent behavior to generate these.

Intangible systems are by their very nature difficult to perceive. Clearly, some things will always remain just beyond our grasp or occur outside of our perception. Nevertheless, we must act despite our limits. And we do. We all act in the face of the unknown that pervades our daily life. We decide on our actions based on things like our past experiences, our gut feelings, our intuition, and the advice of others. All these are helpful to us, but by making an effort to perceive the systems at work around us we can enhance our ability to cope with the invisible. If we understand that we can't see everything that is part of a system we can adjust our decision-making and behavior accordingly. We can act with systems intelligence.

The Bird and the Worm

During her research for *Silent Spring*, Rachel Carson was particularly disturbed by the US Department of Agriculture's decision to eradicate fire ants by aerially spraying pesticides mixed with fuel oil over private and government land. The fire ant had been a minor pest in the US for forty or so years. But, looking for markets for their new products, pesticide companies lobbied to have the insects deemed a high priority menace so they could graciously offer their new chemicals to address the fire ant problem. Carson described the expensive eradication program as "ill-conceived, badly executed, and thoroughly detrimental."[20]

Silent Spring summarized the detrimental effects such pesticide programs had on both natural ecosystems and on human health. It also predicted the long-term consequences of their use, noting that not only would the insects build resistance to the poisons but also that many species would accumulate the toxins in their bodies and weakened ecosystems would develop new problems. In other words, Rachel Carson saw both the immediate impact that pesticides were having on the natural environment and the bigger, more long-term picture that their unregulated use would create.

Unlike Carson, most of us tend to see either the immediate but not the bigger picture, or the big picture without the immediate. This limited perspective, seeing only parts of systems but thinking we see the whole, hampers systems intelligent action. To make better choices in systems we need to be able to attend to both the big picture and the small details of life. Systems perception at its best is thus a combination of a bird's eye view and a worm's eye view. The bird flies above the system and sees the whole, while the worm pokes its head out of the ground and looks at its immediate surroundings. Neither perspective is sufficient alone.

Adopting a bird's eye view puts us outside the systems we are looking at. When we take this perspective, systems become things that exist out there, separate from us and seemingly under human control. Yet, often, we are actually a part of the systems we externalize. When we talk with our friends about how high insurance premiums are and what a good arrangement the insurance companies have going for themselves, we perhaps fail to see that our own actions (inflating a claim, not bothering to put a security alarm in, and so on) contribute to the rise in premiums. We see the insurance system as existing separate to us, and so don't see our own role in that system.

On the other hand, when we take a worm's eye view, we can be limited by our inability to see beyond ourselves. We are blind to the system because we only see what is in front of us. With only a worm's eye view we might feel hurt and worried about our marriage because our spouse has been grumpy with us for several days. We assume their bad mood is all about their relationship with us. Because we haven't seen the other systems at work in their life, we fail to realize that stress at work is generating their unusual behavior. A similar effect occurs when we berate the government for a policy it introduces that negatively affects us, and fail to see that the same policy helps many more people that it hurts, or provides income for implementing other policies that we benefit from. There is a difference between attending to what is around us while acknowledging that there are aspects of the system that we cannot see and know about – which is systems intelligent – and thinking that what goes on around us is the whole picture like the worm does.

We act systems intelligently when we remind ourselves to take the perspective of both the bird and the worm, when we see the connections between ourselves and the big picture. We don't have to see the system as something removed from us, nor as something that we are at the center of. It is possible to see the big  picture at the same time as we understand our own role in creating that picture. That's what Rachel Carson did. She saw the detrimental effects of pesticides on the natural environment and people's health (the bird's eye view) but she also saw her own opportunity to intervene in that systems (the worm's eye view). She knew that by virtue of her training as a scientist and her public profile as a writer, she could act to change the trajectory of the big picture.

We Create Systems

Carson could have an impact because social systems are created by people. They are the product of people's thoughts, beliefs and behaviors. Some powerful and effective social systems have been created by people with shared beliefs. The organization Médecins Sans Frontières (in English, Doctors without Borders), for example, was established in 1971 by a group of doctors and journalists who saw the need for a neutral body addressing international medical and humanitarian needs. Now, on any given day, more than twenty-seven thousand committed individuals representing dozens of nationalities can be found providing assistance to people caught in crises around the world.[21] We create organizations and other systems all the time. When we get married and start a family, when we start a club, when we develop a new group of friends, we bring new systems into being.

We don't only create new systems together, however; we also perpetuate, shape and change existing social systems. Intuitively, we know that human behavior affects social systems; it's just not something that we think about very often. We know, for example, that if the people who make up the system change, sometimes the system itself changes. If a school welcomes a new principal, there are often multiple flow-on effects. The rules may change, the direction and focus of the school may change, the atmosphere amongst staff may change, the response of the pupils may change and so on. At other times, changing the people who constitute a system may not have much effect. If one young child leaves a school, while their friends and the classroom dynamic may be affected, the overall school system may not alter much. Often the impact of change will depend on the position of the person within the system – the more power they have to change the structure of the system the greater their impact. A change in a company's chief executive officer will typically have a greater impact than the hiring of a new junior, for example.

That is not to say, however, that even the apparently least significant people in the system have no influence. In fact, they do; we all do. That's why it is so helpful for us to be able to perceive the systems around us. While we might be a tiny component of an overall system, we are still a component. Without us, and the other individuals likes us, these systems don't exist. Without clients, there are no insurance companies or banks; without voters, there are no governments; without civilians, there are no police or military; without a congregation, there is no church. Our behaviors produce those systems. How a system works arises from how we work; "how people think and act shapes how the system as a whole operates."[22]

Systems are designed and organized by people. They are lived in by people. They are perpetuated by people. Therefore, they can be changed, improved, and reimagined by people. Within any systems leverage points exist where small but significant actions can lead to substantial changes. When we can perceive these, we have the capacity to reshape the systems that shape our lives. Many historical figures – Mahatma Gandhi, Nelson Mandela, Mother Teresa, Rosa Parks – have achieved fame because of their contribution to improving the social systems they perceived. Just because a system is a certain way, doesn't mean it has to be that way. Our systems intelligence gives us the ability to see, understand and influence the systems around us.

Just as we influence the systems around us, though, the systems also influence us. People's behavior helps create social systems, but social systems help create people's behavior. This is a reality we live with all the time. Consequently, part of systems perception is seeing how systems have an impact our behavior as well as how our actions impact systems.

Systems' influence on our behavior is easy to illustrate. For instance, the design of a country's traffic system influences how we all drive. There are different types of roads that we drive differently on. Signs dictate our speed, we are forced to enter and exit at certain points, we can only travel in certain directions. When we join the driving community we undertake to follow the rules of the system. Driving overseas can be challenging as we must adjust to a new system. Similarly, when we go to a restaurant we wait to be seated, we behave in a certain way, we know the order of events. In other words, we know the system of dining at a restaurant. If we go to a fast food outlet, we adjust our behavior accordingly. Unconsciously, we follow the rules of the system. The context determines how we perceive the system and this shapes our behavior.

We are socialized into and attuned to many systems. When we start school, we learn how the day is structured, what to bring with us, how to behave in the classroom, how to be rewarded, and how to get along with our classmates amongst other things. Likewise when we begin new jobs, join new sports teams, participate in new community groups. We unthinkingly accept the authority built into the system's structure and, mostly, do our best to conform to the expectations on us. If we don't, we will likely struggle to get along in the system. We might be fired, benched, or ignored. These consequences help ensure that we produce the behaviors that keep the systems we belong to functioning smoothly.

When we perceive the systems around us and adjust our behavior accordingly, for better or worse, we are in the realm of systems intelligence. This adjustment happens all the time as we move from one context – one system – to another. Sometimes, though, we are unaware of the effect that a system is having on our actions. The social system we are in can shape our behavior at a subconscious level. That may be because we can't see the system, because we have missed the hidden dimensions of the system, or because our narrow perspective limits us.

Take the example of choosing whether to become an organ donor upon our death or not. Most of us would like to think that when we make an important decision like this we are exercising our free will. But Dan Ariely, a behavioral economist at MIT, found something surprisingly simple had an enormous influence on people's decision when he studied research on organ donation.

A comparison of various countries in Europe showed that different countries had quite different percentages of their citizens signing up as organ donors. Not so strange, you might think; however, what was strange was that culturally and religiously similar countries had widely divergent rates. Denmark, for example, had only a four percent donation rate, while in neighboring Sweden eighty-six percent opted to be organ donors. In Germany twelve percent of the population was willing to donate their organs, while in culturally-similar Austria, one hundred percent of drivers agreed to be organ donors. If not cultural and religious differences, what then explained the huge variation in people's willingness to become organ donors?[23]

The answer turned out to be the mechanism for collecting registration for becoming an organ donor. All the countries used the process of registering for a driver's license to ask their citizens to register as organ donors, but they did so in different ways. The countries with low participation rates, Denmark and Germany, asked their citizens to opt in. People needed to tick a box to show their willingness to donate. In the countries with high participation rates, Sweden and Austria, for example, individuals were given the choice to opt out. They needed to tick a box if they *didn't* want to be donors. Something as simple as the design of a form heavily influenced people's behavior. Very few of us would see in the moment of making a decision about being a donor that the system of collecting consent could affect our decision.

The strong, subconscious effect of systems on our behavior can be harnessed by those who understand the power of systems. Governments, for example, often use what is known about systems to change our behavior in ways that have an impact on our lives and the lives of others, as well as the country as a whole. Smoking used to be a structurally endorsed behavior in New Zealand, for example. Many systems in the country encouraged the consumption of cigarettes in public places. Ashtrays were built into cars, into toilets on airplanes, provided in cinemas and restaurants. Cigarettes were cheap, were glamorously advertised, were cool. Workplaces provided "smoko" breaks. Unsurprisingly, many people chose to smoke. The prevailing structure encouraged the behavior. Nowadays, with smoking's health risks exposed, systems have been purposely redesigned to discourage smoking. No ashtrays are provided, anti-smoking signs are common, laws punish smoking, advertising is banned, tobacco taxes are high and so on.

Once we see the systems around us, we can better understand the effects those systems are having on our behavior. Then we can make informed decisions about our actions within those systems. We can choose to act in ways a system encourages, if, for example, we like the system as it is. If we don't like the current system, but we understand how it both shapes our behavior and is shaped by our behavior, we can explore alternatives. When we are blind to the dynamics between structure and behavior, we tend to keep on behaving in ways that produce outcomes that perhaps no one really wants, ironically reinforcing the existing system – and so it goes on in an endless loop. We are in danger of missing what Rachel Carson found, the opportunity to create something different through systems intelligent action.

Cultivate Your Systems Perception

Think of the systems you engaged with today.
Identify the immediate connections you have within those systems.
Try to place yourself and what happened today in a bigger picture.
Now think about what you couldn't see in the systems you experienced today – what relationships might have developed, actions may have been taken, and emotions felt that you were not immediately connected with.

Choose an interaction you have had recently that seemed pretty straightforward (an exchange with your spouse or a co-worker, for example).
What was the purpose of the interaction?
Now think about what happened at the emotional sub-systems level.
What were the inputs and outputs of your conversation, both obvious and hidden?
Did you achieve your goal? What helped or hindered that?

Next time someone in a position of authority asks you to do something that you don't really want to do, think about the effect the request has on you.
Did you feel put out and angry? Did you feel like they didn't care about you? If so, what was it about their approach or your relationship that caused that reaction in you?
If you felt willing to help the other person despite not really wanting the task, consider why. Was it the way they approached you? Was it because you had built up a reservoir of good feelings about that person?

Next time you have to ask someone to do something you know they don't want to do, think about how you might approach them in a way that takes into account the emotional needs of the relationship as well as the task objective.

Imagine some of the unintended consequences of actions that you have taken in systems today.
Does thinking about these possibilities make you wish you had acted differently?

Reflect on an event from your day.
What systems in your life did this event relate to?
What actions taken some time ago might have led to what happened today?
Do you think the outcomes of those actions were foreseen at the time?

Next time you see a social message (about smoking, healthy eating, exercise etc.) think about what kind of behavior the system is prompting from you.
Consider what structures are in place to encourage you to act in particular ways.
Think about what systems the message is connected to. What benefits will there be and to whom from acting on the message?

Seeing What Systems Create

Systems perception gives us the ability to see the obvious and the hidden, the big picture and the details, a system's effect on us and our affect on it, and the multiple systems present in our lives. That helps us to get to the essence of what it is going on in a situation because it gives a broad picture that takes into account the characteristics of systems. In turn, we can start to tackle problems in different ways than we would without the advantage of systems perception.

With systems perception, for example, we understand that effects of actions can often be delayed. If you drop pesticide on insects, they die. The relationship between the two actions is pretty obvious. What's not so obvious is that those pesticides may seep into the food chain and lead to child cancers a number of years down the track. Likewise, if you don't pay attention in school, you don't nurture a positive atmosphere in your workplace, or you don't spend enough time with your children then you might not see the consequences of those actions for some time. We can see this effect with our own bodies – smoking, over exposure to sun and various other bad habits may not show their full impact until many years have gone by.

Not only is the observable impact of actions in systems often delayed, it also frequently occurs indirectly. Whereas some mechanical systems like cars follow a reasonably linear process to operate, human systems, and interventions in human systems, are far more likely to take indirect routes and, over time, produce unintended consequences, both positive and negative. We see this all the time in our personal lives and in society at large. When a child takes up a hobby, they don't anticipate the long-term benefits that activity will have on their confidence and social skills in later life. When we do something to help one person, we are sometimes surprised to learn we have also helped another. When a government implements one policy, it can unwittingly find that it affects a group it had not intended to impact. When a writer publishes a book about one specific pollution problem, they can unintentionally create a major environmental movement.

Deep down we know indirect routes and unintended consequences are a feature of everyday life – plans don't always work out, unthought-of-things happen, goals are achieved indirectly. Despite this, we generally think of our lives as a linear, fairly predictable series of events. On a personal level, we set goals and plan for futures that we want to reach. Within business, many practices are built around seeing companies as stable and predictable systems that will follow a planned trajectory.[24] The problem is that neither economic nor social systems are always stable or predictable. Moreover, sometimes we *prefer* to be blind to systems and not recognize how systems work because it is more convenient for us. That way, we can justify a quick fix approach. Developing our systems perception forces us to approach life differently.

With systems perception we are more likely to consider possible unintended consequences of our actions, unlike the sugar farmers of Australia. When the farmers decided to introduce a new species of toad to Queensland, Australia in 1935 they thought they had found the perfect predator to control the beetles that were eating the region's sugar cane crop. They ignored the warnings of naturalists and scientists who worried that the unimaginatively named cane toad would have no natural predator in Queensland. They should have listened. The poisonous cane toad is now a much-hated pest that has spread throughout much of Australia. Toxic in all stages of its lifecycle, the cane toad is a health hazard to humans, poisons pets and native wildlife, eats honeybees, and competes for food with other species. It is also a prolific breeder and people are now encouraged to kill them on sight, as ineffective a pest control method as their introduction.[25]

With systems perception we are more likely to look beyond the obvious. In the 1920s, many in the US felt alcohol consumption was contributing to an increase in criminal activity. When the government introduced prohibition, banning the sale of alcohol in an effort to create a more sober, healthy and morally upright nation, they didn't realize that they would be fuelling organized crime. Professional criminals largely ran the black market for alcohol. Because liquor could not be bought elsewhere, they made a huge profit off it, which they then used to fund their other illegal activities. The prohibition unwittingly led to an increase in the very law and order problems it was supposed to curtail.

With systems perception we are more likely to think about the bigger picture as well as the immediate issue. DDT was widely introduced because its insect-killing properties had many benefits. It would help farmers produce greater crops; combat lice during wartime amongst soldiers, refugees and prisoners; and prevent the spread of insect-borne disease. In particular, DDT was effective in preventing the spread of malaria. The only problem was, no one understood its long-term effects. They didn't realize that mosquitoes would become resistant to the chemicals and that the pesticide's toxins would linger in the food chain to detrimental effect. The resulting ban on DDT, thanks in part to *Silent Spring*, also had consequences, though, leading to an increase in deaths from malaria. [26] The World Health Organization now oversees finding balance between controlled use of the pesticide and damage to the environment; it juggles the needs of competing systems.

A lack of understanding about systems leads to seeing a problem (a crop-eating beetle, alcohol induced disorder, insect-borne disease), and looking for a quick solution. The story of the cane toad, prohibition, and the unregulated use of DDT are what Peter Senge, the author of a famous management book on systems thinking, describes as "fixes that fail."[27] In other words, there can be negative system-wide consequences to quick fixes. To avoid fixes that fail, it is important to avoid the tendency to be mesmerized by the immediate problem, and to expand our vision to take into account the bigger picture. With systems perception, we can break the habit of looking for a quick fix without thinking of its long-term consequences.

Systems perception tends to lead to more thoughtful approaches to issues. When the US was flooded with illegal Mexican immigrants under his presidency Jimmy Carter did not simply advocate border fences or more guards. Instead, he suggested that illegal immigration would be better curbed by the US focusing on developing the Mexican economy. When the gap between living standards and opportunity in the US and Mexico was reduced, he reasoned, illegal immigration would decrease. Carter's method, that sought to address the cause of the problem, was more systems intelligent than merely punishing infringers. [28] Like Rachel Carson, he was able to see both the local details and the big picture, and to realize how those two aspects of systems are connected. The challenge for us is to do the same.

The Challenge: Adding Feeling to Seeing

Some decades ago, renowned scholar Gregory Bateson suggested that most of the problems in the world are caused by a mismatch between how we think the world works and how it really works.[29] Bateson felt that we needed to transform our thinking away from a fragmented, silo approach to a systems perspective so we could act with the bigger picture in mind.

Rachel Carson valued such an approach, emphasizing people's need to see and understand the systems around them. *Silent Spring* showed its readers that the actions of people had an effect on the natural world, and that the natural world had an effect on people. It opened people's eyes to the interconnections between what at the time seemed unrelated activities – pesticides were dropped, non-pests died, humans got sick. It highlighted the systemic nature of life – the dynamic interconnections between seemingly unrelated things.

Like systems in the natural world, the systems we live in are full of interconnections and inescapably dynamic. They change constantly, sometimes imperceptibly, sometimes dramatically. In addition, we change, so the way we see a system also changes. Systems form and reform. We participate in them and create them. Some systems, and the relationships we have within them, are fleeting; some of them are long lasting. Some are obvious; some are invisible to us. They can produce behavior in unpredictable ways. But once we perceive the presence of systems all around us, we can start to think about how we can better live with them. Within any system there are possibilities of improvement, no matter how large or small, new or old. Armed with that insight we can act more intelligently within the systems around us and so take steps to better them. But there is more – we can open not just our eyes but also other channels as we also learn to feel – to attune to – systems.

Attunement

"A person is a person through other persons; you can't be human in isolation; you are human only in relationships." ~ Desmond Tutu[30]

Archbishop Desmond Mpilo Tutu is a man who has devoted himself to the promotion of peace and social justice.[31] With an instantly recognizable and seemingly ever-present smile, he has accomplished much in his long life. He is a Nobel Laureate, has been a key agitator against apartheid, the first black Archbishop of South Africa, an international mediator, chairman of the Truth and Reconciliation Commission, and more recently has become a campaigner for the human rights of people with AIDS and HIV.

Born in Transvaal, South Africa, even early in his life, Tutu seemed destined for success. He had excellent educational opportunities and he made the most of them by applying himself to his studies, both in South Africa and in England. He had good mentors who guided him, including leading politicians and church figures. He had a supportive and politically engaged wife in Leah. Despite growing up under the regime of apartheid he was able to become a highly educated and well-traveled man.

Beyond his intellect and his work ethic, though, Archbishop Tutu has another gift that contributed to his becoming a beloved leader. He has the human touch. His personality draws all kinds of people to him. A talented and articulate speaker, he is also known to be a sincere and empathetic listener. He has been nicknamed "God's comedian" for his capacity to create laughter in tense situations.[32] He is famous for his warmth and approachability. Once, when a child asked him what you have to do to be awarded the Nobel Peace Prize, Tutu replied "It's very easy, you just need three things – you must have an easy name, like Tutu for example, you must have a large nose and you must have sexy legs."[33] He has a unique ability to connect with individuals from all backgrounds, driven by his belief in the innate wonderfulness of people and his vision of a rainbow South Africa. In systems intelligence terms, he has the gift of attunement, the ability to intuitively sense and connect with the systems at hand.

Systemic perception is not a prerequisite of attunement. We can be attuned even if we don't consciously perceive the system. In fact, at times it is better to be attuned to rather than visually aware of the system at hand. For example, when we are in the state of flow we are essentially attuned. An expert basketball player, for example, is attuned to where the ball and others are and are going to be on the court rather than cognitively stepping through the process of "oh player x is moving there but player y is behind that person so I'll throw the ball here." Sometimes our physical vision actually hampers our sensitivity and performance. When carrying a tray of full glasses, for example, intuitively we want to look at the glasses as we walk to monitor our movement so nothing spills. But actually, watching the glasses is the wrong choice. Instead, we should gaze on where we are going – this keeps the tray more balanced – much as when we cut around an outline on paper we do better if we follow where the scissors are going rather than focus on where they are.

People are naturally systems intelligent with respect to their environment. Just as the tiniest amoeba changes its behavior if its surroundings change or the largest elephant modifies its behavior depending on what's happening in the herd, we also sense what is happening in the systems around us. In fact, systems intelligence may be one of the most important traits of the human species. It basically allows us to live in and adapt to changing contexts. When we change jobs, join a new club, or travel in other countries we adapt our actions to the new system. In some cases, such as when we host a party or start a new relationship, our behavior and the system co-evolve. We even attune to systems without explicitly naming the context as a system. When approaching a horse, for example, we automatically adjust our behavior, our attitude, our body language to interact with the animal, even though we would be unlikely to call the interaction between the horse and ourselves a system. Our instinct that compels us to act differently with a horse than we would a cat or our employer or our doctor.

Our innate ability to attune manifests as soon as we are born. Perhaps while talking to the mother of a young baby you have noticed how she smiles, rocks, and murmurs to her child even while maintaining a conversation with you – and how her baby relaxes contentedly in response. A kind of dance of human gestures takes place. Both the baby and the mother interact with one another intuitively, stepping into a kind of synchronicity. That synchronicity can be good, such as in contended play, or bad, such as when a distracted caregiver leads to a fractious baby. The goal is for us to manage our attunement processes with intelligence so that we create positive systems of interaction.

When mothers and their infants attune well to one another they are connected by what Daniel Stern, a child psychologist and expert in infant development, calls *vitality affect*. The vitality affect is a continuous energetic experience of empathetic interaction that creates a sense of connectedness. In other words, mother and baby in the same room are sensitive to one another's moods and dynamically adjusting to one another all the time, even when they are not overtly communicating.[34] Research also shows that day old babies will cry in response to the tears of other newborns, exhibiting what is known as rudimentary empathic distress.[35] Older children too are naturally attuned to the interconnections, dynamics and patterns of life.[36]

Having an innate ability to attune is hardly surprising when you consider it is all but impossible for us to live our lives in isolation and never pay attention to the people around us. Contemporary life demands that we interact with others. Indeed, human nature is not about seeking solitude but about seeking companionship, intimacy, and affection.[37] We are meant to be part of social groups that are attuned to one another. In fact, evolutionary biologists believe that the brain grew in response to our ancestors living in increasingly large social groups forcing them to both cooperate and compete with one another. The rapid development in the size of the human brain over the last three million years has come about primarily because we are awash in social signals.[38]

Sensing how others were thinking and feeling and what was going on around us were essential to our survival. Primitive humans had to learn to process information about the behavior of others and to react adaptively to that behavior. They also had to develop the brain capacity to keep track of multiple relationships. Modern humans continue to require these skills.[39] In fact, given the demands of our current environment, evolutionary psychologists argue that humans need to develop new capabilities to cope with the increasing levels of interconnectedness and change in modern life.[40] Fostering the ability to attune in systemic contexts is one such capability that helps us flourish.

Opening Attunement Channels

Archbishop Tutu is often described as an impulsive man. In the battle against apartheid, he sometimes frustrated his clerical colleagues. The rational strategists who were carefully considering the church's stance and pronouncements on social issues felt undermined by the man who "operated on instinct and inspiration" in a politically volatile context.[41] But that same openness to impulsivity has led him to dance with delight at a rugby match, cry with victims of torture, and use humor to become approachable. He has also been authoritarian and fractious, even yelling at former South African president P. W. Botha when he felt the occasion needed it. Desmond Tutu does not simply follow the rules of logic and nicety when it comes to interacting with others and systems – he attunes to the situation at hand through whatever channels are available to him.

Attunement, then, is primarily an intuitive process. We unconsciously sense what's going on around and within us at the emotional, cognitive and physical level, and we are capable of doing so as soon as we are born. It is not uncommon, though, for the busyness of our lives to detract from our capacity to attune to our environment. When we are rushing around, when we are preoccupied with the thoughts racing in our heads, when we are focusing on what we have to do next rather than what we are doing now, attunement is difficult. We find it hard to feel the atmosphere around us or we suppress and ignore what our non-conscious registers. Yet, when we are open within systems we free ourselves to attuning to the whole.

That was something Captain Chelsey B. "Sully" Sullenberger was able to do on January 15, 2009, to the overwhelming relief of his passengers. That day, he was piloting an AirbusA320 carrying one hundred and fifty-five people when both plane's engines lost power. Despite being forced to land in the Hudson River, all aboard survived, in large part thanks to the intuitive responses of the pilot who attuned to the situation at hand.

After the bird strike disabled the aircraft's engines, Captain Sullenberg might have stuck to procedure based only on his experiences of flying planes. If he had, he most likely would have handled his unpowered landing differently. But he was also a certified glider pilot. Captain Sully's vision and conscious thoughts told him he was flying a jet plane into a river, but his senses and his gut instinct told him to engage as if he were flying a glider. The basic rules of gliding are universal (push the nose of the aircraft down initially, reduce speed until the wings are no longer producing lift, then pull the nose up for landing). He abandoned the rules for flying powered planes and engaged the rules of flying unpowered gliders, going with his intuition in a moment of crisis.[42]

After the incident, Sullenberg commented during one interview that "one way of looking at this might be that for forty-two years, I've been making small, regular deposits in this bank of experience, education and training. And on January

15 the balance was sufficient so that I could make a very large withdrawal."[43] Part of that experience, education and training was a familiarity with the system of flying gliders. The Hudson river incident and others like it exemplify the phrase "intuition comes to the prepared mind."[44] In other words, the ability to act with confidence based on our gut instinct develops because we understand and are attuned to the system at hand. To hone our intuitive systems intelligence we need to

see systems, but also to feel them so that we act appropriately.

Being able to attune to ourselves, others and systems involves learning to trust our intuition at appropriate times. Neuroscientists call gut instinct or intuition "gist," but the words mean essentially the same thing – an unthinking response to the matter at hand borne of experience.[45] We can and do act intuitively, and indeed, we most often initiate our systems intelligence instinctively. This is despite the fact that some experts like economists have consistently argued for people to ignore their gut and base their decisions on logic, reason, and analysis.[46] Indeed, for many years, western science wanted to separate emotion and cognition, undervaluing emotions or feelings in comparison to the cognitive or thinking processes of the human brain.

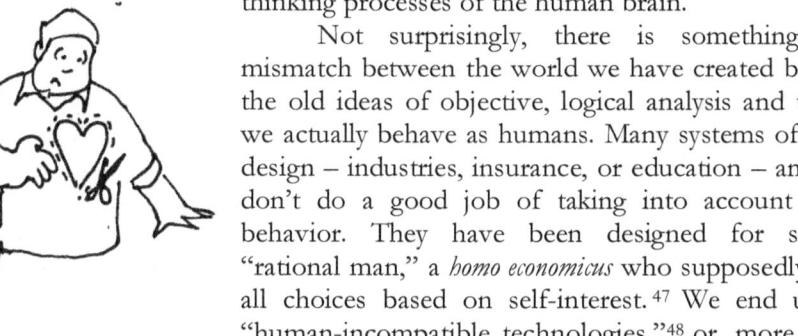

Not surprisingly, there is something of a mismatch between the world we have created based on the old ideas of objective, logical analysis and the way we actually behave as humans. Many systems of human design – industries, insurance, or education – amazingly don't do a good job of taking into account human behavior. They have been designed for so-called "rational man," a *homo economicus* who supposedly makes all choices based on self-interest.[47] We end up with "human-incompatible technologies,"[48] or, more simply, human systems designed in ways that assume we are less emotional than we are. Take for example our belief that rewarding people via large bonuses in their jobs makes employees work harder. It turns out that this is not the case – in fact, end-of-year bonuses can cause stress in workers leading them to underperform.[49] We are as much emotional creatures as rational ones.

Recently, however, scientists have discovered that the processes of feeling and thinking are far more intimately connected than was previously thought. The very categories of reason and emotion, typically kept far apart in the traditional science, are being broken down. In their place, more complex and nuanced understandings of how humans feel, know and decide are emerging.[50] Similarly, not so long ago, humans' ability to feel and be emotion-driven in our acts were seen as weaknesses to be overcome. More recent theories see our emotional aspects as essential to who we are as humans and to how we perceive and interact with our world.[51]

Scholars are increasingly recognizing the contribution of emotion to human life. Numerous studies in neuroscience and psychology have shown the complex interactions between our emotional and rational selves, and the emotional and rational selves of others. We are learning that emotions can override reason, and that, conversely, we can be primed to be rational and so override our emotional response.[52] Processes we thought unrelated we know now to be connected and our understanding of how the human mind works is changing and developing dramatically.

Consequently, there is an increasing body of evidence pointing towards the effectiveness of our unthinking response to situations. Rather than over-analyze situations using our slow, rational and conscious thought processes (type two), we can allow our fast, involuntary and automatic thought processes (type one) to respond intuitively to the dynamic situations we find ourselves in and influence our decisions.[53] The more life experience we have the better we are able to trust our gut instinct.

A combination of the environmental structures around us, our brain's evolved capacities, and the rules of thumb we develop lead to our gut feelings.[54] They are our quick, subconscious responses to our environment, shaped by the capabilities of our brains, and based on rules we barely know we are applying. We combine all the information we receive with our past experience and have a hunch about what to do next. We create an intuitive mental representation of the system and situation at hand. Accordingly, our instincts are a part of our systems intelligence. Even if we don't consciously recognize and consider the systems around us, our unconscious is already taking them into account.

Attunement, then, is about relying on our brain's processing capacity and our life experience to feel the situation. It is our ability to be aware of something that is not yet visible or that we are not able to articulate but that is still there and influential. Living in systems is not a dry, rational, academic experience that we can always plan, manage and control. Life in social systems is dynamic, intuitive, and emotional. Change is constant. People come and go; the nature of relationships transforms; systems are reorganized. Overthinking everything can inhibit our systems intelligence from flourishing as always relying on logical reasoning to dictate our actions can obstruct the functioning of our intuitive channels.

It is important to balance belief in our intuition and the benefits we can gain from considered thinking as we engage with systems. In that way we can attend to wholes as well as focus on parts, processes over time as well as moments in time, and on relationships between individual components as much as the components themselves.[55] Happily, if we open our minds to the combination of perceiving and attuning to systems expansive possibilities occur.

Emotional Attunement

There are moments in our lives when large numbers of people share an emotional experience, when we automatically attune. Connected at a fundamental level by our humanity, we come together in joy, in appreciation, in grief. Particular

events can trigger widely shared emotions, sometimes dependent on our nationality, sometimes transcending all the systems to which we belong other than humanity. Moments like the assassination of John F. Kennedy, the fall of the Berlin Wall, the release of Nelson Mandela, and the devastating 2004 tsunami in the Indian Ocean crystalize how united we are with others on the planet. These events and others like them illustrate how emotionally connected we are as a species. At times like these we move beyond the "me" and join the "we." Even when we are not participants in their unfolding but mere observers, we can feel the emotion of such events deeply.

We experience emotional attunement on a daily basis, too. We share a smile with a stranger, we exchange a glance of understanding with a colleague, we feel empathy for a family member. Imagine walking in your local park one sunny afternoon. You might notice a group of children laughing and playing together. Perhaps one of the children smiles at you as he runs over to fetch a stray ball. You smile back. You can't help yourself. You have "caught" the emotion of the group. Emotional contagion is something almost all of us experience. A smile shared with a stranger, misty eyes of our own prompted by watching an emotional reunion at an airport, and the euphoric feelings generated by an uplifting music concert are all examples of this phenomenon.

Interestingly, emotional contagion is now being understood as having its roots in our biology as much as our social interaction, grounded in the complex relationship between our brains' processes and our emotions. The amygdala, the primitive part of our brain, unconsciously to us, processes our reception of signals like tone of voice, posture and facial expressions, priming us to react to the emotion in someone else. The unconscious information processing that the amygdala's pathways carry out is balanced by the conscious processing our prefrontal cortex, or rational, part of our brain does.[56] We can use our rational processes to override our more instinctive reactions to some degree. For example, if a particular person at our workplace is always in a bad mood, we may consciously tell ourselves that we are not going to let their irritability affect us today – we override our body's primitive response to another's emotional state. Similarly, we can rationally choose to sidestep our initial emotional reaction to someone's tears in order to develop more considered empathy as we explore the reasons for them.

Recently, another part of the brain – the vagus nerve – has also received attention in connection with emotional contagion. The vagus nerve connects the mind and body through the central nervous system. When baseball pitchers take a deep breath on the mound before letting loose a fastball, their vagus nerve is firing, slowing their heart rate and calming their mind. In lab tests, the same nerve lights up when people feel compassion. Hearing another person's sad or inspiring story affects us at a biological level. These findings, and other supporting research, suggest that we are wired to care and that feelings are contagious.[57]

In some ways, the idea of emotional contagion is counterintuitive. Most of us, if pressed, would explain our emotions as coming from within us. We see them as deeply personal responses to events and situations generated by our personality. But emotional contagion tells us that emotions can come from the outside in. That is, other people's expressions of emotion or particular events cause us to feel a certain way, and often that's a process we have little control over. Interestingly, and consistent with the idea of varying degrees of intelligence, some people seem to have more contagious emotions than others. Rousing public speakers, talented singers, and some teachers, for example, have the ability to draw us in and take us on an emotional journey with them.[58]

Desmond Tutu is such a man. He is able to convey and express emotions in such a way that others feel the same emotions as deeply as he does. He connects with others at a fundamental level. A quick glance in the index of the authorized biography *Tutu*, finds the subheading "personal characteristics", followed by a list of words like "compassion," "courage," "empathy," "generosity," "humor," "loyalty," "wisdom" and so on. The biography is full of anecdotes of people who have been moved by the Archbishop.

Not only is Tutu skillful in emotionally attuning himself to his companions and surroundings though, he also has the ability to help others to attune. The Dalai Lama, describes him as playful and jovial but also serious in such a way that "whenever he joins, the atmosphere completely changes."[59] When Tutu spoke at a government dinner in Rwanda after that country's genocide his audience (largely Tutsi) expected a serious speech acknowledging the massacre of their people. But, having toured the prisons that day, Tutu knew he needed to balance criticism of the nation's treatment of accused Hutus with empathy towards the Tutsi people's experiences. To the surprise of the audience he began with a joke about the ridiculousness of racism. Pointing out his own large nose, he made fun of a system that would put large-nosed people in power and require small-nosed people to attend small-nose only universities. The absurdities he shared had the audience laughing, until he said "Oh, I hear in Rwanda you tell whether you are Tutsi or Hutu by the shape of your nose." He went on to describe how those with one shaped nose were treated like animals by those with the other. The emotional impact was powerful, one audience member noting that belly laughs became nervous titters and then silence.[60] Tutu attuned the audience to the negative system created in Rwanda by using humor to first make them receptive to his message, by connecting with them emotionally.

Cognitive Attunement

Few of us are routinely attuned to the processes of our emotions, and even fewer of us to the processes of our minds. We often lack what psychologists call "mindfulness". Mindfulness is a two-part process where we first regulate our attention so we notice how we are feeling and behaving, and then cultivate an attitude of openness to the experience. When we are mindful we are non-elaborative, non-judgmental and present-centered.[61] We are opening our minds. For Desmond Tutu, mindfulness comes through prayer. He regularly takes opportunities to create a space where he can attune to his thoughts, even if that means covering himself with a sheet in a shared bedroom.[62]

In essence, the practice of mindfulness is the process of bringing quality attention to moment-by-moment experience. It involves acknowledging and accepting our current state of mind for what it is. The idea is that we create a mental space between perception and response, so we can observe our thoughts and feelings as they occur but not react to them unthinkingly.[63] That way we can better understand how and why we feel and think like we do. Mindfulness is the opposite of the mindlessness that plagues

most of us on a daily basis, that sense we have of being on automatic pilot as we react unthinkingly to life.[64] It can help us to learn to act in new ways. Consequently, it can lead us to make better decisions for our life in systems.[65]

Part of attunement is the ability to be aware of our thinking. While we don't generally reflect on our thinking processes regularly, we are starting to find out the possibilities this opens us. In part, that's because our thought processes are increasingly at the forefront of researchers' interest. Happiness researchers are finding that we can change the way we feel by changing the way we think. Neuroscientists are showing us how our brain works. Psychologists are figuring out what strategies we might use to interfere with its sometimes-destructive automatic processes. Researchers from a variety of fields are investigating how we can combine gut instinct and logical reasoning to optimize our decision-making.[66]

Physical Attunement

The night before the first Truth and Reconciliation Commission hearing, Archbishop Tutu spoke to journalists of the butterflies in his stomach. He also described a tingling sensation throughout his body, something he believed denoted the positive possibilities ahead. In systems intelligence terms, he was physically attuned. He felt and understood the processes going on in his own body.

Most of us pay only fleeting attention to how our bodies react to systems. We might notice our heart racing before we enter a situation we are nervous about, or we might sense our muscles relaxing as we reunite with a loved one, but on a moment-to-moment basis we tend to tune out to what our body is telling us. The hectic nature of daily life tramples our ability to listen to our physical signals.

Perhaps surprisingly, new technologies are helping to change that. Innovative products are making inroads in helping us to understand and attune to our bodies as systems. The "self-tracking" movement collects data about the human body. While many organizations and governments religiously use metrics to chart their progress towards goals, individuals tend to be more haphazard in their approach. Sure we might weigh ourselves if we are trying to lose weight, or keep a rough tab on how far we run if we are training for an event, but generally we know very little about ourselves in numerical terms. Advances in both software and hardware, however, have enabled self-trackers to gather and analyze data about themselves like never before.

The fundamental belief of the self-tracking or self-quantifying movement is that knowledge is power. If people know exactly how much sleep they are getting, how much caffeine they are drinking, how their mood changes depending on what they do, how much exercise they are getting and so on, they can improve their lives. That's because they can see how increasing and decreasing particular activities affects their overall wellbeing or their achieving of specific goals. In other words, it allows them to see the interrelationships in their lives and how their bodies and their lifestyle work as a system. It allows them to attune themselves to, well, themselves.

Opening Your Attunement Channels

Consider which systems in your life you feel most comfortable in.
What is it about you or those systems that give you this feeling?
How important is gut instinct to you in those systems?
How much do you trust your gut instinct in situations where you feel less comfortable?

Next time you enter a room full of people:
How much does your instinct tell you about the mood in the room?
How does the system in the room affect you physically?
What emotions does joining the group bring up in you?
See if you can sense what the connections are between people.
What are the unarticulated thoughts that come to your mind about the group dynamics?

In an appropriate systems context (perhaps at a family gathering or a work function):
Close your eyes and take a moment to feel the atmosphere.
Open your eyes and check if what you see matches your feel of the situation.
What are the clues and cues that lead you to make your assessment?

During an interaction of your own
Try to notice what your intuition is telling you about the situation.
Are you carrying patterns of behavior from another system to this one? Are they effective patterns in this new context?
Ask *"What is this system right now?"* as opposed to assuming what it is from past experience.
How do you think others feel about your impact on the situation?

Once we have opened our attunement channels we need to orient our senses towards feeling the dynamics of the systems around us. We need to feel what is going on in those systems, and, at the same, time, feel our own reactions and contributions to them. That involves attuning to ourselves, others and the systems we share.

Attuning to Ourselves

Recall a time when you have watched a young child imitate an adult. Perhaps you saw a toddler try to copy a parent as he or she used a computer, drove a car, or prepared dinner. Perhaps you saw children playing house or doctors or shops by mimicking the behavior they have seen in adults. When we experience this phenomenon we are seeing children's natural systems intelligence at work. They are figuring out how context – how being in different systems – alters one's behavior. They step from their normal family system into an alternative system through imitation. In the process, they learn by doing and adjust their mental image of themselves to the imaginary system at hand. In effect, they are attuning to themselves as they work out how their behavior needs to adjust to participate in different social systems.

By the time we become adults, we are so well socialized into the systems around us this attuning process has become automatic. We no longer need to stop and think about how we should behave in different contexts. We pay little attention to the ways we change or don't change from context to context. Yet, what if we did start to attend to our own behavior? While experience in adjusting our behavior to the system at hand provides a great shortcut to action, we are also in danger of dulling our attunement processes. In other words, we adjust so quickly and automatically to the situation as we know it that we don't always see the situation as it actually is or ourselves as we really are. Imagine the benefits of rediscovering our childhood capacity for attunement.

That is not to say that adults don't attune – some people attune to themselves pretty regularly. Before a sports game, for example, an athlete might go through pre-game rituals. Besides practicing, exercising, and eating right – the physical things an athlete does to prepare for a big occasion – there are the mental activities that prepare them for the sporting occasion. [67] Actors, singers and other performers have similar rituals that are about self-attunement. Like athletes, they might pray, meditate, or visualize; they might eat the same meals, wear the same clothes, or carry out the same yoga moves prior to their performance. Whatever they do, the purpose is the same – to build confidence and acuity. They want to be so focused, so attuned, that they give of their best. They want to achieve flow, that state where they are effortlessly absorbed in their activity to the best of their ability.[68]

It's not just famous people or high-level performers that attune to themselves though. Those of us who have performance aspects to our lives do the same thing to a certain extent. Sales people, teachers, and gym class instructors all pep themselves up one way or another before engaging in their activities. Most people who participate in public speaking do the same. It might just be a matter of taking several deep breaths to calm the nerves; nevertheless, it is attunement.

But why limit our sense of mental, physical, and emotional attunement to moments of performance, which many of us do our best to avoid anyway? If we attune to our whole state more regularly, we will be more likely to interact successfully with others and the systems around us. The automatic, subconscious nature of our everyday routines means we pay little attention to the combined state of our mental, emotional and physical wellbeing. We just fall back on set patterns. We say the same things to those who serve us in shops in the same tone with the same lack of attention. We drive our cars in the same programmed way with our minds racing. We do not attend, we do not focus, we do not listen to how our being (mind, body and spirit) is chugging along.

Yet, the limitations of our brains make it very important for us to attune to ourselves as a system. We humans are afflicted with a number of unconscious biases, biases that can make it difficult for us to behave with systems intelligence. These biases detract from our ability to be considerate to others, to take their thoughts into account and approach them with warmth and acceptance. With an increased sense of attunement to our own mental processes, however, we are more likely to be alert to and so able to compensate for our cognitive limitations.

The standard attribution error, for example, is a very common bias. An extensive body of work in psychology research looks at how we make snap, fallible, judgments. Much of it concerns *attribution theory*, which explains how we observe behavior and then reason back to the cause of that behavior – usually in a very rapid, unconscious process. [69] What scientists have found is that most people attribute negative behavior in others to their *disposition*. John slept in and was late for work, therefore John is lazy. My partner never takes me out for a romantic dinner, therefore my partner is unromantic. The woman in the bakery never chats to me when I buy a pastry, therefore she is rude. In contrast, most of us attribute our own negative behaviors to the *situation*. I slept in late and was late for work because there was a power cut. I never take my partner out for a romantic dinner because I am saving money. I never chat with the woman in the store because I am busy.

Attribution involves labeling people with descriptions based on our limited knowledge of them. The process of labeling people is very powerful. First impressions are made in the first few seconds of meeting someone and it is

extremely difficult to change them. Yet, we bristle when people seem to have the "wrong" impression of us, because we can explain our own actions in the context of our lives, in the context of the systems that we live in. When we make attribution errors, we are limiting the potential for systems intelligent behavior because we are not stopping to think about the actions of others in situational, contextual, systemic terms – instead we make judgments about their character. If everybody in the system is doing this, the relationships between the individuals never have a chance to fully flourish. Psychologist Philip Zimbardo stresses that people need to practice "attributional charity."[70] In other words, we need to make a conscious effort to look to the situation rather than the person before we attribute blame and make judgments.

When people first hear about attribution errors, they commonly think of humans as being self-serving – finding excuses for their own behavior while laying blame at the personality of others. However, the situation is more complex than this. Social psychologists have theorized that much of the difference in attribution comes from the available information we have for perceiving ourselves as compared to others.[71]

When we consider our own behavior we are privy to far more information that when we consider the behavior of others. We know our own goals, motivations and intentions. If we happen to be late to work on the day we are due to give a presentation because of a traffic jam, we know whether our intentions were to be on time and it really was the traffic that prevented us from making it or not. We can make a correct attribution about our own behavior. However, if our colleague was late in the reverse situation, we are more likely to attribute their lateness to deliberate avoidance. Why? Because we focus on the end result of their actions. We can see they didn't arrive on time and we assume that their intention was to avoid the visit. When we make judgments about ourselves, we pay attention to our internal thoughts and feelings, whereas when we judge others we rely on what we see externally and what we assume is going on internally (because we cannot ever know what they really think). There is an asymmetry of information that can be detrimental to our choices in systems.

Yet if we are attuned to how our mind works we can compensate for the shortcuts it takes. We can make a deliberate choice to let others have a voice before we rush to judgment. We can cultivate fairness and generosity of spirit in interactions with others. We can practice mindfulness. According to Archbishop Desmond Tutu, incorporating mindfulness into our daily life is a matter of choice. He believes all people are essentially good but continually face a choice whether to do good or to do wrong, such as by participating in oppressive systems. How do people choose how to act? Says Tutu, "Well, how do you learn to swim? You learn to swim by swimming. How do you learn to play the violin? You learn to play the violin by playing the violin. Trust your instincts. Trust your intuitions. Where you would have wanted to give a scathing reply, just try once to bite your tongue. One little victory helps you to get to the next victory."[72]

Tutu practices what he preaches. He attunes to his own motivations and so opens himself up to experience people with fairness, warmth and acceptance. Such an approach has enabled him to be honest about his own shortcomings and so surmount them. He tells of how at the outset of the Truth and Reconciliation Commission, he and the others involved spent too much time jostling for position, trying to impress one another with their abilities and seriousness. He critiques his lack of attunement to the effects of appointing so many white staff to the Commission. He describes his roller coaster emotions and the physical toll the work of the Commission had on his body, and the comfort and renewal he was able to find in his faith.[73]

Being able to attune to ourselves means that we are better able to feel our own response to a systemic situation. We are aware of how our body is responding, our mind's thoughts, and our emotional reactions. Because we are attuned we can combine both reason and instincts to respond to what unfolds. Of course, attuning to ourselves is only part of the story because we are not alone in systems. We share them with other people and so we need to attune with others' experience of systems, too.

Attuning to Others

Some years ago on a television program an interviewer spoke to a female production line worker about her job. The worker explained that she had been at the factory for fifteen years or so since leaving school. The interviewer asked her what she did for her job and she replied that she took packets of biscuits off a conveyor belt and put them into cardboard boxes. Had she always done the same job, asked the interviewer? Yes, she replied. And did she enjoy it? The worker enthusiastically said she did, commenting how friendly her co-workers were and how much fun they had. In a disbelieving tone, the interviewer said "Really? Don't you find it a bit boring?" "On no," said the worker. "Sometimes they change the biscuits."[74]

Most people's first instinct when they hear of this exchange is to laugh at the factory worker's apparent naiveté, but this story is a wonderful lesson in attunement. Just because we personally might find packing biscuits boring, we shouldn't assume that everyone feels this way. We are too eager to assume that others share our motivations, needs, and outlook. We are too quick to dismiss or misunderstand the emotional experiences of others when they are not like our own. When we overcome these impulses towards snap judgments and instead cultivate an empathetic connection, we are attuning to others.

The ability to attune to others, like all aspects of our systems intelligence, is both a gift we are born with and a skill we can improve. Psychologist Barbara Fredrickson's research, for example, has demonstrated that changing the ways we connect changes our capacity to connect by actually rewiring our neural pathways. If we don't make the opportunity or effort to attune with others we diminish our ability to do so. Thankfully, the reverse is also true. The more we attune, the more capable we are of attuning. Studies have also shown that increased warmth and tenderness towards others and ourselves can lead to improvement in our cardiovascular system via the vagus nerve. As a result, the more attuned to others we become, Fredrickson argues, the healthier we become, and vice versa.[75]

This understanding of the mutually-forming and increasingly-connected relationship between others and ourselves is supported by many studies in the fast-growing field of social neuroscience. Social neuroscience is concerned with the study of brain activity related to social interactions.[76] It examines how biology influences behavior but also how social behavior changes biology.[77] The main premise of social neuroscience is that the brain (a biological entity) may develop and operate differently depending on social context. A range of experiments from the 1970s onward, together with the development of new brain imaging technologies, have provided fresh insight into how this occurs. They confirm that what happens to us socially affects us physically. Think of the consequences of hurt feelings, broken hearts, group laughter – we physically feel the results of social interactions. Humans are not only connected emotionally, we are actually physiologically linked. In other words, when we come together we create a system that has a number of different inputs.

Neuroscience research has opened up some amazing discoveries that support the importance of attunement. One such discovery is the presence of mirror neurons.[78] Mirror neurons are the neurons in the brain that become active in response to the actions of others. For example, experiments show that when observing someone reaching for a fresh cup of tea, the observers' motor cortex of the brain will become slightly active, as if they themselves were reaching for the cup.[79] That is, other people's actions communicate directly with our brain at an unconscious level creating a system. If we can alter the processes of one another's brains simply as a result of watching one another, imagine, then, the impact of daily life when we are awash in social signals.

Importantly, people do not always express themselves through words. Studies show that by far the majority of what we communicate is non-verbal. We attune to what other people are feeling by paying attention to their tone of voice, body language, touch, use of personal space, and facial expressions. Most of the messages we receive through these channels, as opposed to the words that people say, are processed without our conscious awareness. In fact, many of the non-verbal messages we receive are messages that the person is not even aware that they are sending. Professor of Psychology Paul Ekman has devoted much of his professional life to understanding micro expressions, the fleeting facial expressions that convey our underlying emotions. Ekman's studies show that these flashes of emotion are not culturally based,  but common to all humans.[80] Some of us are more attuned to other people's micro expressions than others, but Ekman's work demonstrates that we can be trained in reading micro expressions.

Catching people's fleeting expression of emotions is part of our capacity for empathy. Empathy is a natural aspect of our humanity, and the absence of empathy is generally considered to be a personality disorder.[81] It is also an essential component of systems because it creates warmth, acceptance and considerateness in relationships. Empathy is what makes us feel concern for the welfare of others, even when we do not personally know them. For example, children when asked in an experiment if they wanted a sticker for themselves or if they would also like to give one to another person present almost always chose to have both participants receive stickers.[82] As psychologist Gird Gigerenzer notes, we humans not only want to share with unfamiliar people, we even get angry when strangers don't share.

Our ability to empathize with others, however, often depends on how like us they are. The brain is wired to look for confirmatory evidence that our perception is right, and our thought processes help us to cook the facts in our favor, hence our fallibility towards attribution errors. For example, we will retrieve memories that confirm whatever point we are making and ignore those that refute it. In other words, we unconsciously tend to expose ourselves to information that confirms our perception of the world, so reinforcing our beliefs. Nowhere is that more obvious than when we choose the company we keep. Humans want to surround themselves with people who not only like them, but are like them.[83] We befriend people who will mostly agree with us.

Consequently, it is far easier to empathize with our friends. For the most part, they think like us, so to imagine how they are feeling in different situations is not such a stretch. But what do we know about the assistant in the shop, the passengers on the train, the driver in the car next to us? These people, too, are connected with us. When we enter the shop, the train carriage, the car we begin a relationship with others in those systems. Yet they are not people we have chosen to interact with. They neither know nor like us. We don't know if their beliefs and perceptions are close to ours or not. As a result, we have to make an effort to attune ourselves to them.

This is an aspect of attunement that Archbishop Tutu deliberately practices. He has often spoken about the need to cultivate empathy with one's enemies. "If you want peace," he said, "you don't talk to your friends. You talk to your enemies."[84] One of the main tenets of Tutu's life has been his commitment to *ubuntu*, the traditional African concept of interconnectedness. Often poorly translated into English as "community" its richness is perhaps better captured as "a person understands that he or she needs the person in front of them to be who they are."[85] It is an understanding of the systemic nature of human relationships. The reconciliation and forgiveness process he drove in South Africa was about bringing bitter enemies to the table so the truth could set them free to move forward. Many of the blacks who forgave their persecutors did so because of a deep belief in *ubuntu*. For them, perpetrators and victims were inextricably linked and it was important to make the world whole again by having each acknowledge the humanity in the other.[86]

Reading Intentions and Expectations

Reading intentions is part of life in systems. Remarkably we have the capacity to read intentions even as infants. A wealth of research on infant behavior explores how tiny babies develop systemic relationships with their primary caregiver, [87] principally through making eye contact. Psychologist Simon Baron-Cohen argues that eye contact allows the baby to activate his or her "intentionality detector" – the infant's means for reading the intentions of others.[88] Others have pointed out that both the verbal and non-verbal connection between mother and baby equate to a process of co-creativity where they are "working together for the purpose of growth."[89] The infant's innate systems intelligence leads it to seek out connections and inputs from its environment and to respond to those.

We carry that ability into adulthood. In daily life, we are continuously, both consciously and unconsciously, processing how we feel, what we think, what we expect and how we perceive others to be thinking, feeling and anticipating. We are alive to the array of social cues that are thrown at us in any interaction. Most of the time, we make sense of them and respond appropriately. We are especially good at doing so when we are within familiar systems. That's how we figure out how to respond when our co-worker hands us a single red rose. Our reaction will likely be different to how we would respond if our spouse or our parent or our friend gave us the same flower. Without conscious thought, we can sense what is going on and recognize people's emotions. This enables us to generate expectations or predict behaviors, two skills essential for living in systems.

As well as reading the intentions, generating expectations, and predicting behaviors *of* others we also create expectations *in* others. Our own actions within  any system contribute to the rhythm of a situation. We often overlook the power of the unconscious messages we send, but if we stop and think about it we can recall their impact. Think of the difference physically, emotionally and mentally when we go into a workplace meeting excited about what might unfold versus dragging ourselves there out of a sense of obligation, anticipating a negative experience. When we adopt 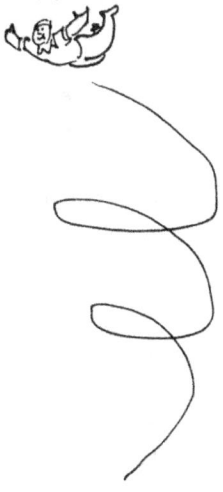 either of these orientations we set the mood for ourselves, but we also affect the system as it unfolds. Others present will unconsciously feed off our energy levels. Acting systems intelligently means attempting to create a positive spiral of expectations rather than a negative one.

The ability to read intentions and create expectations can be something of a double-edged sword. On the one hand, it allows us to get on with life in systems, giving us a kind of short cut to understanding a situation. On the other, it can fool us into believing what really are acts of our imagination. We have to understand that it is possible for us to read situations incorrectly. We have expectations and imagine what the other is thinking, but we have no way of confirming that without interaction. It is important that we do no over-rely on our own answers and treat our expectations and imaginings as fixed and certain. The intentions we ascribe to others might be inaccurate. It is systems intelligent, in other words, to be aware of our attunement process and alert to the traps we might fall into.

Critics of the Truth and Reconciliation process, for example, often complained that Archbishop Tutu put too much emphasis on Christianity. For his critics, Tutu's focus on forgiveness seemed too grounded in theology. But journalist Antjie Krog, who followed the Commission closely, argues that this complaint misunderstands the African psyche. White people tended to misread Tutu as imposing his religious views on others. Black participants understood that forgiveness and reconciliation were needed to restore their country's humanity because they shared his belief in the concept of *ubuntu*. They were more attuned to Tutu's intent and shared his expectations of the process.

While we are busy building our own expectations of others, others are of course doing the same of us. The expectations that we communicate to them affect their view of us and their behavior towards us, and so the outcomes in the system, as the research of Robert Rosenthal shows.[90]

In 1968 Harvard psychologist Robert Rosenthal and colleague Lenore Jacobson conducted a now classic study that looked at how teachers' expectations of children shape how those children perform at school. The researchers tested elementary school children and told their teachers at the start of the academic year that the test scores predicted which children would bloom intellectually during the school year. In fact, the researchers had randomly assigned twenty percent of the children as bloomers. The teachers were deceived on two counts – one, the test taken by the children did not predict intellectual potential and, two, the names they were given of the so-called bloomers bore no relation to the test scores. The teachers then taught their classes as usual.

When the students were retested at the end of the year those who had been identified as intellectual bloomers did significantly better in measurements of intellectual growth than those in the control group. The results showed that those of whom more was expected delivered. In effect, the results indicated that when teachers expect students to do well and show intellectual growth, they do; when teachers do not have such expectations, performance and growth are not so encouraged and may in fact be discouraged in a variety of ways.

Unconsciously, the teachers had responded to the students based on the information they had been given about them. They were encouraging and positive with the "good" students, and more dismissive and perfunctory with the "bad" students. The teachers' opinions about the students affected how they engaged with their pupils, their expectations creating a kind of self-fulfilling prophecy. Rosenthal's results have been replicated in many systemic settings, from elementary school to college and even military academies.

What are the lessons of this research? There is no easy fix to the biases it reveals. It is frustrating to know that teacher expectations affect student performance yet to not have an answer as to how to avoid creating and communicating these expectations. In essence, it seems to come down to the intangible connections involved in interpersonal connection between teacher and student. Somewhere in their interactions, in the system created between teacher and student, expectations are formed and conveyed and the effects of those are extremely powerful. Consequently, many educational and psychology researchers continue to wrestle with issues that will help teachers deal with this effect.[91]

While many studies show the power of unconscious negative expectations, we can take heart from the fact that the reverse is also true. Just as low expectations can lead to low performance, so high expectations can lead to excellence. Employees' work performance, for example, grows across a range of measures when their managers give a genuine, consistent message about their great potential.

Part of being sensitive to the system of interaction, then, is working with expectations and intentions, and understanding how they shape a situation. Instead of assuming we know how others will behave from previous patterns, we can attune ourselves to the moment in the moment. We can make an effort to assess whether we are sensing the system or systems at work, or just what we expect to be there. The systems intelligent recipe for creating an uplifting spiral is to expect a lot from people and reinforce this with positive messages. If we make a conscious effort to form positive expectations of people, we will unconsciously communicate those and they may well instinctually live up to our expectations.

Attuning to Systems

When Archbishop Tutu headed the Truth and Reconciliation Commission in South Africa, the healing process implemented after the collapse of apartheid, he oversaw the creation of a remarkable system of justice and forgiveness. Tutu describes the commission as "a third way" – an alternative to the persecution and punishment model of justice evidenced by the Nuremberg trials following World War Two and the kind of national amnesia that a blanket amnesty would create.[92] Managing the reconciliation process was about the delicate creation of a system, and Tutu was very attuned to the nuances of the process.

The Commission knew the first hearing, in particular, was going to be a momentous event, one that "would shape subsequent hearings positively or negatively" and so they aimed to be fair and take into account the perspectives of the many parties present.[93] The group decided to hold an interfaith service the day before, and Tutu spoke in several languages during the service to stress that the Commission belonged to all. The leadership also chose to hold the meeting in the Eastern Cape because that was the symbolic birthplace of black resistance and correspondingly a place where many of apartheid's atrocities had been viciously enforced. Victims were deliberately invited to speak first to symbolize their being given a voice. The victims selected represented differing political views, both genders, different regions, and young and old. To create an atmosphere of calmness, affirmation and openness, cross-examination of witnesses was not allowed. At the end of the first day, and each day he presided over, Tutu summarized the prevailing mood and its main accomplishments.[94]

The dignity and sensitivity with which Archbishop Tutu ran the Truth and Reconciliation Commission was in many ways a reflection of an ability to attune to the systems around him that he had exemplified all his life. When the young Desmond Tutu attended the mixed race school at which his father was headmaster, he noticed that children of different colored skins were able to get along. He was shocked and intrigued when he saw a white priest tip his hat to his black, domestic cleaner mother. These experiences stuck with him because they were so precisely out of tune with the normal system around him, the injustices of apartheid.

In the mid-1970s, Tutu stepped forward as a leader and became a spokesperson for social justice, at some risk to his own freedoms. In this new role, he attuned himself to the general public's emotional response to the anti-apartheid fight by advocating only non-violent means by which to overthrow the system. He encouraged protests, demonstrations, boycotts, civil disobedience and disinvestment as effective ways to pressure the government, and always renounced violent options.[95] He also constantly wrote and spoke of reconciliation as the path forward. His stance earned him respect at home and abroad, including the Nobel Peace Prize in 1984.

In other words, Tutu attended and attuned to the overlapping systems present and the new system being co-created. As an individual he placed himself in the bigger picture. Interestingly, he described his role as leader of a system to be a servant to that system. By this he meant that he sought to meet the needs of others, did not expect self-glorification, and worked for the good of the system.[96] Archbishop Desmond Tutu exemplifies how even in a difficult situation we can bring about change by attuning to the systems around us.

We don't have to be as gifted or as famous or as respected as Desmond Tutu to develop systems attunement, however. We all have the ability to attune to our environment. Like many aspects of systems intelligence, attuning to our surroundings is something that we do regularly without being aware of it or labeling it such. Recall the last time you walked into a room full of people. Chances are within moments of entering you had unconsciously registered whether the prevailing mood was one of joy, anger, sadness or something else. Consider how you are invariably aware when you interact with people who have just argued even when no argument is referred to. Think about times  when you have felt welcome or unwelcome as you entered a meeting or a store. Something about our receptiveness to the environment conveys to us the atmosphere. We can subconsciously hear, taste, and feel the mood in particular situations. Attuning is an unconscious process that is part of our daily lives, but it is a process that we can draw on more effectively when we understand its impact and application.

Aviation crews, for example, are often trained in what that field calls "situation awareness." Successful flight crews need to be aware of their environment, understand what is going on around them, figure out what is important and accurately imagine what might happen next.[97] This is not as simple as seeing what is occurring in the flight environment as it is a whole body experience. Crews absorb information about the environment via "visual, aural, tactile, olfactory or taste receptors."[98] A change in the hum of an engine, a flickering light, or a vibrating instrument can be crucial clues as to the functioning of the system. In systems intelligence terms, they need to be attuned to the system created in the process of flying a plane.

Just how valuable a skill the ability to attune to a system is can be is perhaps best illustrated by its absence. Autistic people often lack the capacity to make judgments about social contexts. Instead of adjusting their behavior according to a situation as it unfolds, they try to learn and apply rules.[99] But rote application of rules is a poor substitute to instinctually feeling the rhythm of social experiences. Psychologists refer to the inability to make automatic interpretations of events that take into consideration the mental states, desires and beliefs of others as "mindblindness."[100] Few of us suffer from mindblindness, but at times, such as when we experience new situations, we can perceive the social world as somewhat confusing. Because the systems around us are always changing we need to develop capabilities for handling our lives within systems, irrespective of the system. When we can attune and so adapt to the system at hand, that is systems intelligence. We can not only learn to attune to our family, our workplace, our groups of friends, but also the many different contexts and the bigger systems we find ourselves in.

Generally, though, in daily life we participate in a range of systems we are comfortable with – schools, workplaces, relationships, families and so on. Often they have become so familiar and comfortable to us that we take them for granted. Consequently, they slip to the borders of our consciousness. This can be good in the sense that it releases energy for us to focus on other things. We don't spend excessive amounts of time considering all the nuances of the relationships that constitute our workplace, for example. However, there are drawbacks, too, to our inattention.

For one, even where systems are well intentioned and seem to be working well, they can fail in the long run because they are unattended to. Thus when the free-market economies of many western nations went into a recession in 2008, many citizens were surprised. Most of us were happy to allow the system to run its course while we acquired the latest gadgets and saw our housing values rise. We didn't bother ourselves with the details of its workings until we felt the consequence of its failure. Similarly, historically most of us paid little attention to the disposal of waste in our societies until the toxic effects of landfills and the impact of long-lasting plastics and other man-made substances became widely known. It is only when those who are attuned to the consequences of systems, both intended and unintended, manage to inform the rest of us that we become conscious of and can collectively act to change them.

For another, if we are not attuned it is easy to absolve ourselves of responsibility in a system. In the wake of the collapse of apartheid in South Africa many of those who had not opposed the regime claimed that they did not know how bad things were. Tutu allows that many whites grew up knowing no other system, and had no motivation to question a system that bought them privilege and affluence. He notes, too, that apartheid was a very sophisticated system. Black townships and so black oppression were out of sight of most whites. Even more powerful, however, was the way that apartheid ensured that institutions of authority upheld the status quo. Most people were excluded from political decision-making and therefore social and economic influence. The media was used to support the regime. People became conditioned to the system at hand and did not attune to the big picture.[101]

As a consequence each person separately reacted to the system without seeing the cumulative overall effect of the reactive behaviors on others. As a result of this lack of attunement, we end up unable to collaboratively turn our efforts to the system itself. We each do our own individual thing, not realizing we are all dissatisfied with how the system is working.

The wonderful image of a school of fish being chased by a single predator, who when they work together are able to turn on their hunter captures something of this idea. The larger fish is the faceless system at work; the school of small fish illustrates the power of collective over individual action.

From Attunement to Reflection

Attunement is a fundamental orientation process that links individuals to others and to a bigger picture. It occurs on multiple levels – we attune emotionally, cognitively and physically. Attunement is whole of being experience – it involves our minds, our bodies and our emotions. When we attune to others we feel a sense of harmony or resonance with them. We experience empathy and compassion. As a consequence of this connection, we subtly adjust our demeanor, our actions and our reactions in concurrence with the system we experience. We become warm and accepting, considerate, and thoughtful both of others and the situation at hand. That's systems intelligence in action.

But our systems perception and attunement skills – the sensing aspects of our systems intelligence – are just part of the picture. Our systems intelligence can be enhanced further if we also develop our thinking skills, and it is the capacity we have for reflection that we turn to next.

Attunement: What Can I do Today?

Attuning to yourself:
Pay attention to how your mind, body and emotions react to group situations. Think about what is causing the reactions and it might be useful to adjust your responses. How can you be more approachable, warm, fair, considerate?

Pay attention to what you read into the other people's intentions by observing them. Does what you expect occur? Do you think your expectations are affecting how you interpret what you see? Can you practice attributional charity?

How might you change your behavior if you knew people's intentions were different from what you think they are?

Attuning to others:
See if you can sense what the other(s) expect of you.

Watch others in a system interact (e.g. colleagues, family members).
Pay attention to the expectations you develop about how the interaction will go. Ask yourself, *"What expectations am I communicating to others?"*

Consider how your reading of others' intentions is affecting your own behavior. Think of ways to develop and communicate positive expectations.

Take into account how others might be seeing, thinking and feeling about a situation. Let them have a voice rather than assume you know their intentions.
Make an effort to empathize with others, especially those who are not like you. Be generous in your interactions.

Attuning to systems:
Try to get a sense of the big picture. Think about what is affecting your behavior and the behavior of others beyond your interpersonal relationship.

Act in ways that take into account multiple perspectives.
Make an effort to feel how the systems around you are working. Notice if a system is functioning poorly or creating negative outcomes. Attend to the whole, not just your place in it.

Reflection

"We had come to the farmland to eat deliberately. We'd discussed for several years what that would actually mean...we were going to spend a year integrating our food choices with our family values..." ~ Barbara Kingsolver[102]

What are you having for dinner tonight? Meat? Vegetables? Pasta? Whatever it is you are planning to eat this evening, do you know where it comes from? For most of us, beyond the superficial answer of the supermarket, the answer is probably no. The majority of people buy food for their meals without much thought about its origin. We might check the fat content, the best before date, and the price, but we rarely take the time to reflect on where the tomatoes, or lamb chops, or bag of coffee beans came from. We accept the choices put in front of us and make our selection without considering the system of food production we are participating in and how our decisions might be affecting that and other systems.

Our ignorance is in some ways excusable. It seems unrealistic to expect to understand the workings of every system within which we participate. Yet, if we take the time to consider both the system at hand and our own contribution to it – if we take the time to reflect – we open up the possibility of making informed decisions about our behavior rather than simply acting uncritically. Seeing and attuning to the systems around us, enables a better contribution to their constructive flourishing because we have a clearer idea of the impact of our actions. But to accompany a new way of seeing and sensing the world, we also need new ways of thinking. Reflection is a key capacity that helps us to choose systems-commensurate actions. It allows us to ask "what have I done?" or "what is my responsibility?" Reflecting on the systems around us, and our actions in those systems, moves us towards living with systems intelligence.

That's certainly what author Barbara Kingsolver and her family found when they reflected on their role in the food chain, a process that led to a whole new way of feeding themselves. The family had been living in Tuscon, Arizona, a heavily populated oasis in the desert. In Tuscon, almost every foodstuff comes to town in a refrigerated vehicle. Drinking water either comes from a non-renewable fossil aquifer or is siphoned off the Colorado river, via an open canal that traverses some of the driest land in the US.[103] At what environmental, financial and social cost, wondered the Kingsolvers?

As the family reflected on the process of how food was brought to their table, they uncovered some startling information. They learned that the majority of farmed land in the US is now being used for corn and soybean crops, in part because of generous government subsidies. Thanks to the financial incentives and the use of pesticides and fertilizer, yields have increased hugely. As a result, US farmers produce too much corn and soybeans for Americans to eat, so the surplus production has instead become raw material for extractive industries. It is mined for oils, syrups and starches; used to intensively farm beef, produce soft drinks and other junk foods; and even made into packaging materials.

In many ways this is an agricultural success story. But in other ways it is a disaster. The incentives to grow corn and soy mean other food crops are neglected. The over production that diverts the extracts to other industries means that once grass-fed animals are being raised on something that is not a natural food for their species, with unknown consequences for human health. The very sugary excess corn syrup finds its way into many processed foods. This is happening at the same time that the US government is promoting healthy eating and the latest health figures suggest that this generation of children will be the first to have a shorter life expectancy than their parents largely thanks to their diet.[104]

The Kingsolvers knew they couldn't miraculously fix the problems they saw with the industrial food pipeline. Nevertheless, the connections they uncovered between the food they were eating and the environmental and social costs of its production made them want to act in ways that were more aligned with their values. So the family decided to become more conscious consumers. They wanted to see if it was possible to live the values that they espoused and what the consequences of that might be.

In his book *What Intelligence Tests Miss*, Professor Keith Stanovich tells the sorry tales of two smart, educated men who acted foolishly by making repeated bad investments on the stock market. He uses these examples to illustrate that what we understand as intelligence is not enough to explain our ability to make successful and sensible decisions in life. Such foolishness is all around us. Highly educated people make poor financial decisions, our clever neighbors fall for scam artists, bright family members buy miracle pills to cure their baldness. People can be smart but still do dumb things, and the reason for that is because not everyone who is intelligent by traditional measures is fully using their reflective mind.

The reflective mind is the part of cognition that controls the rationality of our behavior. We may well be talented at solving mathematical equations or writing articles for newspapers as Stanovich's two investors were, but that doesn't mean we are talented at adapting our actions wisely to our environment. To be rational, we must have well-calibrated beliefs and act appropriately on those beliefs to achieve our goals.[105] Accordingly, Stanovich argues for the value in measuring people's reflective capabilities when assessing intelligence. For the purposes of Systems Intelligence, however, measurement is not important. What is important is that we cultivate and use the capacities of the reflective mind.

To a large extent, that's what the Kingsolver family did. They contemplated their beliefs, considered many perspectives along the way, and then acted rationally in harmony with their principles. Fortunate enough to own land in the more lush Appalachian area, the family of four (Barbara Kingsolver, her biology professor husband Steven Hopp and daughters Camille and Lily) packed up their things and moved to a more fertile landscape. Their goal was to sustain themselves by abandoning the food industry. They vowed to buy locally raised food, grow it themselves, or do without (with the exception of olive oil, spices and grains). They published the record of their experience, *Animal, Vegetable, Miracle* hoping to inspire others to think about their relationship with food.

We don't have to share the Kingsolver family's values or focus on the system of food production to see the benefits of reflection. Whatever systems we engage with, taking the time to think about how we see, feel, think, and act helps us to understand what drives our behavior. It also enables us to process the connections between seemingly unrelated things and to view situations from many perspectives. Critically evaluating rather than just noticing our thought processes can lead us to think more carefully about the consequences of our actions, and so help us to improve our behavior and live by our values. Unsurprisingly, reflection also helps understanding and the improvement of our interactions with the systems around us. It leads to systems intelligent behavior.

Understanding our Thinking Processes

Given that we can benefit hugely from understanding why we do the things we do, it is important to take time to think about our thinking. Thinking about thinking — what academics call meta-level thinking — is not something most of us typically do. Most of us simply have thoughts and act on those. However, brains have the capacity to not only have thoughts, but also think about those thoughts and analyze where they came from. Humans can reflect on, and change, the processes of their minds.

Daniel Siegel, a clinical professor of psychiatry, coined the term *mindsight* to refer to the mind's ability to see both itself and the minds of others. [106] Using our mindsight is about focusing our attention on the internal workings of our own brains, and by extension being able to imagine how others might be thinking. Understanding how our own thought processes work, what drives our behavior and the values and standards that we live by empowers us in social systems.

By attuning to our experiences, naming them, and taking the time to listen to our own thoughts we can build up a clearer overall picture of how we see the world. Even attending to small details of our thought processes can have a dramatic impact. Consider how you describe your emotions. Do you tell yourself "I am angry," "I am depressed," or "I am sad"? With mindsight it is possible to perceive the difference between saying "I *am* sad" and "I *feel* sad." When we say we *are* sad we define ourselves by the temporary emotion – when we say we *feel* sad we acknowledge a feeling without becoming it, thus giving ourselves the opportunity to transform that feeling.[107] We recognize that our brain is producing an emotion, but we act intelligently instead of reactively.

Learning to see the workings of our minds does more than just change how we act in the moment – it also changes the functioning of our brains. Neuroplasticity, the property of the brain that allows the connections in our brain continue to develop even as we age, means we can shape the pathways of our thoughts throughout our lives. One of the best ways to do this is to take the time to reflect internally, focusing on sensations, images, feelings and thoughts, to help better integrate the brain.[108] Learning to think about our thinking is a useful tool for moving from reactive to reflective behavior in systems.

Adopting a growth mindset, a desire to improve not only our actions but our thinking helps enlighten us about the relationship between our non-conscious and our conscious thought processes. Brain research suggests that more than forty percent of things people do each day are the result of mindless (in the sense of automatic) habits rather than decisions.[109] Scientists have discovered that our non-conscious thoughts are powerful, sophisticated and adaptive, and responsible for much of our functioning as humans. Our non-conscious, what scientists call *type-one thinking*, learns through pattern recognition,

decides what we attend to and select, interprets information, generates feelings that help us make decisions, and even establishes goals. Without it we couldn't do everyday things like divide our attention, process language automatically, or even balance.[110] Being able to size up and interpret our environments by decoding thousands of sensory inputs and acting quickly allows us to navigate our world.

Take, for example, our survival instincts. When we are under threat, survival instinct, such as the flight or fight impulse, can mean the difference between life and death. In situations where we feel danger, human brains are designed to deal with the most important functions first. Were we to see a lion lunging for us, for example, we would feel fear before we would mentally process that the four-legged beast we see is a lion about to attack.[111] Our brains signal what we should do before telling us the finer details of what is going on. Survival instinct is part of the fast, involuntary and automatic processes our brain completes without our knowledge.

But that's not the only type of brain power available to us. We also have the ability to reflect, develop beliefs and make deliberate choices about our behavior.[112] That's our *type two thinking* at work – the thoughtful, rational, conscious processes of our brain. We need both types of thinking to function, and both types of thinking contribute to systems intelligent behavior. However, when we feel under pressure we invariably default to type-one thinking. We become reactive. When survival mode takes over, for example, stimulus plus response becomes our default, even though we are capable of adding an extra cognitive layer and thinking carefully about what response would be best. That's great if we are being attacked by a lion but not so useful if we arguing with a co-worker.

To overcome our tendency to default to type one - thinking under pressure, we need to develop what Stanovich calls "mindware," analogous to software on a computer. With such mindware we can influence our type one with the more rational process of type two.[113] That influence requires two capabilities: the ability to interrupt and suppress our type one reactions and the ability to choose a better response through rational reasoning processes. [114] While type one processes are automatic and often involuntary, we can use

type two to control them when we have to. We experience this when we visit a country that drives on the opposite side of the road, for example. In that situation we can make our conscious selves attend to something (driving) that our unconscious would normally take care of automatically. We are capable of using both types of thinking in harmony. In effect, we get the best out of our brains when we can use them as an integrated system, and this is something that helps our systems intelligence reach its full potential. But, to do that, we need to become more aware of our type one thinking in action.

Mental Models

Imagine you are having lunch with your colleague in the cafeteria at your office. You are laughing and joking around, chatting about what you will all do on the upcoming weekend. Suddenly, over your co-worker's shoulder you see your manager approaching. His hands are on his hips and he has a stern look on his face. "Uh oh," you think, "we are in trouble for something – probably those late reports." You quickly sit up straighter and start preparing your response. As your manager approaches the table, you blurt out "I couldn't finish the reports because I'm waiting on the data from…" But he waves your comment away and says, "I just want to let you know I am heading home early as my back is killing me today." Your brain quickly reassesses the information it had processed. You realize the visual cues you had interpreted as anger (hands on hips, stern look) actually signified pain. Your emotional reaction changes from apprehension to empathy.

A simple situation like this reveals to us the power of our mental models. Mental models are our "deeply held internal images of how the world works."[115] They affect how we understand experiences and are comprised of our ingrained assumptions and the spontaneous generalizations that we make. When we see a non-smiling person, especially if that person is our superior, approach us with their hands on their hips we make assumptions based on our past experiences and how we believe the world works. Those assumptions then shape our behavior, so our interpretation of such body language puts us into a defensive frame of mind. Our mental model has, incorrectly in this case, anticipated a negative interaction.

Mental models, then, influence how we understand the world and so what actions we take within it. Everything from how we interact with our family to what political party we support is shaped by our beliefs and assumptions about the world. It can be difficult to see just how much our thoughts and actions are dictated by our mental models because we rarely articulate or notice them.[116] Why, for example, have consumers come to value pieces of fruit that are blemish free, brightly colored and wrapped in plastic? In *Animal, Vegetable, Miracle* Barbara Kingsolver reflects on this particular mental model that drives the behavior of many shoppers. She notices that with increasing urbanization, American consumers have come to negatively associate dirt with germs. The average consumer has a mental model of hygienic and healthy produce as being pristine in appearance. Many, argues Kingsolver, do not realize that plants grow in dirt. They reject irregularly shaped, unpackaged, slightly soiled produce because it does not fit their mental model of quality food. The growing presence of organic produce with its often-imperfect appearance but pesticide-free production is challenging consumers to change their mental model.

Where do mental models come from? As babies we are born without assumptions about the world so we clearly acquire them somewhere along the way. The social systems we belong to have a powerful impact on our mental models as do our personal experiences.

For example, how we view the system of marriage is shaped by the other systems we belong to – our family, our culture, as well as our own experiences of marriage. So, depending on how and where we were raised and what kinds of marriages we have seen, we might believe that marriage is primarily an economic system rather than a love match. Or, we might believe that getting married is first and foremost about romantic love, so reject the idea of arranged marriages. The beliefs we have about a system then shape our behavior.

Individually we all have mental models of systems, but at times our mental images can be shared across groups of people. Individuals in small groups (like families) and large groups (like nations) will have many ideas about how the world works in common. We often don't realize how ingrained our mental models are until they are challenged. You can probably recall your shock as a child visiting a new family and realizing that the way they lived (whether it be rituals around bed times, or dining or speaking to one another) was quite different from what went on in your household. You thought you understood "family life" only to find there were alternatives. Similarly, the surprise we feel when we visit another country and experience things done differently is a symptom of our assumptions about how the world works being challenged.

Shared mental models help groups to integrate and provide cohesion in systems. However, sometimes when all members develop the same beliefs about how things work a system can stagnate. Peter Senge tells the story of the American automakers in Detroit and their adherence to their mental models. For many years the companies making cars in the US worked on the basis that their customers cared primarily about styling. For a time, that was true, but when Japanese and German manufacturers began to penetrate the market they stressed the importance of quality and consumer attitudes began to shift. But the US automakers stuck to their belief. As Senge points out, they didn't understand the difference between saying "We have a mental model that our customers primarily care about style" and "Our customers primarily care about style."[117]

Several other cases also illustrate the power of even our seemingly innocuous mental models. For years, scientists ran experiments that obtained results that contradicted the widely held beliefs about the laws of physics. Yet, because they were so entrenched in a particular way of thinking and had subsequent expectations of the world the physicists never "saw" the data that would eventually give rise to the revolutionary theories of quantum mechanics and relativity. [118] Likewise, scientists spent many years attempting to elucidate the structure of DNA, based on the erroneous belief that DNA was a protein (it is a nucleic acid that binds to proteins). It was not until the error was detected, after many resources and much time spent, that headway was made.[119] Just because we believe the world is a certain way doesn't make it so, which is why reflection on our beliefs can be an important precursor for Systems Intelligent action.

Reflection helps us figure out what influences our thinking. This is not easy. Our mental models are powerful at dictating what we see and do not see, believe and disbelieve. For example, when we see an unkempt-looking man sleeping on a park bench we might assume he is homeless. But perhaps he is a hardworking city gardener catching a quick nap in his break. While it is impossible to stop making judgments about what we see, we can make a conscious effort to acknowledge that our assessment may or may not be correct – that is Systems Intelligence in action. When we are mindful of the judgments we are making, we give ourselves the opportunity to question our mental models and perhaps reassess the initial conclusions we have made.

Challenging our mental models can be difficult. The difficulties of changing people's beliefs about how the world should be seen are scattered throughout human history. Galileo was ostracized for suggesting that the earth revolved around the sun; Darwin was pilloried when he suggested the theory of natural selection; women were ridiculed when they first sought the vote; Martin Luther King was assassinated for advocating equality for black Americans. Questioning and maybe changing our mental models requires us to consciously reevaluate and possibly reject ideas, values, and practices that we have held to be true.

That is not to say revising how we see the world is impossible. Changes in our mental models can occur as we move towards adulthood, triggered by exposure to new information. Most of us if pushed can recall incidents in our lives when our perspective was challenged. Perhaps we adopted our parents' political views but friends exposed us to alternative ways of thinking and we gradually altered our perspective. Or we had firm ideas about the best way to raise a child but our spouse had quite a different approach. Because the process of changing our mental models occurs within our minds, however, it is almost always accompanied by self-reflection.

More importantly than changing our beliefs, though, self-reflection helps us to *understand* them. Exactly what we believe is not really the main issue. The point is that we need to be able to recognize and articulate our own beliefs about the systems to which we belong. If we can't, we risk creating negative interactions because we tend to project our own beliefs onto others, and then are shocked when they behave in ways that are clearly "wrong" in our eyes. Fortunately, there are ways of reflecting on how we are forming our mental models.

Reflection: What's Your Habitual Way of Thinking?

Read each statement and check "yes" if you agree that it summarizes your typical outlook on life, and "no" if it doesn't

                                               Yes   No

I'm separate and pursue my own agenda.

What I do can change an organization.

I combine logic with intuition and emotion.

Life is unpredictable but patterned.

I advocate my position.

I suppress feelings and hide mistakes.

I attend to processes.

Being good allows me to look good.

Life is about overcoming challenges and solving problems.

I think about the effects of my actions on me.

I believe in logic and rationality.

Life is a linear progression of cause and effect.

The effects of what I do here and now may occur later, and elsewhere.

I try to predict the future.

I see all there is to see.

I am results oriented.

I take what I can from the systems around me.

Systems are external to me.

I act with understanding of the universal "we".

I manage impressions to be acknowledged and avoid looking incompetent.

I look for the obvious.

I expect immediate results when I act.

I try to create a future.

I know I can never see everything.

What I do doesn't matter.

I give what I can to the systems around me.

I am part of the systems I live in.

I see connections between seemingly unrelated things.

I am related and build shared vision.

I am shaped by my environment and connections with others.

I am committed to uplifting others.

I look out for myself.

I learn from mistakes and see how I contribute to my own problems.

I balance advocacy and inquiry.

I am in control of my own destiny.

Life is about creating possibilities.

There are no right or wrong answers – the point of the exercise is to activate your reflective processes. This kind of meta-level thinking helps us to reveal our habits to ourselves and understand the processes of our minds. See the following table to check how closely your current ways of thinking are aligned with a systems perspective.

Check what aspects of your thinking are already oriented towards being Systems Intelligent.

A Systems Intelligent Outlook[120]

Non-Systems Intelligent thinking	Systems Intelligent thinking
I'm separate and pursue my own agenda.	I am related and build shared vision.
I am in control of my own destiny.	I am shaped by my environment and connections with others.
I look out for myself.	I am committed to uplifting others.
I advocate my position.	I balance advocacy and inquiry.
I suppress feelings and hide mistakes.	I learn from mistakes and see how I contribute to my own problems.
I manage impressions to be acknowledged and avoid looking incompetent.	Being good allows me to look good.
What I do doesn't matter.	What I do can change an organization.
I think about the effects of my actions on me.	I act with understanding of the universal "we".
I believe in logic and rationality.	I combine logic with intuition and emotion.
Life is a linear progression of cause and effect.	Life is unpredictable but patterned.
I try to predict the future.	I try to create a future.
I see all there is to see.	I know I can never see everything.
I am results oriented.	I attend to processes.
I take what I can from the systems around me.	I give what I can to the systems around me.
Systems are external to me.	I am part of the systems I live in.
I look for the obvious.	I see connections between seemingly unrelated things.
I expect immediate results when I act.	The effects of what I do here and now may occur later, and elsewhere.
Life is about overcoming challenges and solving problems.	Life is about creating possibilities.

The Ladder of Inference

One useful tool for understanding our mental models is to uncover the steps we are taking on *the ladder of inference*.[121] Developed by academic Chris Argyris, the ladder of inference walks through how our thinking influences our actions. It uncovers the rapid mental processes of our minds that precede our behavior. Generally, we generally have very little awareness of the giant leaps we take to get from the bottom to the top of the ladder. An apparently rational plan for action can be based on the limited data we select and the false assumptions we make. In particular, we tend to skip from observation to assumption, not noticing how we only see part of what is going on and have added our own meanings to that which we've seen.

The ladder of inference[122]

Take for example the issue of feeding the world's inhabitants. Most of us have probably seen plenty of pictures of the starving and malnourished on television. We know that there are people around the world who don't have enough food. Given the images we have seen and the frequent media reports of famine in poorer countries many of us assume that there is not enough food available to feed all the people on the planet. Perhaps this then motivates us to donate to charities that try to alleviate this problem.

In *Animal, Vegetable, Miracle*, however, Steven Hopp debunks the myth that there is not enough food to go around. He presents data from reliable sources that show the world actually produces enough food to feed not just the current population but also the eight billion people projected to inhabit the planet by 2030. There is plenty of food; it is just poorly distributed. In particular, corn, wheat and soybeans are being produced in abundance. But instead of feeding people directly, they are being processed into products for wealthy consumers like fuel for cars and for feeding animals that will be turned into meat.[123]

Why is our mental model around food supply somewhat divorced from reality? The average person selects the data that they see – images of malnourished children – and makes assumptions and takes action based on those images. But what Hopp reminds us is that there is other data out there, and if we think about it we know this. We know that our stores have a huge supply of meat products and if we read the labels we see corn and wheat and soybeans and their extracts as frequent ingredients in our processed products. The problem is, most of us fail to connect two seemingly unrelated things – corn-fed cows and famine, or cornstarch packaging and malnourished people. And so, we don't see how the system could be improved. Consequently, we don't realize that a change in the system for feeding cattle or the system for producing packaging may have more of an impact on feeding hungry people than a donation to charity.

Because our mental models and our thinking processes are so automatic and so entrenched, we often hold on to beliefs about the world (and act on those beliefs) even though we don't really know why we believe what we believe. Reflection can help us break that cycle by encouraging us to look back down the ladder of inference. Say, for example, you see your child holding a tennis racquet standing next to a precious family vase which lies broken on the floor (observe data – the bottom of the ladder). The combination of child plus racquet plus broken vase (selected data) has likely caused you to remember how clumsy this child is or how dangerous swinging a racquet inside is (cultural and personal meanings added). You assume the racquet has broken the vase (assumptions) and are sure your child did it (draw conclusions). Based on your confidence that your child has just broken the vase (belief adopted) you yell at him or her (take actions based on your beliefs – the top of the ladder). Your mind, without you knowing, has quickly accessed a mental model and rushed up the ladder of inference.

If you were in a reflective mode, however, you might react differently. While your automatic response might be to yell, you would take a deep breath and go through the ladder of inference more deliberately. You could for example, take a second look at the available data. You might notice another abandoned tennis racquet on the floor, implying another culprit. Or, perhaps you remind yourself that though this child is clumsy he or she is usually very responsible and it would be atypical for them to have swung a tennis racquet in the house. Or, maybe you reflect that the vase was often near the edge of the shelf and that the vibration of a child running past might have caused it to fall. In other words, with reflection, we take time to understand the situation more fully and interrupt the process of making untested inferences. In the process, we create a better opportunity for constructive interaction in the system. Isn't it much better to thoughtfully engage with our child in this situation than reactively yell at him or her?

Self–Reflection on Mental Models

Every day we take actions based on our beliefs, but we often don't think about the mental models that are behind those beliefs. Answer the following question to help uncover some of the mental images you have about the way the world works.

Your beliefs:
Do you believe prison is for punishment or rehabilitation?
Most people can answer this question pretty quickly. We know our beliefs well. We often have less understanding about why we believe what we believe.

See if you can say why you believe in the answer you have chosen.

Take time to reflect on and articulate the thoughts that shape your belief.

Where do your beliefs come from?
Now take the time to consider why you have the belief you do. In other words, what has helped build the mental models that inform your belief?

Are they inherited from your parents?
Are they shaped by a particular life experience?
Does your religion influence your thinking?
Does your socio-economic status shape your beliefs?
Do you think you would have the same beliefs if you were from Bangladesh?
Do you think you would have the same beliefs if you were born two hundred years ago?
Do you think you would have the same beliefs and values if there was a nuclear catastrophe tomorrow?
Does it make you uncomfortable to think about the reasons why you think the way you do?
Do you feel like just saying "It's just the way things are."
Do you feel apprehensive when you think about having to explain the reasons behind your beliefs to others?

If so, you are not alone. Many people feel uneasy about articulating where their beliefs come from, but asking such questions is an important step to being able to honestly self-reflect and creating the opportunity for self-development. You don't have to change your beliefs – you just need to understand where they come from, and thus be able to understand that others, too, have sets of beliefs that are shaped by their experiences and which they may be reluctant to change.

Have another look at the initial question. Can you imagine someone else answering differently to you? Why might they feel differently?

How do mental models affect behavior in systems?
Think about a social system you belong to, perhaps your workplace or your romantic relationship.

Do you think everyone in that system shares the same beliefs?
What are some of the consequences of having the same beliefs? Of having different beliefs?
What systems in your life provide the opportunity to discuss people's beliefs and the mental models behind them?
How could you introduce conversation about mental models to some systems in your life?

Reflecting on the workings of our minds helps to reveal our thought processes to us. Shaped by our socialization and our life experiences, it is crucial to recognize that our mental models are just that – models. They are approximations of reality, a way for us to describe and classify things, and we shouldn't mistake them for the truth. Realizing that our mental models are constructed by our experiences and socialization does not mean that we have to abandon them and adopt other people's ideas about the way the world works. On the contrary, we do not feel driven to reconcile our beliefs with others because we know both sets of beliefs are the result of unique sets of experience. Instead, we can accept the differences or work to find common ground

Avoiding Self-Deception
The ability to self-reflect does not always come easily – it can be difficult to clearly see why we act the way we do. Often we don't want to see the big picture because that blindness allows us to justify the short cuts we take with our own behavior and responsibilities. That might mean not bothering to put our coffee cup in the dishwasher at work, for example. We tell ourselves that it's the cleaner's

responsibility or that we are simply doing what everyone else is doing. We self-deceive ourselves that our lack of action is justified.

Self-deception is very tempting, but valuable self-reflection depends on our ability to be alert for the things that distort our judgments about ourselves, others and the systems we share. We too easily see ourselves as the victims of circumstances and so justify being unable to act constructively. In fact, people have an astonishing tendency towards self-deception, avoiding seeing mistakes or selfish motives. Our brains go so far as to select and interpret events and situations in ways that tell us we're okay.[124] We so want to feel good about ourselves that we filter out or unconsciously suppress those things that make us anxious.[125] The problem is, we do not realize what it is that we are not seeing. As a result, we miss the opportunities we have to make decisions that can have direct consequences on improving the quality of our lives in systems.[126]

Take a moment to think of a social system you belong to that is not particularly harmonious at the moment – maybe your romantic relationship, your work, your school. What do you see the problems being? Most likely you arrive at a list that includes things like poor communication between members, some overbearing personalities, some conflicts, some ridiculous rules, and so on.

Did any of the problems you come up with start with you? Did you say it was your communication skills that were lacking, your personality that may be a problem, your actions leading to conflict, and your enforcement or breaking of rules that negatively impacted on the system you were thinking of? If you did, that is great. If you didn't then you are like most of us, prone to not seeing our own role in systems. That's not to say that we need to develop a capacity for self-recriminations. Feelings of guilt and self-blame are not productive for systems. Rather it is about reminding ourselves that we contribute to the systems we are in and then critically evaluating what that contribution is.

We rarely set out to deliberately have a negative impact on others or the systems we belong to. When we drive our kids to soccer in an SUV, for instance, we are not trying to contribute to climate change, we just don't typically connect seemingly unrelated things – getting to soccer and fossil fuel consumption. In fact, in most systems, we are usually well-intended. And because our intentions are good, it is easy to slip into self-deception. We tell ourselves that our own behavior is not harmful to the system because we intend for it to be beneficial. Good intentions seem enough. In reality, however, we typically act in our own best interests and fail to take responsibility for how our actions affect others and the systems we share.

Take the example of a meeting. No doubt the majority of us have sat through regular meetings we would rather not be attending. We might make the occasional contribution to discussion, but mostly we shuffle papers, think about what we are doing on the weekend and generally disengage. If we were asked about *our* personal input to the meeting after the event, we might think we did our bit. We didn't interrupt anyone, we contributed as required, we didn't disrupt proceedings. But we would be deceiving ourselves and missing the possibility of finding constructive actions. We may not be solely responsible for the boring meetings, but honest self-reflection would lead us to reevaluate the impact we have.

Just because the default for the meeting is disengagement, for example, it does not mean that we have to disengage. In fact, if we actively break our own patterns of behavior we have the potential to positively impact on the meeting as a whole. If we turned up with a chocolate bar for everyone, for example, we might alter the energy in the room. If we began by saying that the meetings are typically tedious and could the group do things a little differently today, maybe we would spark a positive change. If we made a concentrated effort to be an active participant and smile at people we might change the interaction dynamic. How often have you made the deliberate choice to change your own behavior with the goal of positively affecting the system? Probably not as often as you could have.

Self-deception also often occurs when we pretend that everybody agrees that our individual experience of a system is everybody's experience. If I tell myself that everyone hates the meetings, I justify my disengagement. But it might not be true that everyone hates the meetings; maybe everyone is simply holding back. It's like telling ourselves that everyone cares more about having convenient food than minimizing the burning of fossil fuels to justify our contribution in perpetuating the current food distribution system.

When we reflect in a systems intelligent way we acknowledge that our perception of ourselves and others can be biased. To overcome the biases inherent in our thought processes we need to be mindful of our thinking. Trying honest self-reflection acknowledges that our minds can be fallible, affecting how we perceive ourselves, others, and the systems around us.

One common bias, related to the attribution error that hampers our ability to attune, capable of distorting our perception of life in systems is self-serving bias. This is where we are prone to take credit for successes but deny responsibility for our failures. For example, if we receive a promotion at work we may claim it was due to our hard work, but if we don't get promoted we might claim it is because we have a bad boss or our company has an inadequate career structure. Our successes are internally attributed; our failures are externally attributed. We are also very quick to see bias in others. We find self-interest in the actions of others while we regard ourselves as being fair and objective. Our biased thinking about others can lead to unnecessary conflicts if we don't pay attention to it. In fact, research has shown that we often act to protect our self-image. As a result, we blame mistakes on others, missing the opportunity to learn from what went wrong and also negatively impacting others. In organizations, for example, when members blame others to protect themselves work groups tend to be less creative and perform poorly while those who take responsibility are admired and inspire others.[127]

Furthermore, we are largely oblivious to our own idiosyncratic interpretations of the world. What psychologists call the false consensus bias describes how we assume that others think like us. Accordingly, when people behave as we do we think they are normal and rational, whereas when people act and react in ways we wouldn't, we think they are a bit strange, odd, and perhaps even irrational. For instance, when someone tells you they have quit their job to travel the world because they think they are underpaid, you might think you would never do that. Yet, maybe you turn to your friend and comment about what a risky solution to a problem that seems and your friend looks surprised or disagrees. It is moments like these that our mental models can be revealed to us, moments when we realize not everybody thinks in the same way we do.

Importantly, the biases we have are not entirely disadvantageous. Some biases have evolutionary explanations. For example, they help us filter and make sense of the information we are bombarded with.[128] Being systems intelligent is not about eliminating our individual biases – it is about paying attention to and managing them so we recognize how they might be impacting on our thinking. Only then can we adjust our behavior accordingly. Reflection, particularly self-reflection, cultivates this kind of personal growth in us.

How to Self-Reflect

So far, this chapter has talked about the unconscious, type one thinking processes that govern many of our actions in systems – our mental models, our inferences, and our self-deception. It is now time to turn to the conscious process of self-reflection.

In *Animal, Vegetable, Miracle*, teenager Camille Kingsolver lovingly describes the annual summer task of canning tomatoes. The family had spent summers on the farm in the Appalachians for several years before moving there permanently, and one of the season's rituals was to preserve the bountiful crop of tomatoes that the garden yielded each year. Camille describes how the long days chopping and boiling and stirring heralded the beginning of a new school year and represented a farewell to long days of freedom. You might expect that a teen would be reluctant to spend the last days of her vacation toiling in a kitchen, but she looked on it as a transition back to the routine of school and an "end-of-summer meditation." In fact, Camille valued the physical rhythm the work established as it allowed her to "quiet down and tune in" paying attention to nothing but the task at hand and her own thoughts.[129] American culture, she muses, doesn't typically make space for slow reflection.

Not making space for reflection is detrimental because through reflection we focus our ability to see the patterns that shape our lives. That, in turn, allows us to consider our own individual role in a system as well as the system itself. Honest self-reflection, in particular, can offer valuable insight into how we establish our beliefs and the actions we take because of those. Most of us don't regularly stop and consider what is going on in our own minds. We might let ourselves be bombarded by the chatter of our thoughts, but we seldom pay attention to how and why we are generating those thoughts in the first place. However, we have the capacity to make ourselves aware of how our mind is working.

Life is made up of many experiences, but just having experiences does not automatically lead to awareness. It is through reflecting on the experiences we have and challenging our taken-for-granted assumptions that we can expand our self-knowledge, and subsequently our intelligent participation in systems. There are three common types of self-reflection that we can engage in:

- reflection-on-action,
- reflection-in-action, and
- critical self-reflection.

All three types are valuable for developing our systems intelligence because they help us to critically evaluate our ways of thinking, think about the consequences of our actions, and improve our behavior.

Reflection–on–Action

Animal, Vegetable, Miracle is a descriptive and contemplative account of one family's attempt to live off locally produced food. Barbara Kingsolver shares the story of her family's year on the farm, recounting their cycle of planting, tending and harvesting and what the family learns along the way. She discusses the difficulties in abandoning the industrial food pipeline and the process of becoming a conscious consumer. In other words, the book embodies reflection-on-action as she reflects on the systems in which they participated, big and small, natural and social, as well as the dynamics of the family as a system.

Reflection-on-action is probably the most common type of self-reflection we use in systems. This is where we stop and think about the effects of our behavior after the event so that we can more fully understand them and learn from them. Reflection-on-action is attended to with questions like:

- What was I trying to achieve?
- What actually occurred?
- Where did I do well?
- How could I do better next time?
- What can I take from this experience?

We can direct this type of reflection at our own individual behaviors within systems, or we can ask the same question of the system itself. After a team sports game, for example, we might ask the reflective questions to consider our own contribution, but we can also change the "I" to "we" and reflect on the team as a whole. Organizations, for example, often use this type of exercise to assess their performance. Reflection-on-action is a valuable first step in becoming more self-aware and helps to promote more successful behaviors in future. It is all about utilizing the benefits of hindsight.

Reflection-in-Action

In contrast, reflection-in-action is about evaluating and adjusting our performance in the moment. This is a far more powerful and dynamic reflective skill to have because it means that we are aware of the effects of our actions as they are occurring. Systems often emerge in the moment. We have to act quickly and adapt to changing circumstances. We are constantly adjusting our systemic perspective and attuning to the situation at hand. The strength of reflection-in-action lies in making reflection a cognitive habit. We will not always have the luxury of thinking time before we are called on to act, but if we are already in tune with our thought processes, if we are practiced at reflection-in-action, then we can carry the benefits of that practice to new situations as they emerge.

Imagine you are immersed in the beautiful sparkling waters of your favorite beach. Gradually, you become aware of an undertow pulling you farther and farther out to sea. You are caught in a rip. You need to get to shore, quickly, before you get dragged out too far. Adrenalin rushing, you start swimming hard towards the beach.

Most times in our life the shortest and most efficient route is the best path to our goal. Unfortunately, when we are caught in a rip we need to take the indirect route to shore. The wave system requires us to move sideways, parallel to the beach, to escape from the undercurrent. The best solution in this case is not the obvious one but the counterintuitive response that takes into account the movement of the sea.

If we are experienced ocean swimmers or surfers we might know this system, but if not, then we need to adapt in the moment. We would need the presence of mind to realize that Swimming directly to shore is not working, and adjust accordingly. That may mean swimming in another direction or just waiting and seeing where the current carries us. If we are practiced enough at reflection-in-action then even in a time of threat dynamic reflection and evaluation of the situation rather than panicked reaction is our default.

Reflection-in-action calls on our capacity to modify our actions towards better outcomes in systems. Just as we might need to alter our reactive response to a physical system like the ocean we can also reflect in social systems. For example, in the middle of a family argument you might realize that your raised voice is having a negative effect on your ability to get your message across, so you lower your volume and adjust your tone to encourage others to listen. Reflection-in-action takes a high skill level because it requires us to attune to the system and, at the same time as participating in an interaction, also monitor our own performance by asking

- •What am I doing well?
- •How can I contribute better?
- •What do I notice about myself and the situation?

We attend to ourselves and the system simultaneously. Small and large social systems like couples, sports teams and organizations can also reflect-in-action. It just requires effort and the willingness and flexibility to adapt as circumstances emerge.

Critical Reflection with a Growth Mindset

The third type of reflection, critical reflection, is a slightly different skill. Critical self-reflection involves asking ourselves hard, confrontational questions that challenge our behavior and understanding of ourselves and our world. We are not criticizing ourselves in the sense of being negative, but we are thinking more deeply about ourselves so that we can explain why we live the way we do and value the things we do with clarity. In *Animal, Vegetable, Miracle* Camille Kingsolver, for instance, notices how her relationship with food is different from her peers. Unlike them, she avoids buying convenience foods. She asks herself why she behaves the way she does and finds the answers. Camille's critical self-reflection leads her to make peace with her differences from her friends. Sometimes, however, critical self-reflection will inspire us to change our behaviors.

In effect, critical self-reflection reveals our mental models to us. When we can recognize the thought patterns that shape our own beliefs, we begin to understand more effectively where other people's beliefs come from, thus increasing our understanding of the system we create together. Critical self-reflection also means we engage with systems instead of taking the effects of their structures for granted. We can begin to understand the way systems influence our behavior and beliefs and look for alternative possibilities. Camille Kingsolver, for example, examines the effects of two systems on her behavior – the prevailing system of food consumption in the US and the alternative system her parents adopt and value. In the end, critical self-reflection helps her choose which system best reflects her own values.

The practice of self-reflection in any form is enhanced if we approach it with a growth mindset. A growth mindset understands how the experiences we have can be learnt from or stimulate constructive action. In this mode we focus on monitoring, growing and developing our interpretation of experiences. This stands in contrast to a fixed mindset. In this mode we can be critical of ourselves and judgmental, and in the process we create an internal monologue that tells us how useless/ineffective/stupid we (or others) are. Alternatively, we become too smug and self-satisfied, telling ourselves we have done what we could and so never seeing opportunity for betterment.

But we shouldn't just focus on our internal state. Part of self-reflection is frequently revisiting what is going on both inside and outside ourselves. In other words, are our thoughts and action in harmony or is there a discrepancy between what we feel and think and what we actually do? If there is a gap, then we need to examine why that gap is manifesting. Our beliefs are created in our mind – to address them, we need to become aware of them.

Self-reflection does not always come naturally to us, yet taking time for regular reflection is one of the best investments we can make. We live in a world that operates at a frantic pace, valuing constant action over quiet, reflective time. Effective self-reflection occurs best in a quite and non-distracting environment, both internal and external. It also requires honesty, so demands a conscious effort to avoid self-deception and be alert to our biases. To practice honest self-reflection we must overcome any negative connotations it has for us and give ourselves completely to the process. After all, taking the time for self-reflection means we recognize that complex issues require thoughtful analysis and that we can learn from our experiences. It is about understanding the patterns of feelings, thoughts, and behaviors that limit us and being able to work on transforming those so we can find new ways to engage with the systems we live in. We need to come to know and understand our selves more fully, so we can know and understand others and the systems around us.

Perspective Taking

The effort we make to understand our internal processes is not the only type of reflection available to us – we can also reflect in ways that help us to understand others. Reflection enables us to take different perspectives on events, to remind ourselves that whatever we are seeing in the moment is only one way of looking at the system. We can train ourselves both to imagine how other people might view situations and to broaden our own vision by thinking more widely and deeply about things. Intellectually, adopting different perspectives seems like a pretty straightforward activity, but it takes practice. We have to be aware of our usual thought patterns activating and make a deliberate effort to think in new ways. Of course, once we have become used to doing this, it, too, becomes a normal activity. The challenge is to move from rarely consciously thinking about adopting fresh perspectives to habitually looking at situations and systems from many angles.

Imagine you are playing a game of tennis. You hit a fantastic shot down the line. Your opponent can't return it. The point is yours! Except, the umpire, sitting high on her chair, calls the point against you and your opponent nods his head and indicates the ball bounced out of court. You can't believe it. But when the slow motion replay appears on the big screen you realize they are right – the ball was out. From where you were standing, it looked like a legal shot. But the overview the umpire had and the different position of your opponent on the court allowed them to see things differently.

The imaginary tennis scene is a reminder of the value of perspective taking. Systems consist of many individuals acting together and the view that each person has of the system is particular to them. However, we tend to get caught up in our own, often narrow, perspective in life. We get used to seeing things from one angle, through one mental model or lens. As a result, our thoughts become "shackled by the familiar."[130] It can be extremely difficult to stop the rapid, automatic, and often unconscious processes of our thinking. Developing our capacity for self-reflection encourages us to begin to question, and so open for revision, our perspective of situations. In that way, we can start to explore and understand how to expand our view of systems.

We begin life as children by thinking that everything is as it appears to be. Furthermore, we assume everyone sees what we do. As we age, however, we learn that other people perceive the same events in different ways to us and that we can look at situations for many different angles. By the time we have matured into adults, most of us have learned to adapt to the gap between what our brain first tells us we see and both what others might see and alternative views we can take. We do this by first believing what our eyes convey to us, but then being willing to revise our belief when we have evidence to the contrary. So in a game of tennis we might see a ball as out, but when we watch the slow motion replay we happily revise our initial belief and accept the evidence that the ball is in. "We believe what we see, and then unbelieve it when we have to," as Harvard psychologist Daniel Gilbert explains.[131]

This process is relatively uncomplicated when we are in situations like tennis games, where we have cameras capable of showing us the failings of our own perceptions. It becomes more difficult in social systems when we explain other people's actions or organizational outcomes to ourselves. We are typically less willing to accept our ability to perceive as fallible in social systems. We fail to realize that our perceptions are not the result of our eyes simply transmitting an image of the world into our brains, but rather, are the result of complex psychological process. In effect, we combine what our eyes see with our existing knowledge, beliefs, thoughts, feelings and desires to build up a picture of what we then call reality.[132]

The problem is the brain gathers information so quickly, makes judgments so rapidly, and fills in the gaps so seamlessly, that we tend to accept the version of reality it serves up to us. We have trouble *not* believing what our imagination tells us. We are quite capable of seeing things that are not there, envisaging things that have not happened, and predicting futures that might not be.[133] We can broaden our perspective on life in systems by accepting that our thoughts can be as faulty as they are amazing. If we are mindful of our thought processes, we can consciously overcome the shortcomings of our brain by exerting our type two (conscious and rational) thinking over type one (the fast and automatic processes).

Expanding our Perspective

Have you ever noticed how much easier it is to give advice to others than solve your own problems? One of the main reasons we experience this phenomenon is that our perspective limits us – when we are in the system we are the worm who can only see its immediate surroundings. When we help others, we are often the bird, seeing issues from the outside. One of the challenges we face for developing perspective taking in systems is to learn to zoom in and zoom out, that is, to see the issues at hand but also to try to see the big picture. Of course, we can never escape the worm's perspective entirely because we are part of the system we are trying to see, but we can explore viewing things from new angles.

It is easy to become stuck with one perspective because first impressions are powerful. We tend to grow inordinately fond of our initial interpretation of events,

forgetting we have the mental ability to take more than one view of something. Whenever we have an experience we view it from a particular perspective, much as if we are viewing life through a window frame. When we look through a window what we see is colored by the size of the frame, the opaqueness of the glass, the position we are standing in, the weather, the light, our height and so on. That is, we never see everything there is to see and we never see exactly what someone else sees. The same applies to our mental images. Our different experiences and our different mental models affect what we see, and that affects the choices we make in systems. The challenge is for us to reflect on our perspective so we can expand it, and so act more intelligently in a system.

Framing and Reframing

During an official reception during the US Civil War, Abraham Lincoln spoke of Southerners as erring human beings rather than enemies worthy of extermination. An attendee, an elderly Union patriot rebuked him for speaking kindly of his enemies when he ought to be thinking of destroying them. "Why, madam," Lincoln replied, "Do I not destroy my enemies when I make them my friends?"[134]

In effect, Lincoln reframed how the woman understood their Southern adversaries. Reframing encourages us to adopt fresh perspectives by forcing us to see a situation differently. Where his compatriot had a particular understanding of what destroying an enemy meant, Lincoln showed her a fresh perspective –

befriend rather than annihilate. It was an approach that was to serve him well in his efforts to unite the North and South after the civil war.

Our frame or our perspective is shaped by the experiences we have had but it is not fixed. New experiences can alter our frame, and we often think and feel differently about events over time. We all also have the capacity to put aside our initial perspective and adopt a new frame – it just takes a bit of effort. Take a look at the following scenario and consider your response.

> Your company has just finished building a fantastic new high-rise hotel. The rooms are great, the service is wonderful, the price is right. Everything is running smoothly except for one thing. Customers are consistently complaining about the amount of time they spend waiting for the elevators.

How might you solve this problem?

In this example you would be amongst the majority if you came up with a list about what to do that read something like this:

- Let guests use the stairway
- Build a new elevator
- Add an external glass elevator to the building
- Develop a software program that optimizes the elevators' service to calls
- Encourage people travelling a few floors to use the stairs with posters promoting exercise

Almost everyone frames this problem as one to do with the elevators and makes suggestions accordingly – but is it really? Couldn't the problem be reframed as being about waiting times? It is the length of time that people are kept waiting for the elevators that is causing them to complain. Rather than changing the elevators, wouldn't it be easier to change people's perception of how long they are waiting? Once the problem is reframed in this way, new solutions emerge. The hotel could provide comfortable seating near the elevators, could have TV screens or mirrors near the elevators, could have free magazines placed near the elevators, could have water coolers or complimentary snack machines installed near the elevators, and so on.

Reframing makes people see, feel, and think differently about an issue. Barbara Kingsolver, for example, wants to reframe American people's relationship to food from negative (focused on calorie counting, labeling, rules and regulations) to positive (connected to nourishment, comfort, and ritual) so they are more inclined to buy organic produce.[135] Reframing is a useful skill because it helps us to recognize both that others see the world differently from us and that we can learn to see it differently, too.

How then can we foster our ability to reframe situations so that we see from many perspectives? There are a few things we can do. First, we can cultivate mindfulness. Mindfulness is the process of paying attention to the moment in the moment, a kind or reflection-in-action.[136] It is the difference between automatically saying no to our child's request because we are in the habit of refusing, and really attending to how our child is feeling and considering their point of view before providing our considered answer to this *particular* request.

Another way to attend to framing and reframing is to pay attention to initial messages – those that we receive and those that we give. If a family member approaches us saying "I want to talk to you about your behavior" a frame has already been set for the conversation to follow. We tend to feel that they have already decided that our behavior is bad and that the conversation will not be pleasant for us. From their choice of words, we have an expectation that the frame is negative – and what follows is likely to result in conflict. It is in our interests, and probably theirs, for us to reframe the situation into something more positive. Instead of responding with "What have I done now?" or some other antagonistic phrase in keeping with the initial frame, we could say "I'd love to sit down and chat about what is bothering you." Immediately, we have reframed things more positively. We have welcomed their approach, we have agreed to discussion, and we have acknowledged that something has upset them – without accepting blame.

Conversely, when we initiate a conversation, we need to think about the frame that we are introducing and about how we are creating expectations in the person we are talking to. We automatically attune to situations and develop expectations of them, but sometimes we need to reframe those. When we have high expectations, they can be too easily disappointed and when we have low expectations they can become self-fulfilling. The Kingsolver family, for example, changed the language that they used in connection with food to help change their frame: "We just wanted to stop pushing pampered fruits and vegetables around the globe on our behalf, so we changed our thinking. Instead of starting every food sentence with "I want," we began with "right now we have…"[137] The effect of the new frame was to make their project of doing without processed foods seem less like an exercise in deprivation and more like an adventure.

It is also important for reframing to pay attention to the interaction as it unfolds, to use reflection-in-action. This way we can attune to when the interaction becomes stuck or negative and make an effort to reframe at this point. Reframing mid-interaction can be achieved by really simple interventions. Using an overt signal like "This isn't working. Why don't we try a different approach" or "Let's put aside these issues and think about things from a different angle" can have an enormous impact. It reminds us that we are becoming too narrowly focused and helps us to widen our perspective. Reframing can be about both process and content. Suggesting that the group tries a different approach is a process reframe. It might mean moving from something like listening to speakers one-by-one to breaking into small groups. Putting aside some issues and moving on to others is more of a content reframe. It's the ability to say let's stop talking about the hotel's elevators and think about customer service.

Walking in Another's Shoes

There's a famous scene in Woody Allen's movie *Annie Hall*. In the film, we see Allen's character visiting a psychiatrist, who asks him how often he makes love with his partner. "Hardly ever" he complains. "Maybe three times a week." Moments later we see his lover, played by Diane Keaton, also at a psychiatrist's appointment answering the same question. "Constantly," she bemoans, "I'd say three times a week!"[138] The two characters see the same situation in different ways.

Understanding our own mental models is a great first step in developing perspective, but it is important to attempt to understand others' mental models too. In other words, everyone in the system has their own idea about how things work and bases their actions on those ideas. A black American businessman from New Orleans will see life differently to a Hispanic American student attending Harvard who will see life differently to a white American factory worker from Indiana. Even if we take a group of culturally similar Americans attending Harvard, though they will have many perceptions in common, there will also be significant differences. The scholarship student will likely have a different lens to the wealthy student. The Christian student will likely have a different lens to the Buddhist student. The Democrat student will likely have a different lens to the Republican student. Even though we share participation in large social systems with many others, we also have differing values and combinations of experiences at the individual level.

We are most conscious of the differences in our individual mental models or perspectives when they conflict. The Democrat and the Republican know they see the world differently, as do the Christian and the Buddhist, and because they see things from different perspectives they believe different actions are called for. Sometimes we are very accepting of these differences. We agree to disagree, realizing that we each subscribe to a different way of understanding human experience, or that we belong to different value systems, and so choose to live differently. At other times, we struggle to accept that there is an alternative perception to ours. Or, if we accept that the alternative exists, we struggle to understand why – we think that the other view is clearly wrong and ours is clearly right. Ironically, both sides can think they are pursuing the common good and that the other side does just not understand this. Consequently, we sometimes try to impose our perception of the world on others. History is littered with conflicts that have arisen because people were unwilling to accept different perspectives, as are our own lives.

Leaving our default point of view entirely behind, a point of view influenced by our socialization and our emotional and cognitive make up, is impossible. Our own perspective is just that – our own – and so has value to us. While we can never step outside of ourselves entirely, we can work to develop the skills that allow us to briefly walk in one another's shoes. An important aspect of Systems Intelligence is having the willingness and goal to see life from someone else's perspective. By taking a different perspective we can not only see how the other person experiences the system, but also increase our own understanding of it. That in turn offers us the opportunity to change our interaction within the system in some way that benefits everyone.

Every system we are part of consists of us, the other members who make up the system, and the system itself as a structure. Each person has a different perspective on the system. Take a simple family system as an example. In a family with a mother, a father and two children there are four perspectives. Each individual will have perceptions about how the parents are as individuals and as a couple, the siblings/children, their own role in the family, and the family unit as a whole and how it functions.

The intricacies of even a small system are suddenly apparent. Even just a few connections between people dramatically increase the competing perspectives of the system. As social systems increases in size and complexity, that range of perspectives also increases.

To act with Systems Intelligence we need to be aware that alternative perspectives to ours exist within every system. While we cannot ever fully know what others see and think, we can be attuned to the likelihood that their thoughts will differ from our own. Then we can start to ask ourselves why people might be behaving in certain ways rather than simply react to their actions.

We can do more than just imagine how others might see the world, however. We can actively engage with them to explore their perspective of the systems we share. We all know about the parts of the system we are in but other parts remain invisible to us and we can only understand those parts by communicating with others. Instead of simply acting on the basis of our own beliefs (which we know can be fallible) we can ask others to describe their worlds, their feelings, their view of the system, and their understanding of everyone's role within it. In turn, we need to be willing to share our own experiences. This process can be illuminating. We are used to seeing other people's actions, but we rarely seek to understand the feelings that motivate those actions. Expanding our view of the system in conjunction with others increases everyone's ability to depersonalize issues and see the influence of the structure on people's actions.[139]

The Kingsolver family explored alternative perspectives as they reflected on their role as consumers of food. Sure it was convenient to buy whatever they felt like eating whenever they wanted it, but they began to consider what the consequences of their purchases might be for others involved in the system. What were their perspectives? They researched how much an individual farmer is paid compared to a distributor and why a farmer might choose to grow corn crops over organic vegetables. They began to look at who owns the land and reaps the profit when products come in to the US from developing countries. They noticed that living in Appalachia meant living in an area where bad weather meant the loss of people's livelihoods. A major storm, they saw, could affect school enrolments, local businesses, changes in land use and tax structure. If developers come in buying the land from struggling farmers, the environment would also be affected. By exploring a variety of perspectives in the food production system, they were able to better develop their own standards and values, and act based on those.

Improving Behavior: From Reflection to Action

Barbara Kingsolver and her family spent many years reflecting on how they could integrate their food choices with their values. They knew that opting out of the dominant food supply system in their country was not going to be easy. Uncomfortable with the environmental costs of agribusiness and the health costs of junk food, however, they became motivated to do something. Their ability to reflect on the practices of the system as a whole, and the consequences of their own actions in it, led them to identify the main change they could make to both limit the detrimental consequences of their actions and to live by their moral code – consume locally produced food.

Kingsolver recognized her family's decision to jump off the industrial food wagon would not change the US food system. But she also knew that change starts one family at a time. She wanted her children and their children to be able to feed themselves without relying on mass production. From a personal perspective, the family also believed that living for a year on unprocessed food would likely increase their enjoyment of their meals as homegrown food tastes better. The whole year was not an experiment in abstinence, hardship and gloomy morality but a chance to celebrate the cycles of life and enjoy food from beginning to end.[140]

Animal, Vegetable, Miracle is the story of the family turning reflection into action. They consciously chose to modify their behavior and critically evaluated their thoughts and actions as they did so. The book could have been preached to its readers, telling them to adopt the same values, but it doesn't. Because they have considered many perspectives and recognize their values as their own, the family doesn't present the information as a one-size-fits-all recipe for how to live your life. Instead, Kingsolver acknowledges that most people do not live on large tracts of fertile land and that for many growing food is impractical and not necessarily appealing.[141] By presenting alternative systems of food production, she simply hopes to educate readers so they are at least aware of the different food options available to them. It is, according to the Kingsolvers' experience, not so very hard to be a more conscious consumer of food, to be reflective in this system.

Reflection and its subsequent action doesn't need to be confined to serious social issues, however. We can also use reflection to improve ourselves as systems as much as to improve the systems we live in. That's what Gretchen Rubin set out to do when she decided to devote a year of her life to figuring out what made her happy. Her happiness project grew out of a moment of realization that even though she wanted to be happy, she spent very little of her life actually thinking about how to achieve that goal.[142] Unsurprisingly, during the year, Gretchen spent a lot of time reflecting on her beliefs and values and her mental models of the world. The end result was a continually evolving set of practices that made Gretchen happy. Neither in her book nor on her website does Rubin attempt to come up with a formula for others' happiness. Instead she suggests that everyone needs to reflect on their own nature. It is self-knowledge, she argues, that leads us to learn what truly makes us happy.

The Happiness Project is Rubin's exploration of how a person can find happiness through self-reflection. Animal, Vegetable, Miracle is the story of the Kingsolver's family's reflection and action in a system that we all participate in. Whatever level of system we wish to focus on, being reflective makes it easier to act with systems intelligence. Tempering our automatic processes with self-reflection and the adoption of different perspectives, helps us attune to how we, and others, think and behave in systems. Once we have opened our senses and our minds to life in a systemic world, the challenge becomes to interact in systems in ways that foster beneficial outcomes for everyone. The next chapters address the positive actions that can spread from individual to family to community to workplace to government. We can inspire others, as the Kingsolvers hoped to do, through well-thought-out engagement in systems.

Positive Engagement

"But it doesn't matter what you're doing, it matters how you're doing it."
— Dan Savage

Positive engagement with others involves creating and sustaining connections within systems that are uplifting, open, and mutually beneficial. Communicating with respect and empathy is key. Positive engagement may include play and humor, but we can also be seriously positive. We can listen intently, ask questions, show interest and focus on the moment at hand. We can work to establish constructive patterns of communication as we relate to others in systems.

Billy Lucas was fifteen when he hanged himself in his grandmother's barn. Clearly different from his mid-western classmates, Billy had been bullied at school. In particular, his tormentors delighted in calling him a "fag" and "queer," telling him he didn't deserve to live. He took their message to heart. Even in death, Billy couldn't escape their taunts. The Facebook page set up in his memory was defaced by homophobic comments.

Billy's story is a depressing and all-too familiar one. Lesbian, gay, bisexual and transgender (LGBT) kids are among those most cruelly treated in small town USA.[143] Billy's tormentors did not make him feel appreciated. They didn't support him. They didn't bring out the best in him. Billy Lucas's school life lacked positive engagement, with devastating consequences.

Billy could have become just another casualty, one more kid who couldn't cope with life in an intolerant and narrow-minded society. But he didn't. Instead, Billy Lucas's short life proved to be a spark for change.

Widely reported in the media, Billy's story caught gay journalist and blogger Dan Savage's attention. It saddened him. It angered him. He decided to do something about it. Less than two weeks after Billy died, Dan and his partner Terry Miller posted a video to YouTube. In it, positively engaging LGBT youth directly, the couple of sixteen years spoke of their own experiences of being bullied at high school. They acknowledged the misery of those years, but, they told their audience, it gets better. Get through middle school and high school, and your world will change.

Dan recognized that without openly gay adults and mentors in their daily experience, people who could support and bring out the best in them, many gay youth cannot envisage a future where they will be accepted. He saw the video as a way to tell the teens that they were not alone. Dan sought to relieve some of the difficulties LGBT teens experience by making sure they knew they were valued. He wanted to show teens bullied about their sexuality that they would be able to experience happiness, enjoy a life of positivity, and reach their full potential if they just survived their adolescence. They could find love, acceptance and have an amazing life.

That video was the beginning of the It Gets Better project.[144] Provided with a model of and an avenue for positive engagement, thousands of others were inspired to follow Dan and Terry's lead. They, too, wanted to inspire, comfort and uplift teens struggling in communities that sent them negative messages. Within a year Dan's idea to help at risk youth had turned into a worldwide movement, supported by gay and straight alike, by celebrities, companies, politicians, activists, and ordinary people. The It Gets Better project provided a brand new forum that encouraged all kinds of people to stop holding back.

There are now more than fifty thousand videos of people showing youth how it does get better, simply by talking about their own lives or by demonstrating acceptance of the LGBT community. The website, http://www.itgetsbetter.org, positively engages with LGBT youth by providing a place that shows how love and happiness can be a reality in their futures. It also helps by providing resources to alleviate the difficulties of their adolescent years.

Dan Savage saw a sector of society that lacked support, that needed a system that nurtured instead of crushed it, and he set about creating that system. Rather than be a concerned bystander, Dan chose to positively engage with both the problem he saw and the people affected by it. We can all positively engage with systems. The challenge for us is finding effective ways we can consistently bring positive engagement to each situation.

Creating and Sustaining Positive Relationships with Others

Dan and Terry could have posted a video that expressed their anger at the bullies who tormented Billy Lucas. They could have incited bullied teens around the US to fight back, to stick up for themselves. They could have complained about the nature of a society that rejects and torments LGBT people. They didn't. Instead they chose positive engagement. They shared the very personal stories of their own lives. They spoke of being called names, physically attacked and left to fend for themselves by the adults in charge of their care during their adolescence. They told how their families struggled to accept them as gay at first, but how eventually they were embraced. They spoke of a loving relationship, happy memories and the chance to raise a child together. They showed that the suffering of their school years was just a moment in time in the brighter, happier picture that is their lives now. They spoke from the heart.

Dan and Terry understood the power of creating a relationship with the teens to whom they were speaking. They didn't focus on their own needs, but on what the teens needed from them. It can be hard for us to focus on the other. We become so immersed in generating our own thoughts, feelings and perceptions that we don't always consider how someone else is thinking, feeling and seeing things. And we often fail to realize how much of an impact our interpretations have on our interactions within systems. Because we don't notice the way we are thinking and behaving, we miss opportunities to make minor adjustments than can have major effects.

Respect, openness, interest, listening and so on are all obviously beneficial to communication. Yet, think about the systems you engage with – your work, your family, your peers, your community groups, your sports team. Can you put your hand on your heart and say that the communication in these systems embodies these characteristics? Can you even say that you always engage in these systems in this way? The honest answer is probably no. Despite intellectually knowing what good communication is, we don't necessarily consistently put that into practice. Despite our good intentions, it is easy to slide away from positive engagement.

Some systems intelligent actions that this book discusses seem almost trivial in their simplicity (apologizing, being positive, and so on), and yet, we do not take them. What prevents us from acting in systems intelligent ways even though it is obvious it would make life easier for everyone around us? The answer lies in the powerful phenomenon called *holding back* introduced in Systems Perception. The outcome of holding back is a perpetuation of the status quo that most would prefer to change. If there is no individual willing to make the first uplifting move within a system then it will always remain diminished and unable to flourish.

We also don't often notice that doing nothing creates something. Not acting can be just as influential as acting; not engaging can be just as powerful as engaging. Repeatedly not listening to our spouse, not praising our children, and not managing conflict in the workplace create systems just as real as their opposites. In fact, they can become systems that are even more entrenched because it is harder for us to see what it is we *aren't* doing than to realize what it is we *are* doing. So, we might congratulate ourselves for not arguing with our spouse, but never realize that nor are we really listening to him or her.

Even when we intend to create systems of positive engagement, there is a danger of the positivity fading under the burden of overfamiliarity, as happens in many romantic relationships. We feel so comfortable in our habitual interactions that we miss the opportunity to put life and spark back into our engagement with others. So, in our romantic relationship, one of the most important systems in our lives, bit by bit, our joyful connection can erode into something more mundane. We believe we are acting well, but because we are not fully attuned to the other person and the system, we are actually failing to see the small things we could change that would uplift the situation.

We can overcome our tendency to slide into non-positive engagement through reflection, attuning to the system and seeing things from different perspectives, the systems intelligent behaviors discussed in earlier chapters. However, we can also exercise specific communication skills that promote positive engagement in systems. Psychologist Martin Seligman and his colleagues, for example, have worked on resilience training with soldiers by getting them to think more carefully about their interactions with others. [145] During a program, one trainee told the following illuminating story:

> I talked to my eight-year-old son last night. He told me about an award he won at school, and usually I'd just say something like "that's nice." But I used the skill we learned yesterday and I asked a bunch of questions about it – Who was there when he got the award? How did he feel receiving it? Where's he going to hang the award? And about halfway through the conversation he interrupted me and said, "Dad, is this really you?!" I knew what he meant by that. That was the longest we ever talked, and I think we were both surprised by it. It was great.[146]

The impact that genuine interest and thoughtful responses have on the parent-child system is immediate. Something as seemingly trivial as changing from the reactive "that's nice" to the engaged "how does that make you feel?" attuned parent and child to one another. By positively engaging, the soldier changes the dynamics of the system and both parties value the difference.

Exploring the dimensions of systems intelligence awakens us to similarities between systems. Because systems share many characteristics, it is possible to transfer successful attitudes and approaches from one system to another. Of course, specific actions won't always carry well. For example, we might speak in a motivating manner at work with positive effect so we import the same tone of voice at home. It feels like positive engagement but may actually be irritating our family.

But transferring our understanding of how systems work can open up new actions for us. Say, for example, you and your spouse have a disagreement. Both of you are tired of talking about the issue and both of you are pretty entrenched in your own perspectives. Typically, without an understanding of effective intervention in systems, it is hard to break the negative spiral. The disagreement just spirals out of control. But if you think about how a system of engagement has evolved, you might also think to suddenly dash outside to pick a flower from your garden and present it to your spouse. This unexpected gesture – maybe it will make you both laugh, maybe it will remind you of the bigger picture of your love for one another – is likely to change the tone of your interaction. It is a form of *positive engagement* that intervenes in a negative system of conflict with the intent of breaking a pattern.

Now imagine a conflict at work. You and your boss disagree on an issue and you feel the discussion escalating into an argument. Running outside to pick a flower is probably not a great option as that action is not appropriate to the work system. However, some other kind of positive engagement could be effective. Perhaps you could offer to make a cup of coffee for both of you, a gesture that in the setting of a disagreement reminds both of you that you usually get along pretty well and perhaps a break would be good. Or maybe you realize that you have been so busy telling your boss your side of the issue that you haven't really listened, so you offer to be quiet for five minutes and make sure you clearly understand his or her perspective. The point is that when we act systems intelligently we are orienting our attitude and actions towards the system at hand and, though the individual behaviors necessarily change from system to system, the higher-level intention remains the same. Our goal is always to improve what is happening in the system and our engagement with it.

What opportunities and prospects might we open up when we choose to positively engage? Dan Savage stopped holding back when he heard Billy's story, and the It Gets Better project became something bigger and more amazing than he ever imagined. With an awareness of systems and an understanding of how our behaviors affect them, we, too, can positively engage with the systems around us.

Advocacy and Inquiry

An effective way to begin or renew our positive engagement is to choose constructive communicative styles that attend to others and so contribute to an uplifting atmosphere in systems. Take a look at the following exchange:

"I think we should go to the beach today."
"We need to go visit my mother."
"But it's a beautiful sunny day and we haven't been to the beach in ages."
"We haven't visited my mother in ages either."

Just four simple lines tell us that these two people are in advocacy mode. Advocacy is about fighting for a perspective, holding one's ground, and converting someone to a point of view. Now look at the following exchange.

"It's a beautiful day. What do you feel like doing?"
"I'd love to do something fun, but we need to go visit my mother."
"Is it possible we could manage to do both those things?"
"I guess we could visit my mother this morning and then go somewhere." "Where would you like to go?"

Look how this conversation starts – with a question, not a statement. It is not about imposing one's will on someone else. It is about communicating in such a way that explores options. This is inquiry mode. Inquiry involves flexibility, responsiveness, and questioning. It is about the genuine sharing of perspectives. One way that we can achieve positive engagement is to pay attention to our mode of communication, particularly whether we are adopting an *inquiry* mode or an *advocacy* mode.[147]

Both advocacy, where we stand up for our position, and inquiry, where we are open to other perspectives, are useful modes of engagement at times. The problem is we tend to spend much more time in advocacy mode than we do in

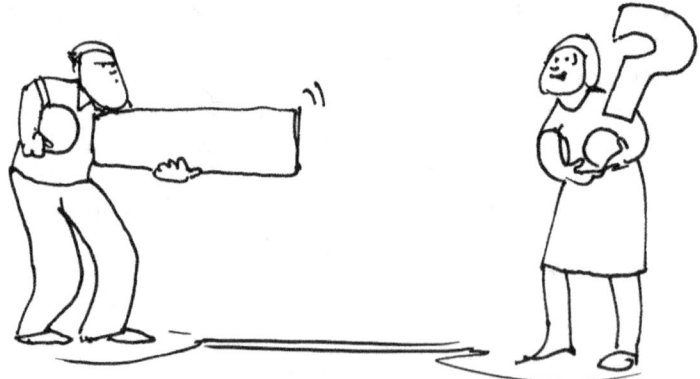

inquiry mode, with detrimental results on social systems. Why? In part, we want to be efficient, so we offer our opinions and solutions as if they were the only sensible possibility. We also tend to trust our own judgments, perceptions and interpretations and so fight for them. Invariably, others do the same and potentially a system of escalation develops. This can be exacerbated in cultures that place particular value on standing up for yourself, being firm in your beliefs, and being articulate. Finally, advocacy mode is a kind of defensive routine; it feels safer to come out telling people how things are than asking what they might be.

The difference between advocacy and inquiry is especially relevant when we are problem solving. Imagine your workplace is wrestling with how to cut costs. You're certain rescheduling the work roster is the way to go and you have the numbers to back up your claim. It's so obviously the solution you are excited to present it to your colleagues. During the discussion you end up making statements like

"As you all know..."
"Clearly the answer lies in changing the rosters..."
"Look at these numbers that back me up..."
"I've done all the research, and the results show..."
"Other options just don't stack up compared to this..."

In other words, you enter the discussion with a specific outcome in mind. You are there to advocate your position and convince others that it is the only sensible solution. It might feel like positively engaging because you are offering a solution, but the process of engagement itself is not positive – it is adversarial.

Imagine the alternative, inquiry mode that you could adopt. You would still share your idea about the rosters, but you could do so in a way that invites others to contribute their ideas too. You might say

"I'd like to offer an idea for discussion..."
"Let me tell you why I ended up focusing on changing the rosters..."
"Can anyone see weaknesses in my plan that I haven't considered..."
"It would be great to hear some other ideas..."

These kinds of statements invite others into the discussion and show your willingness to accept fresh inputs. They are constructive contributions to communicative interactions that positively engage with systems.

Inquiry mode encourages us to remember that there are as many perspectives of events as people involved in those events and so helps us to approach interactions with an open mind. In this mode we are more willing to listen to the other person's answer and to learn from it. Inquiry helps reassure other people that it is safe to share with us in a trusting and open way. One of the simplest ways to do this is by using questions. Instead of taking an advocacy approach that is about cementing our own position and influencing the other person to think like us, we might say "Please describe how you see the situation" or

"Can you share with me your experience on this subject?" Inviting others to offer their perspective shows our commitment to listening and learning, and suggests it will be possible to move forward jointly.

It is not always necessary to abandon advocacy altogether in favor of inquiry. There are times when we are communicating with others that we need to put forward our own point of view. Such situations call for "reciprocal inquiry," a combination of advocacy and inquiry. In this mode of communication, every party makes their position explicit but also responds to inquiry. In this way, everybody's view is open to scrutiny and the focus becomes less about winning an argument and more about finding the strongest position. Rather than simply selecting confirmatory evidence to support our argument people are exposed to all the evidence and reason through it. In the process of reciprocal inquiry, people feel their opinions are appreciated and they have an opportunity to contribute – they feel positively engaged.

Naturally, following a reciprocal inquiry mode doesn't always end with perfect agreement. Sometimes we feel very strongly about our positions and are reluctant to change them. People can have very determined views in some topic areas. Maybe you and your sibling are diametrically opposed on many issues, but, like their views or not, you are part of the same family system. It's OK to agree to disagree – the important thing is that you both feel that you have been heard, that you have been able to positively engage.

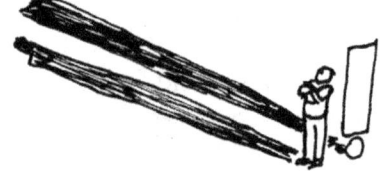

Reflection: Advocacy and Inquiry

At the next meeting you attend, whether it is in your family, your workplace or some other group, take a blank sheet of paper with you. Divide the sheet into two columns: advocacy and inquiry. As the meeting progresses, check the appropriate column after you speak.

Beginning statements with "I think…" "In my opinion…" "We should…" typically reflect advocacy mode. Saying things like "Tell me about…" "How might we move forward…" "What makes you say…" are examples of inquiry mode.

Which mode do you use the most?

Do the same thing in other settings. Does your mode change depending on the system you are in? Or who is in the room? Is there room to include more inquiry in your communication?

Alternatively, you could work with a partner. Record each other's contributions as either advocacy or inquiry and give each other feedback after the meeting.

If you can, follow this up with the group. Let them know what you are doing and enlist their help. Perhaps everyone can check a sheet for himself or herself. Or, you might have everyone classify all the comments under one or other heading so the group gets a sense of how much advocacy and how much inquiry goes on in its meetings.

Use the results to spark discussion about the kind of communication the group would prefer. Have people volunteer to be in inquiry mode only for the next meeting and see how that changes things. Experiment with positive engagement in this system.[148]

Creating a Positive Atmosphere

Think of a time when you have been involved in a productive team, be it sports group, volunteer association, workplace team or something else. Remember how everyone was involved, pulled their weight, and got along well. If an outsider had come along and asked anyone in the group how they felt about the team, each person would have had positive things to say. The shared atmosphere of this type of group is supportive.

In contrast, a team where people are not getting along and team members are fearful, apprehensive and argumentative has a defensive atmosphere. Members will be reluctant to get together, likely have high absenteeism, and develop factions.

The atmosphere of a system emerges from the many behavioral and communication choices each member makes and experience day after day. Making conscious decisions to constructively communicate can profoundly influence our experience in systems. Ongoing positive engagement has a contagious effect, shaping the long-term relationships between people in systems. It builds a supportive atmosphere, and a supportive atmosphere tends to bring out the best in everyone. Without positive engagement in a system, people feel underappreciated and tense, and the general feeling of the system is low. There is little chance for individuals or the systems as a whole to flourish.

Consider your own workplace. How would you characterize the atmosphere there? In a workplace where stories are shared, praise is actively given, and support is provided in times of trouble, positive engagement is practiced. But if colleagues barely communicate, if people are not attuned to one another's needs, and if there is neither the time nor inclination to support one another, then positive engagement is lacking. The resulting atmosphere is produced by our actions in the system and at the same time affects how we continue to act. It has a huge consequence on how we feel about the system overall.

Importantly, a system's atmosphere is not determined by the actions of any one individual. It is a systemic phenomenon. Atmosphere is the relatively enduring mood that is the outcome of the process of interaction between all individuals in the system. Naturally, if one worker arrives at the office grumpy and bad tempered it will affect the general mood. But if the workplace already has established a supportive atmosphere through positive engagement, the other members might be able to cheer the grumpy person into a better mood or will respect their feelings, understanding that everyone has an off day. In a defensive atmosphere, a grumpy colleague is more likely to be attacked, complained about or ignored.

As individuals, while we cannot control the atmosphere of the systems we belong to, we can recognize our own contribution to the prevailing mood. We can attune ourselves to others' feelings, offering support where needed. By offering praise and encouragement we can help everyone live up to their potential. Where we see negative patterns of interaction developing we can intervene and break the patterns. If we are the grumpy one, we can pre-empt our potentially negative effect on the systems dynamics by acknowledging and explaining our bad mood and asking to be given some leeway.

In other words, we can positively engage within systems and so set the tone for the kind of system we want. Look at the many videos posted on the It Gets Better website and you will see that they perpetuate Dan and Terry's original message of hope and uplift. That's because Dan and Terry established from the outset what kind of contributions and conversations would be welcomed in the It Gets Better Project. They did their part in creating an atmosphere that allows other people to take risks without fear of ostracism. With positive engagement, we can do the same in the systems we live in.

Conflict Management

Of course, even groups that generally get along will not agree on everything all of the time. The difference between a supportive and defensive atmosphere often lies in how people cope with conflict. Where a defensive atmosphere will lead to open disagreements, threats, judgments, and controlling behaviors, a supportive atmosphere will be characterized by empathy, inquiry, spontaneity and flexibility. A commitment to positive engagement builds large enough a well of positivity and goodwill that momentary negativity doesn't destroy the system's synergy. [149] Scientist and relationship expert John Gottman's research shows that what matters most in human relationships is not avoiding conflict but having the ability to repair relationships when things go wrong. [150] It is hardly surprising, then, that acting intelligently in systems involves managing conflict, and that positive engagement helps us to do that.

Conflict can be a stressful and emotional experience. One reason that we find conflict psychologically demanding is that many of us become self and settlement-oriented. We want our own way; we want to achieve the objectives that we have. Often, we think we know better than the other person. We forget that we are connected to the others involved in the conflict via the systems that we share. We don't notice that the

conflict itself creates a new system as it unfolds. Likely the other person is experiencing the same emotions and desires that we are. Like us they feel they are not being listened to or appreciated and like us they have too much pride to back down. So the focus of our interaction becomes argument, persuasion, and influence – on doing everything we can to bring the other side's perspective closer to ours. In this advocacy-based approach, we can become adversarial or manipulative.

Alleviating Tension

There is another option. We can seek to bring out the best in people even when we have a difference of opinion. Conflict does not preclude the ability to positively engage. In fact, conflict makes positive engagement all the more essential for the system. That means asking what our own role is in the emergence of the conflict, what we can do to resolve things, and how we might be able to create trust. It is possible to choose positive engagement rather than spiral into patterns of negativity. With positive engagement we can move through the differentiation phase calmly and respectfully, then focus on integration.

Systems are all about relationships. Adopting a systems lens makes us mindful that after the disagreement we will still be connected to our colleague, our friend or our family member. Our focus subtly shifts from being settlement oriented (where we aim to get what we want) to relationship oriented (where we care about maintaining the connection we have with the other party). This motivates us to look for a mutually beneficial resolution instead of wanting to succeed at the expense of the other person. We can actively seek consensus, finding a decision is acceptable to all parties, rather than compromise, having everyone walk away somewhat dissatisfied. We can also look for outcomes that help improve the system rather than just meet our or the other party's needs.

Roger Fisher discovered how positive engagement could change conflicts.[151] Fisher spent forty years on the faculty at Harvard Law School, but he also took a central role away from academia, introducing himself into major disputes to fix problems. His focus was on getting to yes, a saying that became his catchphrase. Fisher had a knack for separating the people from the problem, for exploring the deep issues for either side, and for thinking through many possible options. He

wanted those involved in disputes of even the greatest magnitude to see the humanity in each other, to listen to one another, and to really understand what each other was thinking. He wanted them to positively engage.

Fisher was so skillful those in high positions adopted his methods – Ronald Reagan, Mikhail Gorbachev, Golda Meir, Egyptian President Gamal Abdel Nasser, and Israel's Menachem Begin all experienced his method of negotiations. It was Roger Fisher who suggested to Reagan that rather than confront Gorbachev over policy he sit and chat with him in relaxed surroundings. He knew how to change the nature of the system of conflict by focusing on relationships.

Developing bonds rather than focusing on issues is also a key skill for hostage negotiators. Hostage negotiators need to make a connection with hostage takers that allows them to influence them away from destructive behavior towards constructive action. They have to change the mindset of the person holding the hostages from negativity to positivity, and they do this by creating an emotional attachment. By using techniques such as initiating conversations about something other than the situation at hand to connect with the hostage taker, the negotiator brings about a magical transformation and dissipates the hostility of the situation. In other words, they create a relationship, a system of positive engagement, during the stand-off.[152]

Where we are connected by strong systemic ties to people who we disagree with it is especially helpful to positively engage in ways that alleviate tension. The main goal becomes not bringing someone around to our viewpoint but about treating the other person with respect, understanding, caring, and fairness as we communicate our opinions. It is not about us winning and them losing (or vice versa) – it recognizes that *us* and *them* form part of the same system. Communicating in this way helps us to understand what it feels like to live in a different world of experience – we learn to see the system through someone else's eyes and to engage with them positively.

Naturally, the people we are in conflict with may resist efforts to positively engage. They may well remain in advocacy mode, arguing strongly for their position. Even if this is the case it is worth persevering with positive engagement because it changes the dynamic of the system of conflict. Conflict usually escalates because both people remain stubborn, so even if just one person approaches the interaction differently the process changes. It becomes hard to fight with someone who is not fighting back.

It is possible to alleviate tension in a conflict situation by using specific techniques for positively engaging. We can, for example, use the three phases of ethical persuasion to create a positive conflict system: they speak, we speak, then together we integrate.[153] We begin by inviting the other person or persons to speak first. This is pretty unusual because when we are in conflict we typically are eager to explain our perspective first. To show we are listening, it is important to then restate their message back to them.

Once we have heard their perspective, and they agree that we understand what they are saying, the next step relies on their sense of obligation. In allowing the other person to have had their say first, we hope that they will allow us to speak freely in return. By calling attention to the process we modeled ("I allowed you to speak without arguing, please do the same for me" "Can you tell me what you think I just said?") we can also encourage them to engage respectfully in the positive system we are trying to create.

When both parties have understood each other's point of view, they can see exactly what their differences are and what everyone does agree on. Then the task is to respectfully explore options that might bring people together on the points of conflict. Emotions need to be restrained so that smart decisions can be made about what to say and how to say it. Decisions about a solution should not be hasty or bullied. Being willing to take responsibility for concrete actions that bring change and improvement will help to advance the process. Of course, sometimes two parties may never agree with each other. The focus then becomes on finding a way to move forward despite the differences. It is possible to respectfully agree to disagree and still maintain healthy and open systemic relationships.

Attending to Emotion

Canadian musician Dave Carroll and his band mates were understandably upset when they looked out of the window of their just-landed plane (the first leg on a multi stop journey) and saw their musical instruments, their livelihoods, being thrown with abandon by the airline's baggage handlers. When Carroll finally took possession of his guitar at journey's end, he found, unsurprisingly, that it was broken. What happened next was to have an enormous impact on the airline. The company persistently gave Carroll the run around as he tried to initiate a claims process to recover just over a thousand dollars in repair costs. He was shunted from one customer service agent to another, dealing with employees as far flung as Chicago and India, with no department or individual taking responsibility for looking after his claim. Faxes were lost, phone numbers disconnected, paperwork vanished into thin air. Finally, eight months after he initiated the process, Carroll was informed via email that his claim had been denied. He tried for another month to obtain compensation, until finally admitting defeat.

But then Carroll had a bright idea: "The system is designed to frustrate affected customers into giving up their claims…but I realized then that as a songwriter and traveling musician I wasn't without options."[154] Carroll did what he knew best and wrote a song about his troubles with the company, posting the accompanying video on YouTube.[155] When the video went viral the airline had a major branding issue on its hands. Astonishingly, its stock dropped ten percent in the aftermath, dramatically raising corporate awareness about the power of social media in the process.

Resorting to revenge, even the amusing kind that Carroll used, is not positive engagement, but it is a common reaction to perceived wrongs. The cycle of revenge is one of those irrational yet predictable loops we get caught up in. When we feel we have been wronged without justification we build up feelings of resentment towards others or systems and look to take revenge on either individuals or the organizations that wrong us. This may play out as simply as taking our business elsewhere after poor service, or as elaborately as Dave Carroll's response to the airline that damaged his guitar. Revenge is a kind of last resort for dealing with unacknowledged negative emotions. It is far more systems intelligent to attend to the emotions that develop during conflict, and we can do that by making the choice to positively engage.

That is not always easy. At times strong feelings develop in us during conflict and override our ability to act thoughtfully and calmly. Swept up in deeply felt emotions, we may fail to see alternative thoughts and courses of action available to us. In fact, being dominated by our emotions is a physiological phenomenon known as an "amygdala hijack."[156] The amygdala is the part of the brain that governs our emotional reactions. Under normal, non-threatening conditions it works in harmony with our pre-frontal cortex so we live with a balance between our reasoning and emotions. Sometimes, though, we experience an amygdala hijack. In response to a perceived threat, our amygdala overrides our ability to reason and triggers a flight-or-fight response in us, working for our emotions much like type-one thinking does for our cognition. In the absence of the calming influence of our pre-frontal cortex, we rely on habitual responses and the influence of stress hormones. No problem if a rabid dog threatens us, but somewhat less helpful if our partner tells us we are lazy.

An amygdala hijack is less useful in social situations (like arguments) than it is in physically dangerous situations (like meeting a sick dog) because the amygdala is prone to making mistakes. What it perceives as a threat is not always a threat – consequently, our immediate reaction may turn out to be out of proportion to the original event. Many modern threats are symbolic rather than physical. Criticism, unfair treatment, disrespect and job insecurity can all result in amygdala hijacks. The problem is that the amygdala responds to limited data, gaining a sloppy picture to which it reacts instantly. The richer data travels to other parts of the brain at a much slower rate.

If we react on the basis of only our amygdala's interpretation, we run the risk of taking actions we might regret later. It's far more sensible to wait for the rest of the brain to catch up and make a considered response. We need to attune to our own body's processes and thoughts and say to ourselves "I'm upset now – I will walk away and respond later" or "I'm overreacting here. I need to calm down and engage more positively."[157] Behaving less reactively means we are more likely to be able to pause and consider the systems affecting the generation of the perceived threat, something it is difficult to do when our physiology makes us feel we are under personal attack.

It's important to engage cognitively with our emotions as the long-term effects of reacting based on short-term emotions can be costly. The intense emotions will pass – deep down we know this – but the consequences of decisions made in the heat of the moment can linger.[158] They can set up repetitive patterns of negative interactions, a kind of emotional cascade as we react, trigger amygdala hijacks in others, and then react to their reactions again. Breaking this default pattern of emotional response takes effort, but allows us the opportunity to create more positive ways of engaging within the social systems we are participating in.

The amygdala is part of our evolutionary history as a species. We cannot eliminate its reactions altogether, nor should we want to, but we can learn to recognize them and so live better within our own limitations. We can attune to ourselves as a system so that we can get along better in the social systems we live in, including when we are experiencing conflict. When our emotions get the better of us, or we recognize the person we are talking to is experiencing strong emotions, we can call time out until those feelings have passed. It is important that we also respect other people's desire to take a break. It can be infuriating to have someone insisting that "we need to talk this through" when you know that you are in the grip of an uncontrollable emotional reaction.

Saying Sorry

While ideally we seek to positively engage with systems, in times of conflict we occasionally forget our skills in the heat of the moment. When we are drawn into a conflict and do rash things and make stupid statements that hurt others, our behavior helps escalate the system of conflict. Fortunately, there is another positive engagement technique we can tap into that has enormous potential for improving the quality of engagement within systems, alleviating tension and attending to people's emotional needs – the apology.

Take the case of Dave Carroll and his guitar. Carroll's frustration was less to do with the damage to his instrument and more to do with the poor response of the company to his complaint. The airline's systems let him down. Had they simply apologized and paid the twelve hundred dollar cost of repairing the guitar, Carroll would not have chosen to vent his frustration in such a public manner. Acknowledgement and feedback is important to humans, and apologies can dampen our instinct for revenge.

Acknowledging our mistakes and the pain we have caused others by apologizing is a simple but effective way to acknowledge the emotional system of conflict. A sincere apology is a soothing balm to hurt emotions. It admits the hurtful impact of actions or words on a relationship and helps diffuse anger. It even has a physical effect on the recipient, decreasing their blood pressure, slowing their heart rate and calming their breathing.[159] Emotionally, receiving an apology helps override the workings of our amygdala – we no longer perceive the person who hurt us as a threat. We feel able to move past the perceived injury when our pain has been acknowledged.

But it is not only the recipient of the apology who benefits. Conflict is a system and apologizing changes the experience for both the person apologized to and the person who makes the apology. If we acknowledge our wrongs we shed the guilt and shame that often attends hurtful actions, and in the process hopefully are reminded of the benefits of positive engagement. We also increase our empathy and connection with the other person, and because it makes us vulnerable, it prevents us becoming distanced from them.[160] Behavioral economist Dan Ariely's research has shown that apologies have a huge impact in counteracting the cycle of revenge that people are prone to fall into. One study showed people were less likely to sue doctors who took responsibility for medical mistakes and apologized.[161] In part that's because offering and accepting an apology nurtures forgiveness. It is easier for us to forgive someone who acknowledges their actions have been hurtful, so an apology introduces the possibility of forgiveness to the system.

Often people need their emotions acknowledged more than they need to be right about the facts, and when we positively engage with others we are attending to this dimension. When Dan and Terry posted that first video for the It Gets Better project, they didn't turn it into an argument with those who bully homosexual youth. In other words, they didn't create a system of conflict. Instead, they made the primary focus of the It Gets Better project providing emotional support to LGBT teens.

Managing conflict through positive engagement is a skill that takes practice to master because it runs counter to most people's automatic and emotional responses. It requires us to be self-aware and aware of the other simultaneously. In other words, it is about attuning to the system that we create with others and looking for ways to better the relationship within that system, to positively engage. We can avoid holding back and waiting for the other person to make the first move, instead taking the responsibility to change the dynamic to a more positive one ourselves. We can step away from advocacy and adopt inquiry mode as well as alleviate tension and attend to emotions. We can do our part to build a supportive atmosphere even if we disagree about something. Positive engagement helps turn conflict into a manageable process instead of a stressful experience and cultivates constructive and respectful relationships in systems.

Elevating Others

On February 14th, 1984, in the historic city of Sarajevo, an insurance book clerk and a policeman from England mesmerized the world's television audience for four minutes and twenty-eight seconds. Jayne Torvill and Christopher Dean became, well before the advent of YouTube, household names. Their haunting ice dance to Ravel's Bolero was emotionally uplifting and inspired the judges to award them the highest ever score for figure skating. Perfect synchronicity, graceful flow, and complete harmony elevated their performance beyond the ordinary. The television commentator noted at the end of their routine that it was perhaps not the most difficult, perhaps not the most dangerous routine, but it was without question a beautiful emotional experience. [162] All who watched it felt the moment. The audience was carried on an emotional journey with the ice dancers.

When we witness others being emotionally uplifted or spontaneous act of

kindness, courage and compassion we experience what psychologists call "elevation."[163] Elevation is the warm feeling that suffuses us when we watch a beautiful ice dance, a child offer another child comfort in the playground, or a stranger telling an LGBT youth they are valued. The experience of elevation is a fundamental phenomenon in life, a phenomenon made more likely through positive engagement.

Just like other human emotions, elevation can be contagious. Witnessing, and, psychologists speculate, even just hearing about such acts may inspire us to want to perform in similar ways.[164] Emotions and actions diffuse in systems, and positive engagement encourages the spreading of positivity rather than negativity. A social system in which members are striving to perform elevating acts is likely to be peaceful and nurturing. The more elevating actions we witness, the more likely we are to elevate others in turn. But it has to start somewhere. Instead of holding back, we can take the opportunity to be a Dan Savage, to assume responsibility for initiating the lifting of our own attitude and the spirits of those around us.

Reciprocity

During the Christmas of 1914, in the trenches of Flanders during World War One, something astonishing happened. It was the beginning of the war, the middle of winter, and a brief strip of no-man's-land littered with dead bodies separated the German and (mostly) British armies. On Christmas Eve, as dusk fell, the German soldiers lit candles sent to them from home and began to sing Christmas carols. Moved, the British spontaneously applauded. Hearing the German soldiers caroling had momentarily elevated them beyond their grim circumstances. Then the British, too, began to sing. When they finished, the Germans clapped for them.[165] Each side impulsively appreciated the others' efforts and that small act of positive engagement led to an extraordinary few days.

By Christmas morning, a spontaneous and instinctive truce emerged. Soldiers from both sides came out from their trenches and met in the middle ground. There they exchanged things like tobacco and rations, and worked unimpeded to bury their dead. Some soldiers fashioned soccer balls out of materials at hand and played friendly games with one another. The simple sharing of Christmas carols had reminded the soldiers of the humanity they shared.

Ultimately, the system of war reasserted itself. The high commands of both sides ordered the soldiers to go back to fighting else face court martial. Briefly, the ordinary men at the front stepped outside of the roles – soldiers and enemies – that the army ascribed them and chose to engage with one another positively. In doing so, they inadvertently drew on the idea of reciprocity, a useful concept that helps us to initiate elevation in systems.

Reciprocity is driven by the innate human impetus to respond to one another in kind. When people are nice to us, we treat them nicely. When they are not so nice, neither are we. Research into the system of marriage, for example, has shown that nice-nice behavior is implicit in any marriage contract – we expect the kind things we do for our spouse to be reciprocated with equally kind actions on their part. Those couples that frequently use nice-nice, or positive reciprocity, even in conflict, have happier, longer-lasting marriages. Unsurprisingly, those who go the nasty-nasty route became unhappy, leading to even more nasty-nasty interactions.[166] When people act with positive engagement within systems they help everyone to be the best they can be because others are drawn into acting reciprocally. To initiate this positive engagement cycle, we need to be willing to be nice first.

This is not as difficult as it might sound as humans are actually hardwired to be kind to one another. According to the latest research on happiness, being kind to others is crucial to a person's wellbeing. We often try to take shortcuts to moments of happiness – through chocolate, alcohol, shopping and so on – but the rewards are fleeting. This is because it is not just the feeling of happiness that we want but also the feeling that we are *entitled* to feel happy.[167] It is through enacting our strengths and virtues that we achieve emotional satisfaction. When we volunteer to drive cancer patients to the hospital or babysit so our friends can have a night out we feel virtuous. These actions lead to feelings of elevation and gratification that are far longer lasting than the temporary joys that a nice glass of pinot noir or a new TV bring. These kind acts bestow on us an "afterglow"[168] and the effect of that feeling is to generate even more kindness in us.

Interestingly, psychology research shows that people act charitably towards others even when they don't have to for any reason. We are usually generous even when we don't think we will ever see the recipient of our kindness again. It seems that acting to help others without foreseeable self-gain emerges naturally from the evolution of cooperation.[169] From a systems intelligence perspective this makes sense. We live our lives immersed in social systems, the connections we have with others not always visible or apparent to us. It is far more intelligent of us to positively engage with people because they may well turn out to be connected to us by some not-visible-right-now system. Tellingly, people who help others only when they see a gain for themselves do worse over time than those who are generous without thinking about what might come in return.[170]

Our impetus to be generous and kind, and so foster reciprocity, can be harnessed for the betterment of systems. Both the "Pay it Forward" and the "Random Acts of Kindness" movements, like the It Gets Better project, draw on the idea of benefitting others to create benefits in the wider system through positive engagement. In the Pay it Forward concept, people who benefit from an act of kindness are encouraged to pay it forward by doing three good deeds for others. Inspired by the movie based on Catherine Ryan Hyde's novel, a grass-roots social movement emerged encouraging this philosophy in life. The idea is that if recipients of kindness follow this simple tenet then acts of kindness will increase exponentially for the betterment of society.[171]

Random Acts of Kindness is a movement with a similar focus.[172] To counter the negative feelings generated by the frequent mentions of "random acts of violence" in the media, people began to promote random acts of kindness. The intent is to elevate and inspire individuals to live a life of kindness so that overall society as a system is uplifted. The movement relies on reciprocity and the uplifting feelings that the recipient of a kind act feels to encourage them to act kindly in future. At the same time, it rests on the hope that the positive feelings generated in the person who is kind encourage them to perform random acts of kindness more often. A US-based foundation promotes random acts of kindness through its website, even providing free resources for promoting and teaching kindness in schools.[173]

Movements like these that promote acts of kindheartedness are about moving from a transaction-focused life to a more systemic understanding of experience – where reciprocity and elevation ripple through a system, contributing to the shared atmosphere. Instead of keeping tally of what we do for others or expecting quid pro quo we give freely without any expectation of being paid back. Clearly such actions have a positive impact on systems in an indirect but intuitive way. By performing an act of kindness without any expectation of immediate, tangible, *individual* payback, people are demonstrating their understanding that we are all connected, even if those connections are invisible to us. Like Dan and Terry when they posted that first video, they act kindly because they trust that by encouraging acts of kindness in others, overall, eventually, we will have a better society. They are trying to improve the systems we live in for the good of the systems, others, and themselves.

The only immediate reward for an act of kindness may simply be a feeling of satisfaction at having done the right thing. But we should not underestimate the power of this feeling. Feeling positive emotion, as we learned earlier, is not only its own reward; it also causes greater success in life.[174] The more positive we feel, the better our friendships, health, love relationships, and achievements. Altruistic acts help us to strengthen social ties and develop the means we have for expressing love and care. Such outcomes often endure long after the initial positive emotion has faded away.[175] Stimulating reciprocity by acting being the first to positively engage is one way we can act intelligently in systems.

Praising People for Their Achievements

Human life is a struggle for recognition. We thrive on affirmative attention. Given this, a very simple but effective way to improve the relationships within systems, and thus the quality of the overall system, is to acknowledge the efforts of others. There is no need for us to be miserly with our praise, especially when we know that acknowledgement reinforces positive behavior. A former employee of Al Gore, for example, remembers that he always took time to thank staff when they had just finished a major task for him, noting he was one of the few senators who understood how important just a few words of gratitude could be to a junior staffer. [176] That realization inspired loyalty in Gore's team. The simple act of verbalizing appreciation of others, of congratulating them on their successes can have an enormous impact.

The systems intelligent person seeking to positively engage will acknowledge beyond the obvious. Of course we should thank and praise those who clearly deserve it, but we can cast our eyes wider, too. By taking time to look for the connections we have with others in systems, we will find many people who have helped us whom we have never expressed our appreciation to.

Charles Plumb, a former navy jet pilot in the Vietnam War had this brought home to him in a chance encounter. When a man kept staring at him and then approached his table in a Kansas City restaurant, Plumb, now a motivational speaker, didn't recognize him. But the man knew him and knew the details of his service. When Plumb asked the man how he knew so much about him, the man replied that he had packed Plumb's parachute for his final mission, before he was shot down and had to parachute into enemy territory. A surprised Plumb offered his hand and words of thanks to the person who had indirectly saved his life all those years ago. Plumb recognized that the prevailing social system that separated pilots and sailors prevented him from seeing, let alone, positively engaging with those whom he was connected to. It had never occurred to him how much he relied on the sailors to keep him alive and so it never occurred to him to appreciate, praise or thank them.[177]

Joann Jones had a similar thought-provoking moment when systemic connections were opened up for her. During her second year of nursing school a professor gave the class a quiz. Jones answered the questions easily until she reached the last one. It asked her to write down the first name of the woman who cleaned the school. Jones wondered if the question was a joke and handed in her paper at the end of the class with a blank space where the answer should have been. Another student asked the professor if the final question counted towards the grade. "Absolutely," the professor said. "In your careers, you will meet many people. All are significant. They deserve your attention and care, even if all you do is smile and say hello." Jones recounts that she never forgot the lesson. She also subsequently made the effort to learn the cleaner's name – it was Dorothy.[178]

We all have the equivalent of the parachute packer and the school cleaner in our lives. They are the people who we are connected with within larger systems who barely register on our radar, the people we forget to praise and to appreciate. Yet, making the effort to positively engage with these people by acknowledging their actions may elevate both them and the system.

That acknowledgement can be as simple as verbalizing the positive things we think about people. It is easy to *think* positive thoughts like "he looks nice today" or "she did a good job with that project" but more difficult to regularly turn those thoughts into words. Praise is not always an automatic part of our script. Nor is affirmation, which is just as valuable as praise. Letting people see that their contribution is noticed and valued is powerful, as the It Gets Better project has shown. Praising and affirming others in meaningful ways are simple but effective means of engaging positively that enhance the systems we live in.

Reflection and Action

'Think back to the last time you were acknowledged – by a colleague, a family member, a lover, a stranger.

Remember how good it felt to have someone recognize your hard work, or even just compliment you. Think about how warmly you felt towards that person and how it put a smile on your face.

Now think about when you last praised someone – how did it make them feel? How did it make you feel? When did you last offer praise?

Practice acknowledgement today:

Does the server at the supermarket work efficiently, smile nicely, act friendly?
Thank them.

Has your spouse or parent or child done something kind today?
Tell them.

Has a recent change at work been successful?
Let the person who implemented it know.

Look for the opportunity to acknowledge at least one person's efforts everyday.

Whatever praise and acknowledgement we give needs to be genuine. Trite, insincere, or undeserved comments do more harm than good. They make people suspicious of our motives and cause a breakdown in trust. In fact, the contagious nature of emotions means that emotional feedback overrides the content of our message. In a study where people were given praise with a cold, critical and judgmental tone and given criticism in positive, happy and upbeat manner, those who were criticized felt good about the interaction and those who were praised didn't.[179] Unsurprisingly, praise and affirmation need to be authentic to generate positive responses in others. Wanting to be acknowledged is part of the human condition, and why positive engagement through praise can have such a large impact in systems.

Bringing Out the Best in Others

Elevation of others is not only achieved through acknowledgement or praise. We can also create opportunities for others to flourish in systems through other positively engaging actions. Often, very simple acts, such as being kind to a stranger or posting a supportive video, can make a real difference in people's experiences in systems. There's a great story about a British shoe store company, Bally's, wanting its employees to enhance their customers' retail experience. Instead of ordering its workforce to be nice to the public, top management decided to model the behavior it was seeking from its employees. They used people's natural tendency to reciprocate and took the opportunity to acknowledge their staff, hoping it would have a flow on effect in the overall system.

Managers at this shoe company were taught to look after their employees' needs. By allowing staff to have time off to go to the doctor or being flexible with childcare arrangements they helped develop a happy and appreciative workforce who wanted and were able to treat customers well. In addition, the company acknowledged their employees by rewarding not just the high sales achievers, but also those who did other helpful things, like work on their day off to cover a sick colleague. Bottles of champagne and bunches of flowers – acknowledgement – made their staff feel valued, and in turn led them to go the extra mile for their employer.[180] As a result of feeling appreciated and respected by their employers, staff felt the value in similarly acknowledging their customers. It was not unusual to send thank you notes to customers to acknowledge their purchase, for example.

Many companies use a similar approach and offer health and wellbeing perks for employees and their families.[181] Such companies hope that by paying attention to improving the organizational systems for everyone in them, they are sending a message to their employees that they are valued. Organizations experimenting with these new ways of positively engaging with their employees try to change the typical structure and expectations of a workplace to bring the best out in their workers.

While changing how we positively engage within an existing system can be helpful, sometimes creating a new system can be a productive way to bring out the best in others. That's what Dan Savage did when he launched the It Gets Better project. It's also what Muhummed Yunus, the father of microfinancing, did.[182] In the 1970s, economist Yunus discovered during his visits to extremely poor households in Bangladesh that exorbitant interest rates charged by moneylenders were preventing the poor from making a living from their limited skills and resources. Women weaving baskets in the village of Jobra, for example, were forced to borrow money to buy materials and then sell their product back to the moneylender for less than US two cents profit. Yunus famously reached into his own pockets to offer twenty-seven American dollars to forty-two women in the village to free them from a cycle of poverty.

Freeing the women from their indebtedness had an enormous impact on the lives of the workers in Jobra. But Yunus saw that a charity dollar only had one life: once spent it was gone.[183] His determination to find an alternative method to help the poor led to Yunus spending the next forty years immersed in the world of microfinance. He developed a banking system that aimed to facilitate the needy elevating themselves from poverty and teach them financial principles, and in the process opened a new model of lending. Microfinance, or microcredit, as it is also known, is the provision of small loans to poor people who would otherwise be unable to establish creditworthiness and thus struggle to gain financial self-sufficiency. By 2006, Yunus and the alternative bank he had founded, Grameen Bank, received the Nobel Peace Prize for their contribution to economic and social development from below.[184]

Grameen, as a non-profit system where the borrowers are also the shareholders, has a particular microcredit philosophy.[185] It sees credit as a basic human right and purposely aims to help underprivileged individuals overcome poverty. The credit it provides is based on trust, not contracts, and is given for the creation of income producing activities rather than to buy things to own. This system of microfinancing considers poverty not to be the result of poor people's lack of skills but the result of the institutions and policies – the systems – that govern the poor. Eliminating poverty requires structural change or the creation of new systems; hence the goal of non-profit microfinancing is to provide service to the poor and an alternative to the systems that produce the poverty in the first place. By lending rather than giving the money, Grameen also affects the recipients' thinking processes, generating a sense of responsibility towards paying the loan back and a sense of pride in their ability to become independent.

The success of the Grameen model of microfinancing has inspired similar efforts in many countries throughout the developing world. Crowdfunding, for example, allows many people willing to donate small amounts of money to participate in funding a project they find worthwhile, and to track the project's progress. Kiva (www.kiva.org) is a crowdfunding website that allows individuals anywhere in the world to lend as little as twenty-five American dollars to individuals or groups in developing countries through established microfinancing partners. Once a loan seeker has raised the finance for their project, they begin work and start to pay back the loan, the progress of which is trackable on the website. The lender, in the majority of cases, is paid back and then may reassign their original funding to another borrower or withdraw the money if they desire. Established charities like World Vision have also founded not-for-profit lending schemes, allowing people in New Zealand, for example, to loan money to Tanzania through VisionFund.[186] The hand-up rather than hand-out nature of microfinancing has even inspired related movements in developed countries.[187]

Positive Engagement: What Can I Do Today?

Born of tragedy, the It Gets Better project spreads hope by creating a system of positive engagement. When Dan Savage started the project, he had no idea how his willingness to positively engage and create a system of support would flourish. He did it because he felt the need to do something to make people feel appreciated and loved. He wanted to make a difference in a social system that was overwhelming LGBT youth.

In engaging positively with the issue at hand, he brought out the best in others, inspiring people from all walks of life to join him. Collectively, the actions of the contributors to the It Gets Better project have created a new system of support and flourishment to counteract the effects of the negative system of bullying and non-acceptance. And they have done that primarily by positively engaging with those who are oppressed by the existing system. In the process, they also uplift those of us who don't have direct experience of bullying but who empathize with those who do. We all have the potential to be a Dan Savage or a Muhummed Yunus. Making small but significant changes in our engagement with systems can have an enormous impact.

Creating and Sustaining Positive Relationships with Others

Try out the power of reciprocity by making the first positive move.

Reflect on the things that you don't do and don't say. Are you holding back?

Monitor your communication style – check whether advocacy or inquiry is appropriate.

Reflect on what your contribution to the climate of the systems in your life is and what it could be.

Managing conflict

Think about how you are contributing to the common mood.
If conflict arises, be relationship rather than outcome oriented.
Consider how people's behavior, including your own, is shaped by the system they are in.
Think about how you might change the system by changing your engagement.
Apologize if you hurt someone.

Be alert for your next amygdala hijack – notice it happening, notice its effects on your reactions, and notice how long it takes for it to be over. Try to avoid taking any rash actions or making any reactive statements while it's going on.

Pay attention to the emotional life of others. If you think they are in an amygdala hijack, try to postpone your interaction. Alternatively, govern your own reactions to their behavior. Instead of being provoked, be mindful of why they are acting in the way they are and mindful of how you handle that.

Elevating others

Acknowledge what someone else has done for you.
Verbalize the positive thoughts you have towards others.
Give a compliment or offer a spontaneous act of kindness.
Create an opportunity for someone else to succeed.

Spirited Discovery

"Be Adventurous, Creative, And Open-Minded" ~ Zappos Family Core
Value #4

One day in 1999 Nick Swinmurn traipsed around a San Francisco mall looking for a pair of shoes. It proved to be a frustrating experience. Right size but wrong color, or right color but wrong size, he just couldn't find what he was looking for. Having returned home empty handed, Nick decided to try online.[188] Back then online shopping was in its infancy. Connection speeds, inefficient check-out processes, and a limited range of options all stymied the online shopper.[189] For Nick, the lack of choice was the biggest issue. While a few small shoe stores were selling over the web, there was no large marketplace that provided a comprehensive selection of footwear. An idea was born – Nick quit his day job and set out to become an online shoe retailer.

The only problem was he needed some capital. That's where Tony Hsieh came in. By the age of twenty-six, Hsieh had achieved more financial success than most of us dare dream about. He'd just sold the internet advertising network he'd co-founded to Microsoft for a cool two hundred and sixty five million.[190] Yet, while celebrating his success by taking his college friends on a cruise, he was beset by doubts. Just where, he wondered, was his life going? What was success? What was happiness? The questions plagued him for the weeks following the cruise. With more money than he could spend, and more free time than he was used to, he began to reflect on his life. He figured out that what he really enjoyed was creating, building, and feeling passionate about projects.

The revelation inspired him into action. He walked away from his highly paid position at Microsoft and founded a venture capital company with friend and colleague Alfred Lin. A few months later, Nick Swinmurn came calling. Hsieh almost erased Swinmurn's initial voicemail thinking no one would want to buy shoes without trying them on first. But as his finger reached for the delete button, he heard Swinmurn's statistics – footwear was a forty billion dollar industry in the US and already five percent of sales were being done by catalog. If paper-based mail order shoes were worth two billion it suddenly didn't seem so far fetched than one day internet sales would be at least that big.[191]

Hsieh and Lin's business incubator ended up investing in Swinmurn's idea to sell shoes online. The plan was they would provide the seed money then pass the growing company – named Zappos – off to a bigger investor. The plan didn't work. Larger investors just didn't buy the online shoe sales industry as anything more than a niche market. Hsieh did, so he took of his investor hat, rolled up his sleeves and joined the company as CEO. Within ten years, turnover had skyrocketed and Amazon bought Zappos for over one billion US dollars, retaining Hsieh at the helm.

Zappos' tale would be just another entrepreneurs-make-good-story if it were not for a particular point of difference. The company, under Tony Hsieh's guidance, deliberately set out to try new things. Its founders, successful as they were, were disillusioned with business-as-usual and wanted to create a new kind of company. A company they and others would enjoy working for. A company that would make people happy. They wanted to build a new kind of business system, and they were willing to take risks to do it.

And they did. Informed by the latest science on happiness, a field that Tony had personally been interested in since being disappointed with his own reaction to financial success, Zappos developed a philosophy that combined profits, passion and purpose. The company began by conceptualizing itself as delivering "happiness in a box," focusing on making customers happy by exceeding their expectations. Within ten years Zappos' vision had become the much broader and more ambitious goal of "Delivering Happiness." [192] In articulating delivering happiness as their mission statement, Zappos gave its staff a higher purpose. Work became more meaningful for the employees when it was not just about getting the company more profits but about their own and others' wellbeing, too. Zappos was no longer just about pleasing customers, but about cultivating happiness as a primary purpose of the business, happiness for its staff, customers and investors.

Creating a different kind of business was not always an easy process. The organization went through hard times. Bad decisions were made; things didn't always work out. But by deliberately cultivating an atmosphere that encouraged innovative ideas and experimentation, Zappos was able to work through its problems and learn from its mistakes. Hsieh and the organization learned that happiness can be neither bought nor manufactured but rather is a by-product of flourishing systems, and that the right attitude – an attitude of spirited discovery – plays an enormous role in creating and sustaining such systems.

With spirited discovery, a boring, business-as-usual mindset can be ignited into an adventure by the actions of an individual or, as in Zappos' case, a group of people. Amazing things can happen in systems but we just don't know what they will be until they occur. Therefore, it makes sense to engage with the unknown with energy and excitement about as-yet-unthought-of possibilities. Focusing energy appropriately allows us to unfreeze stagnant systems and sharpen issues.

Consequently, it makes sense to be open-minded, creative and courageous – all elements of spirited discovery.

Open-Mindedness

In the classic family movie *ET: The extra terrestrial* ten-year-old Elliott discovers an alien in the family tool shed. Instead of being afraid, he engages the creature, smuggling it back to his bedroom where the two spend a day bonding. Their mutual interest in one another and embracing of adventure sets the scene for an emotional movie. Director Steven Spielberg captures wonderfully a child's approach to life where everything is new and exciting and full of possibilities waiting to be explored.

That attitude is something many of us lose as we get older, and it doesn't take long. Just contrast the exuberance with which a group of six year olds head off to school as compared to a group of twelve year olds. They become stifled by

convention and develop an aversion to taking chances or showing excitement. Something about the organizations, the structures, the systems we create dampens our spirit of adventure. We see the same thing too in adult relationships – couples in the first flush of love seem so much more interested in each other than those that have been in relationships for a long time. Yet we know it doesn't have to be that way. If pressed, most of us can identify long-term couples who still have that spark between them. Why are they the exception rather than the norm?

The same dampening phenomenon occurs in larger, more formal systems. Once exciting sports teams lose their flair. Innovative field-leading organizations become stale and stagnant. Newly elected governments have their ideals and principles crushed under the weight of power and bureaucratic machinery. What happens?

The answer in part lies with the challenge of maintaining an open-minded approach to life in systems. Few people intend to be close-minded, but if we are not alert it is easy to let systems constrain us. Our perception becomes hampered by familiarity with the way things are done. Instead of being open to new ideas, we get stuck in old, entrenched patterns, whether created by us or the system. As a result we unwittingly anchor ourselves in the past and close off possibilities for the future to be different.

It can be difficult to counter the effects of such a mindset because there are benefits to living a life of business as usual. A patterned, structured life does not challenge our default modes of thought or the systems around us so is undemanding. It feels safe, comfortable, predictable. We don't have to think too much. We can do things on automatic pilot. We can save our energy. In a stable environment, this strategy can be useful, allowing us to form habits and routines that help us get by in the world.

But circumstances change, sometimes dramatically (a new baby in a family), sometimes imperceptibly (a gradual rise in global temperatures). Not only does the external environment alter, we also change. We might develop a new interest in healthy living or spirituality that our family may not share. We might want to swap careers or live in a new country. In today's environment new opportunities and threats, new social conditions, new systems emerge at a frantic pace. In addition, social systems themselves are not static – they are dynamic and emergent, re-enacted constantly as we go about living. This is something we tend to forget, or at least not pay much attention to. The challenge is for us to adapt intelligently to those changes.

Fresh Eyes

International artist Vic Muniz is used to seeing the world in interesting ways. He attributes his unique perspective on life to his early years as a Brazilian citizen under a military dictatorship. It was an environment in which people soon learned that information was slippery and untrustworthy and everything that was said could have more than one meaning. As a result of living in such circumstances, Muniz's art has developed multiple layers of meaning. He takes photos of famous artworks, recreates them with unusual materials, and then photographs the new product. Things that seem familiar when studied closely turn out to be strange – a Manet painting is faithfully recreated with torn pieces of magazine, portraits of children are found to be made in sugar, the Mona Lisa is rendered in peanut butter and jelly.[193]

Muniz sees the world differently and makes others see it differently too. His vision is not constrained by convention or expectation. He wants to be surprised, and stimulated and challenged, and he wants to surprise, stimulate and challenge his audience. Vic Muniz seeks to open minds using art.

Being open minded is more multifaceted that the term suggests. With its use of the word "mind," open-mindedness suggests a cognitive skill, a willingness to think about alternatives, a receptiveness to new ideas. Certainly, these are aspects of having an open mind but it is also a much broader capacity. Being open minded is not always a rational, explicable thing. At times, intangible aspects of life – like mood, emotion, and chance – can come together in ways that challenge and inspire us. It is not just our minds that can be open, but also our eyes and our hearts. Being fully open to varied experiences increases the likelihood of moments of breakthrough when we see things with fresh eyes or feel unexpected emotions.

Spirited discovery means not becoming stuck with one way of perceiving, thinking about and doing things. Sometimes even if we think we are open-minded we are often only willing to entertain ideas that fit within our existing mental models. So if our spouse suggests moving house we might think about it, but if he or she suggests abandoning all our worldly possessions to live in a cave we would likely not seriously consider the proposal. Moving house fits within our expectations of life; living in a cave does not. It's an extreme example but the point is that our open mindedness typically doesn't extend to the deeply held beliefs we have about the world. The ideas we are willing to change are like the tip of an iceberg, but below the water line are the deeply entrenched patterns of thought and behavior, the beliefs and the mental models that drive our actions.

This plays out in all kinds of systems – marriages, families, workplaces, governments and so on. For instance, even though much research shows that teenagers don't learn well in the morning, most societies continue to send adolescents to school early in the day.[194] The alternative, letting them sleep in and stay up late, is just too much of a challenge to fundamental beliefs about what's appropriate for children to be acceptable. And of course, societies' systems are structured around those beliefs. Imagine the outcry if high schools were actually designed to best meet the requirements of adolescent brains instead of the expectations and values of the adults who establish, run and enroll their children in them. Yet, if we are truly cultivating spirited discovery as a key dimension of our systems intelligence we would approach a problem like poor morning performance in adolescent students with an open mind that includes a willingness to question what we think we know and how we think things should be done.

One of the issues is that people often treat systems – like a school – as if they were natural, physical constructs rather than the product of many human actions and interactions. They think systems can't be changed. Or they worry about what change will bring. Fear, discomfort, and clinging to old values even when we don't truly understand where they come from, undermine the energy needed for spirited discovery. We need to have the mental and emotional freedom to seize opportunities without worrying about our supposed role, the system's history, or the expectation of others.[195]

Take the example of the environment. Most of us agree that the environment is being damaged by human activity and something should be done about it. Things need to change; business as usual is not good enough. Despite this, as a group we seem a long way from achieving a green, sustainable economy. We have changed our thinking about the environment from "no need to worry" to "it's being damaged" but that change has only affected the behavior of a few people. At the individual level, even when we know our activities add to the damage, we continue with them – by driving big cars or being lazy about recycling, for example. The systems of our society – around transport and product packaging, say – have created in our minds a kind of "operating system" that sets our patterns of living and makes behavioral change difficult.[196]

That's because, for most of human history, the dominant perspective has been to see a world without limits. That is a view that has served us well while we have lived in small, localized groups with plentiful resources. Now that there are billions of us and we have had a major effect on our environment we need to evolve. Our success as a species means we need to do things in new ways. But to make changes in our behavior we need to change our mental model. Instead of seeing growth as unlimited and desirable, humans as ruling the earth, resources as free because we find them, and things as replaceable we would have to think differently.[197] Thinking differently needs an open mind.

Systems flourish when members bring an attitude of spirited discovery. Such people are effective at disrupting the normal scripts of systems because they are the people who allow idiosyncratic spontaneous actions that unlock potential. Rather than seeing life as a series of problems needing to be solved through identification, analysis of causes, exploration of solutions, and planning, they take an alternative perspective. They are the people who don't mind risking embarrassment as they try to make an impact. They are the people who remind us to see the possibilities of life rather than the restrictions. The good news is it's never too late to learn to be open. Because our relationships, our experiences, and our roles in life are constantly changing, how we think, feel and act can change too.

Fresh Actions

An open mind is one that is intellectually curious, flexible, willing to be changed and thirsty for new ideas. But in the service of systems intelligence an open-minded person is more than that. They also take action. They are willing to experiment with those new ideas. They are willing to play and look for opportunities to be creative. They go through life asking not just "How might I think differently" but "What might I do differently?"

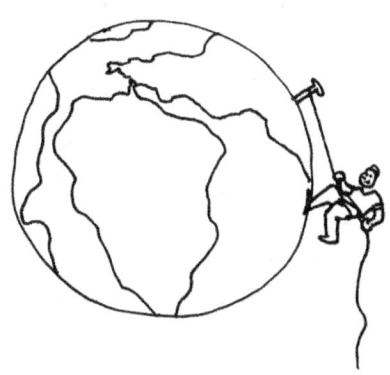

Typically, this is not something we ask ourselves regularly. We think we know how things work. We think we know the right way to see and do things. We think if there were a better way we would have found it by now. Imagine how life could be if we were not constrained by these kinds of thoughts. Perhaps we could have the vision of a Leonardo da Vinci, a Martin Luther King, or a Steve Jobs, making major differences to the world around us? Even if we are not able to change the world on a grand scale, we at least can improve systems we have some expertise in, like Dick Fosbury did.

At six feet five inches Dick Fosbury would seem to have been fated for the basketball court, but it was the high jump he ended up specializing in. An average athlete throughout high school, he had trouble clearing the required heights using the standard techniques of the day. Neither the old-fashioned scissor jump nor the so-called western roll (a face-forward straddle) seemed to suit his frame. His highest jumps were an unimpressive twenty-three-and-a-half inches off the world record. It seemed he was destined for mediocrity. Until, as a sixteen year old, Fosbury began to experiment with alternative jumping styles.

In 1963, Fosbury threw himself over the bar at a new angle, and made the jump. In one afternoon, he improved his height by half a foot. In a sport where records tumble by fractions of an inch, he was clearly on to something. He honed his technique, succeeded at meets, and earned himself a partial scholarship to Oregon State University. A local newspaper described him as looking like a fish flopping in a boat, and the name Fosbury Flop was used from then on to describe his unique style. The moniker appealed to Dick Fosbury as he liked the irony that his flop was also his success.

While he was a talking point in athletic circles and in his home state of Oregon, a year before the 1968 Olympics Fosbury only ranked sixty-first in the world. He was the final qualifier for the US at the Olympic trials. He was not expected to do anything special. Consequently, his attitude at the games was pretty casual. He hung out with other athletes, even missing the opening ceremony to sightsee. But during the competition his unusual style made him a crowd favorite. They loved his differences from the other jumpers – the long run up, the rocking motion he began with, and the final backward flight through the air. Fosbury used the support to motivate and focus himself. He took gold.[198] He set a new Olympic record.

Dick Fosbury changed the system of high jumping. When he started, high jumpers landed in a pit of sawdust. His revolutionary technique hastened the move towards providing an elevated cushioned landing. When he started, people laughed at him. By the next Olympics, twenty-eight of the forty competitors used the Fosbury Flop. When he started, the Fosbury Flop looked bizarre. Now, it looks normal.[199]

Many changes in systems come about in a similar way. Open-minded individuals try something new. They innovate. They develop a better way. Gradually, others see the benefit of their actions and the change spreads and a new system emerges. By engaging in different ways, it is possible to make small differences in the systems we live in. We just need to be open to opportunity or, even better, opportunity seeking. If we just ask ourselves during the day, "What can I do here that will make a positive difference to this person or this situation?" we might be surprised how often we see an opening.

Take something as simple as smiling. For most of us, non-smiling is the norm. We smile only in response to particular stimuli – a joke, an amusing thought, a familiar face. Yet, most of us would not hesitate to say that when someone smiles at us that action uplifts us. We also see the person who smiled in a more positive way. For just a moment, we experience elevation. We feel good. We smile in return.

Why then, despite the benefits that a smile brings, do most of us choose non-smiling as our default? Perhaps we think other people would think we are silly for smiling all the time. Perhaps we want our smiles to be for special occasions. Perhaps we just don't feel happy. Yet, deep down we can probably admit that we don't smile as often as we could because we have been brought up not to smile. We have been socialized by the systems around us into non-smiling, even when a tiny, inexpensive gesture can add joy to both our and others' day.

With an attitude of spirited discovery, we can be willing to try something new. We can smile more often and see what changes that simple act brings to the relationships we have in systems. And even if we try to enhance a situation and fail, it doesn't really matter. Experimentation is crucial to learning and trying new approaches is a core component of spirited discovery. Experimenting can help us to solve problems and improve systems in the face of constantly changing circumstances.[200]

Part of being open-minded is also remembering that others are affected by systems in the same way we are. They, too, find change hard. They, too, tend to follow scripts. They, too, struggle to transfer skills from one context to another. These are eye-opening revelations. The colleague that is obnoxious to you at work may be totally different at home or to others. Perhaps there is something in the way the two of you are interacting that has created a negative connection. The sister that you stopped speaking to ten years ago is no longer the same person that she was then, just as you are no longer the same person. There is hope for reconciliation. The person you disliked as a roommate may turn out to be wonderful as your doctor. Within different systems our relationships are different. We need to be open-minded enough that we recognize our own behavioral changes across systems and accept the same in others. Being open minded helps us to avoid developing entrenched opinions, assessments, and evaluations that hinder our own adaptability and recognition of the potential of others.

Embracing spirited discovery means believing that, nine times out of ten, we can be much more effective if we approach life with an open mind and orient ourselves to a promising future. We can change patterns of behavior and rules and structures – this is an undeniable capacity in us. We can benefit from remembering that many of the patterns, rules and structures we live within are arbitrary, capricious, and based on assumptions we often aren't aware of.

Just take Richard Branson's idea of introducing space flights to the general population. Prior to Branson publicizing his plan, most of us assumed that space flights were only attainable for astronauts who had trained for years and were handpicked by elite organizations. That was just the way things were. Instead of assuming how things should be based on the past, Branson got busy creating a future he wanted.

Similarly, just because no other company was making happiness a focus of their business, that didn't stop Zappos from building their business around that goal. Like Branson and Hsieh, with an open mind we can build an image of how we want a system to be and be pulled towards that vision by inspiration, commitment, positive energy and creativity.

Creativity

There's a great story about William Pitt, the British Prime Minister in the late eighteenth century, addressing the recalcitrance of one of his fellow parliamentarians to agree to a particular bill. Visiting the Chancellor of the Exchequer at home in an effort to persuade him, Pitt found the man confined to his bed suffering from gout in a poorly heated room. The Chancellor complained about the cold conditions and the state of his health. He refused to attend parliament, which meant there could be no discussions on the bill that Pitt wanted to pass. Pitt quickly sensed that his colleague's misery was the bigger impediment to the progress of his policy than his political objections. Attuned to his colleague's state of mind, he saw an opportunity to create a new system. Instead of giving up on the idea of a discussion, Pitt removed his boots, climbed into the other bed in the room and pulled up the covers. This single, unexpected, creative act changed the dynamic of the room. It put both men on equal footing, uniting them in discomfort and stripping away the norms of their stately offices. Surprised and amused, the Chancellor engaged with the Prime Minister. The two discussed the matter at hand and soon agreed on a united way forward.[201]

Another similarly interesting anecdote involves Mahatma Gandhi. Apparently one day while boarding a moving train one of Gandhi's shoes slipped from his foot and landed on the track below. Unable to retrieve it, Gandhi calmly removed the shoe from his other foot and threw it towards where the first shoe had fallen. That way whoever found the shoes would have a usable pair.

Half a century later, as a not very dedicated Harvard student, Tony Hsieh tried to do the least amount of work necessary to achieve good grades. One course required no ongoing assessment so Hsieh soon figured out he could skip classes. He only needed to pass the finals. Unfortunately for Hsieh, at the end of the course the professor set a final exam that required answering five questions to be randomly selected from a list of one hundred.

With only two weeks before the exam, Hsieh realized there was no way he could prepare answers for a hundred topics that he had no familiarity with. Instead of being overwhelmed and resigned to failure, he got creative, putting together a virtual study group. He invited all students taking the class to submit answers for three questions he would assign to them, making sure he covered all hundred possible topics. He then compiled the model answers into a binder and sold them individually for twenty dollars. Only students who had contributed answers were eligible to buy the binder. The end result was profit for Hsieh, the creation of a substantial study guide for the many students who signed up, and a lesson about crowdsourcing – not to mention a pass in the course.[202]

What the stories about William Pitt, Mahatma Gandhi and Tony Hsieh have in common is the illustration of the power of creativity. Not creativity in the sense of artistic ability, although that is useful too, but creativity in the sense of being able to do something extraordinary in response to something ordinary. These three people responded to three very different events in ways that would never occur to most people. They threw away the script for the system they were in.

Let's face it. Most of us would have reacted to a sick and grumpy colleague

by leaving him alone. Most of us would have cursed our bad luck at losing our shoe but never have thought to throw the remaining one with it. Most of us would have resigned ourselves to repeating the course we hadn't attended and probably told ourselves we had learned a lesson about taking risks. The alternative responses of the Pitt, Gandhi and Hsieh in the stories demonstrate the power of innovative, creative actions to make us think differently about the systems we live in. Their simple actions show us it is possible to step outside the normal social scripts in everyday life with constructive results.

Creative Individuals

In stable, slow-changing environments most people happily take on the role of good, solid, functioning members of a system. They don't want or need to be rule breakers and innovators. And why not? The need to explore ways of changing and improving systems isn't always obvious. Everything seems to be working fine so we settle for the status quo. It is not until someone with vision comes along and tries something different that we realize how much better things could have been. Waiting for the visionary to improve things for everybody is one option. Another is to instigate change ourselves.

Even if we don't consider ourselves particularly creative we can still seek opportunities for innovation. Creative experimentation in systems doesn't have to be complicated – we all have the ability to change how we behave and what we do. In *The Tipping Point*, Malcolm Gladwell tells the story of San Diego nurse Georgia Sadler and her battle to spread knowledge about breast cancer and diabetes. Gladwell uses the story to illustrate how to start an epidemic by concentrating resources but there's another way of looking at it – as spirited discovery in action.

Sadler's goal was to help improve disease prevention for San Diego's black community. To reach her target community, she set up a series of meetings to be held after services in black-attended churches. The turnouts were disappointing. Sadler realized that after church people were tired and hungry and just wanted to go home. She needed to reach women when they were receptive to new messages and relaxed. The church network was not the right system to use. So Sadler got creative and, in an inspired move, she decided to disseminate her information through beauty salons.

But she didn't only change the venue to one where women were a captive and social audience. She also changed the messenger, enlisting the help of the stylists to spread the information she wanted in the community. The beauty salon workers had the ear of their clients and were natural conversationalists. She trained a group of them to introduce the topics while they were working on the women, and regularly updated them with new findings and the latest advice. An evaluation of her program showed Sadler she had been effective in persuading the black women to go for mammograms and be tested for diabetes. Her creative approach and experimentation resulted in the success of her intervention.[203]

Company executive Jürgen Link also acted creatively when he invited union leaders to attend the same negotiation training course as management prior to the scheduled round of wage talks. Link was new to the large timber company and found himself in an organization with a history of deep and often violent hostilities between workers and management. Union members, he recalls, used to throw stones at managers who came too close during protests. Strikes and protracted wage negotiations were the norm. Before Link's arrival the previous wage round had taken over a year to reach an agreement.

Link decided he had to do things differently and he was systems intelligent enough to realize change would have to start with him. He believed that if he treated the workers differently, they would treat him differently. He started by inviting them to attend negotiation training. His managerial colleagues were horrified. Why would he invite the enemy to learn the negotiation techniques and strategies that they wanted to use against the workers? Link told them that if they planned to win based on manipulation and strategy they had the wrong mindset at the outset. The workers, too, were suspicious of the move, but they eventually sent their leaders along to the training session. Union and management negotiations took two days that year. According to Link, once the posturing was removed from the equation, and because they had studied side by side for several sessions, negotiations were much simpler. Everyone got to the heart of the matter quickly and dealt with the issues instead of falling into patterns of confrontation.[204]

The gift of creativity is an often overlooked and undervalued human capacity. All these examples of unusual and innovative actions in systems demonstrate that people have imaginations. Amongst other things, our imaginations allow us to keep one eye on the future. Whereas most animals can only imagine a future twenty minutes away, we can plan decades in advance.[205] We use our vision of the future to guide our actions in the present, such as when we don't eat the piece of chocolate cake in front of us because we are trying to be

healthy. We can use that same vision to guide our actions in systems, imagining possible outcomes to possible actions instead of reacting in the moment, as we are apt to do.

Our imagination also helps us to anticipate possible outcomes of our behavior and, thus, in theory, respond to events with intelligent action.

The proviso "in theory" is necessary because we can also use our imaginations to misread situations. We imagine how we think we feel about a future event (say an upcoming work meeting or family gathering) and then adjust our behavior to create that reality. That works well if our projection is positive (It's going to be a great occasion full of energy) but not so well if it's negative (It will be so boring I hope it's over quickly). If everyone is unleashing negative imaginings then the future event cannot help but be diminished because everyone will turn up less than they could be. Conversely, if everyone is imagining great things, the chances of it being a great event multiply. Life is better if the mental process of creative imaginings is used wisely.

Unleashing the power of our imagination helps search for a better experience of the systems around us. People who think and act outside the square often have the ability to creatively improve existing systems or generate new systems. Entrepreneur Sir Richard Branson has done both. When a flight he was taking from Puerto Rico to the Virgin Islands, the only flight of the day, was cancelled he didn't react like most of us would have. Instead of complaining about the efficiency of the airline or being angry at the staff member at check in, he thought about how he could change the situation. His idea? He walked to the nearby charter counter and booked a plane. Then he walked back to the check-in area with a sign advertising cheap seats to the Virgin Islands. It didn't take long for him to recover the costs of the charter flight, and he, and many other happy passengers, made their trip that day after all.[206] That experience became the inspiration behind Virgin airlines.

For most of us, often our behaviors are so bound to the setting that triggers them we feel unable to change them even if they are poor and ineffective. Part of being open to new, creative behavior within systems involves loosening the often-arbitrary system boundaries we feel. When in particular systems we fulfill the expectations and patterns of those roles and we may do it very well. But when faced with a fresh situation, we may struggle to realize that we can either import effective skills from one context to the other or abandon ineffective scripts in the new environment. It's about being willing to try to transfer what works for us in one system to another. Sometimes that process will be habit born of experience, as when Captain Sullenberger transferred his gliding skills to the context of a disabled Airbus, but at other times we need to consciously make an effort to use our existing skills in new ways.

Finnish photographer Miina Savolainen, for example, deliberately transfers her skills between systems in a creative way. She imports her talents from her professional context to intervene in others' negative social experiences. In one case, she worked with abused and neglected girls from a children's home. She took beautiful photographs of the girls, helping them to develop a sense of identity, self-acceptance and worthiness. Girls who had experienced the world as a chaotic place where bad things happen and people do bad things to each other learnt to see themselves and their environment differently by being subjects of stunning photographs. Savolainen's technique of empowerment has been used in Finland in social work, healthcare and education as a method of intervening in social systems to improve the quality of life for marginalized people. She offered a new approach for an old problem.

Creative Systems

Creativity is more than just the responsibility of the individual. Organizations and other systems can be put together in such a way as to foster creative impulses. When a system actively encourages spirited discovery by its very structure, interesting things happen. Take young Finnish company Supercell, for example. Like at Zappos, the mobile gaming company founders wanted to create a fun place to work. They deliberately set out to avoid corporate bureaucracy trampling creative passion, creating a workspace and work practices that encourage innovation. Where most gaming studios have an executive telling designers and programmers what projects to work on, Supercell works in small self-governing teams. After they develop a game, they let another team play it. If they like it, the game is tested in a small market. When it flies in that forum, it is opened up for global release.[207]

Not all games make it to the final stage. When a game is consigned to the scrapheap, the company breaks out the champagne. The juxtaposition of champagne and failure is a symbol for the organization's philosophy. As co-founder Petri Styrman explains, "If you try to avoid failure and make safe decisions then what you do becomes contrived. And you can often learn more from mistakes than from successes."[208] Supercell is not the only company recognizing the value of trial and error.

Charles Schwab, a leading financial services company, for example, distinguishes between noble failure and stupid failure, encouraging those employees who try new things to learn as they go.[209]

Organizations that invest in developing an atmosphere where failure is neither a threat nor a disaster are more likely to have employees who take creative risks. For Supercell, nurturing a system that encourages spirited discovery means deliberately combining three essential ingredients: talented and creative people, unrestricted freedom, and great team chemistry.[210] Their approach has worked. Supercell had phenomenal success in just two years, with two of the highest grossing games in Apple's App Store in 2013.

Zappos fosters a creative atmosphere in other ways. Zappos' values include statements like "Embrace and drive change"; "Be adventurous, creative and open-minded" and "Create fun and a little weirdness." The organization lives the values it asks of its employees. Hsieh, for instance, famously offers to pay all staff for their time and gives them a bonus after the four-week compulsory training program if they *leave* the company. Paying people extra to quit after you have just hired and trained them is counterintuitive to say the least, but it makes sense in systems terms. If new recruits feel that the company is not for them they have an easy and beneficial way to move elsewhere, and Zappos makes sure it only has people who are passionate and committed to the company joining the staff. Less than one percent take up the offer.[211]

The company does other creative things, too, offering its staff happiness and "laughter yoga" classes, encouraging individuality (not scripts) in its call centers, and letting employees manage their own training. The success of Zappos' approach has been borne out by more than just financial success. In 2012, Zappos was ranked number eleven in *Fortune* magazine's annual list of best companies to work for, with *Fortune* highlighting the positive culture at the company.[212]

Of course, building innovative systems and acting creatively to bring about a better future can be challenging. The ability to act creatively but effectively in systems doesn't magically develop overnight. We need to try out different actions to discover what works and what doesn't work. Small, innovative behaviors can breathe new energy into stale practices, much in the same way adding a new node to a cognitive network will initiate an update of the entire network. With experimentation it is possible to find the right ones. Of course, we will never be able to know before we act the exact outcome of any new behavior, so we have to be willing to stumble. We can't allow ourselves to be disheartened by one apparent failure. It takes effort to redraw boundaries, to realize that there is more to the environment than meets the eye, and looks for a greater possibility than the obvious. But if we are willing to explore then we may better envision what might be, talk about possibilities, and more often innovate through creative experimentation.[213] All we need is the courage to try.

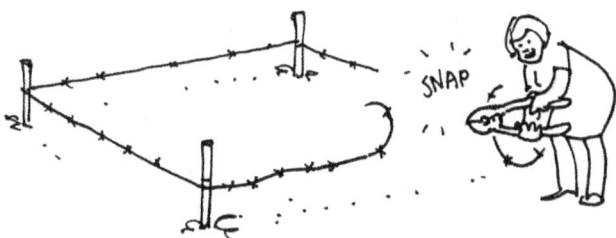

Courage

Tony Hsieh and Alfred Lin began as angel investors for Zappos, but when the time came to call for more funds the dot-com crash and economic recession had a major impact. Despite their credibility with online business, an approach to other investors for a second round of funding yielded nothing – "exactly $0."[214] Hsieh still believed that the online shoe store was a good bet. Rather than abandoning the young company, he joined Zappos full-time and put his own money on the line. For two years, the company focused primarily on survival.

Despite the team's efforts, the company struggled. Staff began to leave. Ironically, through the hardship Tony realized that Zappos had coalesced into a tribe. Everyone who remained involved was there because they were passionate, and they had all made sacrifices. He stopped seeing Zappos as a failing organization and began to regard it as a family. The change in his framing affected the staff. Their focus became "all-for-one and one-for-all."[215] Hsieh put many of them up free of charge in his own properties and staff willingly took pay cuts and worked long hours. Eventually, even Tony's money began to run out. He had sold many of his properties to prop up Zappos and his once-deep well was running dry. Because everyone was committed to and believed in what they were trying to do – because the prevailing attitude was one of spirited discovery – Hsieh had the courage to invest the last of his money in the company.

Conventional wisdom would say that Tony Hsieh's actions were reckless, but Hsieh had always been willing to take risks when his gut told him to. He is entrepreneurial by nature, describing himself as having always enjoyed "being creative and experimenting"[216] He was willing to break the rules of good business and defy expectations because he sensed the possibilities that were just out of reach.

It is not systems intelligent to take risks for the thrill of it, or to make change for change's sake. Instead, it is about being more attuned to the scripts that we are following. If we are aware of the scripts driving us we can then see opportunities to deviate from them when it would enhance the outcomes for the system. When we are attuned with the systems around us we see beyond simple and obvious choices and give ourselves permission to engage in extraordinary ways. We allow ourselves to change the script. Our systems intelligence enables us to glimpse or feel the structure that is shaping a particular response in ourselves and others, and sense that the response the system is eliciting is not optimal. Then, with courage, we can choose to defy expectations as we try to improve things.

That's what Emmeline Pankhurst did when she formed the Women's Social and Political Union in 1903 to fight the election rules of England and earn women the right to vote. Impatient with the slow progress of the peaceful campaign, Pankhurst and her group of suffragettes took more strident action to publicize their cause.[217] They actively sought new ways to protest and disrupt the established system. They suffered greatly for their courage, imprisoned and vilified, but they also ultimately achieved the system change they were seeking. It's what Tony Hsieh and Dick Fosbury and many other entrepreneurs and innovators have done in systems big and small as they have refused to conform to "normal" behavior.

It takes courage to move beyond the scripts given to us by our social groups because an essential part of being human is our desire to belong. We want people to like us. We want to feel part of a community, and that involves behaving in ways that others expect us to, even if those ways are just habitual rather than effective. Unity brings pressure to conform and be uniform. [218] Intervening in poorly functioning systems often requires us to go against social norms and open ourselves to the judgment of others. But we can be more fully alive, more energized when we put ourselves at risk and go beyond our normal limitations and routines. Life can be much more than the systems we live in seem to dictate.

The actions of Nelson Mandela illustrate the potential benefits of this courageous and systems intelligent approach to life. While he was imprisoned on Robben Island outside Capetown in South Africa, Mandela had the courage to make expectation-defying choices. Incarcerated for more than two decades, often in solitary confinement, Mandela deviated from the script ascribed to a prisoner. Instead of treating the guards as his enemy, Mandela saw them as humans caught in the same flawed system of justice in which he was embedded. He understood the guards were sticking to the scripts that the systems they participated in (jail, apartheid) allocated their role. Mandela chose not to follow the expectations of his own role. Instead of being stoic and antagonistic, as one might expect from a prisoner, he allowed himself to be gentle and vulnerable. He chose to reach out the hand of friendship to his jailers. In doing so he showed them that though he was politically and ideologically opposed to their system, he was human just as they were.

Mandela particularly befriended a pro-apartheid eighteen-year-old guard, Christo Brand. Mandela, then in his sixties, was down-to-earth and courteous in his dealings with the young guard, treating him with respect. Brand's experiences with the dignified prisoner led to him bending the rules to bring him small comforts, such as allowing him to hold his infant grandson. Mandela expressed concerned that Brand might be punished for his favors. He also wrote to Brand's wife asking her to encourage the young man to study. Eventually, inspired by Mandela's human touch, Brand revised his views not just on Nelson Mandela, but on the system of apartheid and his country. Mandela's deviation from expectation inspired Christo Brand to deviate from his own role in the South African system. Brand now works in the museum shop on Robben Island, alongside former political prisoners and prison guards.[219]

Mandela's unexpected actions within the system of prison also had incredible secondary effects. Not only did he touch and influence many of the individual guards who dealt with him on a daily basis, the stories of his behavior added to his legend beyond the walls of his prison. One man's courage to step outside of the role he was cast in helped many to question the script itself. He awakened others to the flaws of the systems he was fighting against not by violent action but by defying expectation.

The important long-term effect of Mandela's actions can be seen in the establishment of the Truth and Reconciliation Commission in South Africa in the 1990s. A committed few (including Archbishop Desmond Tutu) noticed that the old systems of justice were not working effectively and were brave enough to try new ways of dealing with social issues. Instead of working on the traditional punitive model of crime and punishment, they decided to create a system that worked at restoring the relationship between the victim and the perpetrator. It was a bold example of spirited discovery in action as the tried a completely atypical approach to justice.

Victims of crimes and atrocities spoke of their experiences and the impact they had had on their lives in front of the offenders. It was hoped that the perpetrators would experience a shared humanity and develop some empathy with their victims. The perpetrators were then invited to fully and truthfully disclose their actions and were given the opportunity to ask for forgiveness. The idea was that both parties experienced a form of catharsis in a safe environment, thus providing them with an opportunity for healing and reconciliation.[220] People are more likely to forgive injuries against them when they feel they have a voice and have been heard. Bringing out the truth of people's actions made sure that history was recorded but at the same time created a platform for rebuilding relationships.

The Truth and Reconciliation Commission and other systems like it, such as the restorative justice program used in New Zealand, provide an alternative model to the retributive justice programs most countries use. These efforts demonstrate it is possible to break free from the risk-averse revenge/punishment mindset we have as humans in the social world. With courage, we can escape the automaticity of imposing a kind of cost-benefit rationality on our every action that makes us ask "what's in it for me?" instead of "how can I improve this for everybody?"

The Infectiousness of Spirited Discovery

Powerful change is possible in systems thanks to the unpredictability of humans, but to exploit that possibility we need to let go of our focus on expectations. Too much time is spent imagining, anticipating and expecting certain

things to happen, in the process often unintentionally creating those things.[221] It is systems intelligent to allow for the possibility of something other than we can imagine occurring. The past is not always an accurate predictor of the future; people can surprise us. They are more likely to surprise us if we act in

ways that encourage that prospect. We need to give ourselves and others the space to interrupt their normal patterns of behavior and try new things. We never know what might emerge from a simple change in behavior.

Most human minds are generally attracted to "straight lines and not curves, to whole numbers and not fractions, to uniformity and not diversity, and to certainties and not mystery."[222] But we have the capacity to celebrate the weird, the wonderful, the unique. It's that capacity we tap into to live with

spirited discovery in systems. Systemic environments, on the whole, reward open-minded curiosity, imaginative actions, and the willingness to take risks. When we nurture the capacity for spirited discovery we focus on the benefits of an open-minded approach. We relax our assumptions about how we (and others) think we should behave. We get creative. We give ourselves permission to defy expectations, and break social norms. We have the courage we need to be vulnerable in our participatory, highly connected world.

What the stories of Zappos, Dick Fosbury, Nelson Mandela and a myriad of other similar anecdotes demonstrate is that it makes sense to engage in spirited discovery because when we go looking for ways to make life better we usually find them. Most of us live with the realization that we do not know everything that is going on around us. Some things in life remain hidden. Whatever problems are present in a system, there are likely to be causes and solutions that are yet to be revealed. An attitude of spirited discovery infuses us with the assumption that there are good things waiting to be realized and worth finding. When it comes to that discovery process there are no predetermined criteria for what will work to improve the system. How can there be when we don't know the possibilities until we explore? That's why spirited discovery is such a common sense approach to life in systems.

Spirited Discovery: What Can I Do Today?

Open-mindedness

Notice the boundaries of the systems around you. Experiment with redefining them and see what new possibilities for action emerge.

Work at being open minded below the tip of the iceberg, that is, to ideas that challenge your mental models.

Believe in people. Be open to the potential of others.

Try to recapture a childlike belief in the possibilities of life.

Imagine the system you want and work towards creating it.

Try importing skills you have in one context or system to another.

Creativity

Try doing something differently – break a routine and try something new.

Experiment with creative micro-behaviors that might bring effective change in a system's patterns.

Seek opportunities to innovate.

Be playful and energetic.

Purposely use your imagination to better the systems you live in.

Courage

Step outside the script. Look for an opportunity to do something differently for positive effect.

Be prepared to face the judgment of others.

Be willing to face failure.

Think "how can I improve this system so that everybody benefits?" Change the focus from yourself to the system.

Effective Responsiveness

"At the time I was arrested I had no idea it would turn into this. It was just a day like any other day. The only thing that made it significant was that the masses of the people joined in."
~ Rosa Parks[223]

It's a familiar story. In 1955, well-respected seamstress Rosa Parks refused to give up her seat to a white man on a Montgomery city bus. Positioned just behind the ten seats reserved for white people, the forty-two-year-old African American spontaneously ignored the driver's directive to change to a seat further back in order to enforce the laws of segregation. The bus driver called the police, and the small black woman was arrested. And so, on a non-descript December evening, the civil rights movement reached a tipping point.[224]

Parks was not the first African-American to fail to give up her seat in Montgomery, Alabama. Nor was she the first to be arrested for the crime. None of the earlier arrests, however, had resulted in mass boycotts and protests. So what was special about that Thursday night? The difference was the systemic reaction ignited as people responded to the situation.

When she was arrested and convicted of breaking the so-called "Jim Crow laws" Rosa Parks called her parents from the police station. Her mother subsequently called a friend of Rosa's who happened to have a husband involved in the NAACP – the National Association for the Advancement of Colored People. He, in turn, knew of a white lawyer who would be willing to help both Rosa and the cause. Both men asked Rosa if she would let them fight her arrest in court and make an example of her case.

The activists who wanted to use her arrest to make a stand thought carefully before making the request. They had considered using the earlier arrest of two other black women on the buses in Montgomery to initiate court action against the segregation laws, but felt that those women were less likely than Parks, who in so many ways was a model citizen, to appeal to the public. Civil rights activists had also tried bus boycotts in other cities, but gave up before real gains were made.

Fortunately for the Montgomery campaigners, the politically aware Parks agreed to be a test case and challenge the legality of the Jim Crow laws by appealing her arrest.

News of her detention traveled fast through the activist network, and within twenty-four hours local civil rights campaigners organized a boycott of the Montgomery bus system, printing fliers to spread the news. Parks was well known in the wider community, her networks cutting across racial and economic lines thanks to her activities as a volunteer in many community groups, a secretary in the NCAAP, her sewing work and her church. Because of her ties to many groups, large numbers of people were willing to support the boycott, encouraged by the support of the town's ministers including a twenty-six-year-old Martin Luther King, Jr.

On the Sunday after her arrest, Montgomery's newspaper published an article about how the local Negroes were all planning to boycott the buses on Monday. Having laid hands on a flier advertising the boycott, they exaggerated its scope to inflame the white community. Ironically, when the black citizens of Montgomery, most of whom had not heard about the planned boycott, saw the story, they assumed everyone else had, so they felt pressure to participate.

When Monday dawned, five hundred African Americans showed up in court to hear Rosa Parks convicted of breaking the segregation laws. That same day, a jubilant Martin Luther King Jr. drove around town noting bus after bus empty of black passengers. He was soon chosen as the leader of the group organizing the boycotts, the Montgomery Improvement Association. A mass movement had begun. The Montgomery bus boycott lasted 381 days, ending only when the U.S. Supreme Court ruled that the segregation law was unconstitutional.

Rosa Parks' refusal to give up her seat on the bus that day triggered the beginning of an era of non-violent mass protests in support of civil rights in the United States. Eventually, the entire system of race distinction in the US would be reshaped by the consequences of this one small incident. The enormous impact of her act was extraordinary, but it was not pre-planned. Rosa Parks did not know her action would change the laws of an entire country; she just couldn't take a particular injustice one more time. "It was not pre-arranged. It just happened that the driver made a demand and I just didn't feel like obeying his demand. I was quite tired after spending a full day working."[225]

Rosa Parks simply took action on the spot when an opportunity presented itself. She made a small, personal change in her behavior because she wanted to make a stand against an unjust system. It wasn't planned in the sense that she knew what the outcome would be, but she did know there would be consequences. It wasn't just dumb luck either, as she was astute enough to know there were structures in place – organizations and individuals – who would support her and maximize the effect of her actions. In Systems Intelligence terms, Rosa Parks and the activists who made a test case of her actions exercised effective responsiveness. They utilized rather than just responded to the dynamics of a system, exposing the unjust rules of bus travel to highlight the inequities of the larger social system.

Effective responsiveness is about taking the initiative to fix things when they don't work. Systems can be changed by challenging the negative, being prepared and proactive, and using leverage. People often get caught up in tracing the causality of events, but for Systems Intelligence causality is not always of prime importance. Figuring out how things came to be can have limited benefit. It is often better to focus on making things happen. When we respond effectively from a Systems Intelligent perspective we create new actions, reformulate systems, look for new inputs and we do it because we are seeking improvement of the system at hand.

Unlike spirited discovery's notion of exploring a system for unknown possibilities that might unfold, effective responsiveness calls for action when we already have some kind of criteria for success. We know what needs changing, and we are trying to make an immediate difference to the system we are acting within. Sometimes we can spot practical and effective places where small interventions will have positive effects in systems intuitively. But we can also learn to recognize, implement and create inputs more consistently – we can live actively with systems. Purposely and successfully intervening within systems with the intention of improving them is effective responsiveness in action.

Challenging the Negative

It would have been much easier for Rosa Parks to acquiesce to the bus driver's demands that she change seats, or to refuse to allow the civil rights activists to fight her arrest. In other words, it would have been simpler not to be the person whose actions challenged the existing system of racial discrimination. Unlike Rosa Parks, many of us choose the easy path because we feel trapped to the point of inaction by social pressures and expectations, and the structure of systems. As a result, we choose inaction over action, even in negative systems.

Negative systems also tend to perpetuate because it can seem impossible to change them – think about the failure of the US to address the problems of illegal immigration and gun violence. Most people feel that the existing systems are ineffective, but few can agree on an alternative. Or, consider how ordinary Germans struggled to resist the Nazi party's policies and how long apartheid was legally entrenched in South Africa. It is generally easier to go accept the status quo than to instigate change. But easy behavior is not necessarily intelligent behavior, particularly in the face of repressive or poorly functioning systems. It is important to respond in ways that challenge negative systems.

Systems, by their very nature, structure and influence our behavior without us even realizing or thinking about it. For many Americans, black and white, conforming to the requirements of segregation was automatic. Much as we currently automatically follow traffic rules, behave in certain ways in a hospital, and get jobs without question, they simply sat where required in the local bus. We all unconsciously act in ways encouraged by whatever system is at hand. Even if we don't like the system, complaining about the security screening at airports or the tax breaks given to large corporations, most of us still conform to the role required of us.

Serious research has been done on the power of systems to dictate our behavior. Perhaps the most famous study of all is what has become known as the Stanford Prison Experiment, led by psychology professor Philip Zimbardo in 1971. For Zimbardo's research, a group of pre-vetted twenty-four male students was randomly divided into prisoners and guards, with the prisoners held in a mock jail in Stanford University's basement. Zimbardo himself took on the role of the prison superintendent.

Zimbardo was interested in studying how inherent personality traits in prisoners and guards might explain abusive prison situations, and he imposed a number of conditions that were intended to promote disorientation, depersonalization, and de-individualization. The guards were dressed in uniforms, wore mirrored sunglasses, and carried batons. The prisoners had uncomfortable clothing, were assigned numbers sewn to their clothing instead of names, and wore a chain around their ankles.

Zimbardo instructed the guards that they were not to physically harm the prisoners but did tell them how they could create a sense of powerlessness in the prisoners by disrupting their routines and instilling fear. To add to the realism of the experiment, the students playing prisoners were arrested at their homes, taken by the local police (who were cooperating with the experiment) and booked at the police station. They were strip searched and imprisoned.

The "prison officers" quickly adopted extremely authoritarian attitudes and sought to punish and torture the "prisoners." They used exercise, the withholding of bathroom facilities, the refusal to empty sanitation buckets, the removal of bedding and the removal of clothing as means of controlling and punishing prisoners. The guards' levels of sadism increased as the experiment went on. In contrast, the prisoners rapidly became passive and submissive, accepting their abuse and inflicting punishment on those of their number who questioned the authority of the guards. As the experiment went on, however, some prisoners rebelled, others talked of escaping, and several became traumatized and were removed. The experiment was meant to last for two weeks, but was brought to a halt on the sixth day because the students had embraced their roles in an alarmingly enthusiastic manner.

The Stanford Prison Experiment provides an illuminating, albeit somewhat frightening, example of how compelling and influential systems can be. Instead of the day-to-day individual personalities and beliefs of the guards and prisoners driving their behavior, the experiment revealed the powerful influence of the situation and social structure on their actions. The collective power of the system seemed to override the beliefs and morality of the individuals. The students quickly internalized the roles they had been assigned and those roles, defined by the system, dictated their behavior. Zimbardo realized that the experiment's main lesson was that situations – systems – matter: "Social situations can have more profound effects on the behavior and mental functioning of individuals, groups, and national leaders than we might believe possible."[226] Given the formidable influence systems can have on our behavior, our capacity to resist the power of negative systems is an important component of effective responsiveness.

Questioning the Status Quo

One day, a research scientist locked five monkeys into a cage with a ladder leading to a bunch of bananas hanging from the ceiling. Naturally, one of the monkeys immediately headed up the ladder towards the bananas. Much to its surprise, the monkey was sprayed with ice-cold water before it reached the top, as were its four companions below. Some time passed before another monkey decided to try for the bananas, but as soon as it reached the same spot it, too, was sprayed, along with its fellow captives. After several attempts, the wet and angry monkeys gave up on trying to reach the bananas.

Next, the researcher replaced one of the original five monkeys with a new monkey. Unsurprisingly, the newcomer spied the bananas and headed towards the ladder. Instead of allowing it to climb the ladder and lead to another soaking, however, the other four attacked the new monkey and beat it up. Needless to say, the battered newcomer didn't try climbing the ladder again.

The same pattern unfolded when another original monkey was replaced with a fresh face. The new recruit headed for the ladder and took a beating for its temerity. Interestingly, the previous recipient of the beating, who still had no knowledge of the cold water dousing, was an enthusiastic participant in the second new monkey's punishment. The pattern repeated every time a new monkey joined the group, until eventually none of the original monkeys were in the cage.

Finally, to complete the experiment, a pluckier monkey was introduced into the cage. It ran towards the ladder only to get beaten up by its companions. Unlike the others, this monkey turned around and asked "Why are you beating me up when I'm trying to get the bananas?" The other four monkeys stopped, looked at each other slightly puzzled and, finally, shrugged their shoulders and said, "We have no idea. That's just the way we do things around here."[227]

This humorous story about monkeys makes us smile because we see the kernel of truth in the tale – sometimes we do stuff just because everyone else is doing it. Over time, all systems, whether they are families, workplaces, educational institutions, or social groups, develop routines, habits and practices. Systems encourage us to behave in certain ways, and reward and punish us to gain conformity. Programs, policies, and operating procedures all work together to govern our behavior within a system.[228] That in itself is not necessarily a bad thing. Where things start to go wrong is when we fail to realize that the context in which these routines, habits and practices were developed has changed and they are no longer the most effective or appropriate way with getting on in life. Systems need the equivalent of the new monkey – the people who come along and question why things are done the way they are, or see opportunity for doing things in new ways. The effective responsiveness dimension of Systems Intelligence is about training ourselves to be the new monkey.

As the Stanford Prison Experiment showed, it is easy to let systems dictate our behavior. That is not to say, however, that we cannot override the influence of systems. Once we are alert to life in systems – once we are consciously using our Systems Intelligence – we can act in ways that attempt to improve how systems function. Where a system is functioning poorly, refusing to conform without first questioning the status quo is one way we can effectively respond.

Typically we conform to the behavior that a system expects from us in two ways. First, we conform when we want to be liked and accepted (normative conformity). Second, we conform when we are unsure with the situation so we mimic the behavior of others (informative conformity). For example, when we start a new job we likely experience both of these conforming pressures as we try to build relationships and learn how our new workplace functions. Even if we think the behavior is stupid, we do it because we don't want to seem different from everyone else. We cannot avoid these pressures to conform, and they are not always harmful to us. Without the desire to conform to the norms around us we would struggle to integrate into systems like workplaces, airline travel, the local gym, or supermarket shopping. The impetus to conform keeps many social systems running smoothly. [229] The problem is, conformity also keeps ineffective and negative systems from improving.

We all have the ability to challenge the status quo when we see that it is having a detrimental effect. That's what Sherron Watkins, an executive at Enron did when she wrote an email detailing her company's elaborate accounting hoax. It's what Jeffrey Wigand did when he told current affairs show "60 Minutes" that the tobacco company he worked for not only knew their cigarettes were addictive but were deliberately enhancing those addictive properties. [230] It's also what basketball coach Ken Carter did.

Some years ago, in working-class San Francisco, Ken Carter took a job as head basketball coach at his old high school, Richmond High. Carter knew that most of the kids he coached would likely never graduate, attend college, or work their way into a more financially secure future. Carter believed he could use sports to motivate his students to better academic performance. His method was to get the boys he coached, and their parents, to sign a contract agreeing that they would attend all classes, maintain a respectable grade average, never be late, study for at least ten hours a week, sit in the front row in classes, and wear a tie on game day. He was determined to instill a work ethic and a sense of discipline and self-pride in the students in his team.

Carter might have been just another coach trying to help a group of unruly and disadvantaged teens to achieve if he hadn't made a notorious decision that caused an outcry. At a time when the Richmond High basketball team was undefeated, Carter locked the school gym and forfeited two games because fifteen of the forty-five players were not fulfilling their contracts. No contract, no games. Tough love.

Coach Carter went from hero to zero in his local community. Some of the parents were outraged that basketball, the one thing the boys were successful at, was being denied them. The team was shocked and angry at his actions, which punished the innocent as well as the guilty. Carter refused to back down. A contract was a contract and he was determined to stick to the rules he had put in place and the students and their parents had agreed to. He was prepared to risk his job and reputation to break the cycle of an ineffective system. He was prepared to persevere because he had criteria for success. Ultimately, Carter won everyone's respect for his unwavering stance that prioritized the students' long-term futures over short-term gain.[231] The team didn't win the championship that year but several players, against the odds, went on to graduate and attend college.[232]

Like Rosa Parks, Ken Carter decided to make a difference in his community. He saw a bleak future for the kids in his care – a future dictated by economic and social pressures and a feeling of being oppressed by those systems. The wider community – students, parents, supporters – were holding back. They expected and accepted poor academic performance from their students; they did not believe that impoverished urban kids could make it out of the neighborhood. They thought the problem was "out there" in the unfair way the world worked, not realizing that they individually and collectively were part of the systems that resulted in half of the students not graduating. Coach Carter saw what wasn't working and took action to fix it.

In part, Carter's response was so effective because he showed remarkable insight into the systems at work in the school environment by getting not just the players but also their parents to sign the contract he developed. His attention to the parents showed he understood that the boys were not isolated individuals, but that they were embedded in and took their values from their families as well as their peers and the institutions around them. Rather than just being systems aware, though, Coach Carter saw an opportunity for taking action. He saw that success in the game of basketball, itself a social system, could be leveraged for success in scholarship. If the kids could develop discipline, take on hard work, and work together in sports, they should be able to bring the same characteristics to their scholarship.

Ken Carter clearly challenged the assumptions of his community when he demanded academic and social discipline from his talented basketball players. He disputed the Richmond High community's belief that sports success nullified the need for academic success. Some in the school community felt that the boys' success at sports should be celebrated no matter what because it was the one social system they were likely to flourish in given their economic and social environment. Carter felt that if they could succeed at basketball they could also transfer their system skills to education. Coach Carter's radical response to the team not meeting the contract requirements showed the school community that by elevating and celebrating sports skills as a replacement for academic achievement they created the poor scholarship from their students and thus perpetuated a cycle of low achievement in the community at large.

Resisting negative systems and acting with the good of everyone in the system in mind, as Ken Carter and Rosa Parks' experiences show, is rarely easy. Carter's intervention was within a stable system accepted by the community. The beliefs about the value of sport he was challenging were long-held, and sanctioned and upheld at many levels and in many quarters of US society. The segregation system that Rosa Park intervened in was upheld in law. Both their actions led to anger and conflict as they defied the status quo, but they also opened up conversations about what might be. They showed the community an alternative system was possible.

Reframing the Negative

There's a great story of an old blind man who sat on a busy street corner during rush-hour begging for money. At his feet, propped up against an empty upturned hat, was a cardboard sign that read: "Blind – Please help." Passers-by ignored his plea.

A young advertising writer noted the beggar's empty hat and the pedestrians' disregard. She asked the blind man if he minded if she rewrote his sign more clearly. Dispirited, he told her to go ahead. Taking a thick black pen from her briefcase, she turned the cardboard sheet over and wrote a fresh sign, smiled to herself and moved away. Immediately, people began dropping money for the man.

After a while, with his hat overflowing, the blind man asked a stranger to tell him what the new sign said. "It says," said the stranger, "'It's a beautiful day. You can see it. I cannot.'"[233]

A similar tale is the often-told story of the young boy auditioning for a part in his school's play. This boy had his heart set on being given a role, and his mother was worried how he would react to the disappointment if he was not chosen. On the day the pupils found out whether they had made the cast, the little boy's mother went to the school gates to collect her son. She was relieved to see him come running towards her eyes shining and face beaming with excitement. "Guess what!" he shouted. "I've been chosen to clap and cheer."[234] The boy's teacher framed rejection (from acting) as selection (as a member of the audience), turning a negative into a positive.

Both anecdotes are great examples of the power of reframing. Reframing changes the way we see the system at hand. Framing, as you might recall, is what we do when we interpret information, and reframing is the process of abandoning our initial frame for a different perspective. Purposefully reframing can be helpful for resetting our expectations or creating new comparisons and so extracting more happiness from the same reality.[235] With a positive attitude, instead of complaining when things don't go our way, it is possible to reframe situations more optimistically and work creatively to improve circumstances.

An effective response to a negative system can be to reframe issues for others, changing the way they look at a situation and its possibilities. Martin Luther King, for example, did just that when he reframed the civil rights movement in a way that brought people together for change.

Prior to King's rise as a spokesperson, the language of battle had characterized the civil rights movement. Blacks were *fighting* for their rights, *contesting* racial laws, *demanding* to be heard. They had *triumphs* and *defeats*. They were *at war with* the dominant system. Such a way of thinking led to a particular way of acting, characterized by aggression and violence. Influenced by both Jesus and Gandhi, King began to change the frame. He reframed the civil rights movement as one of love in the name of God. Instead of meeting violence with violence, King preached that blacks should turn the other cheek, pray for their enemies, and forgive their attackers. Even when his own house was bombed, he exhorted the angry, vengeful crowd that gathered to love rather than fight the assailants.

By changing the frame from war to non-violence, King opened the way for supporters of the movement to take new actions and develop different responses. They would not have to be angry and violent protesters – they could quietly stand their ground in solidarity, affirmed by the belief that they were doing what was right. The sense of community this shift created meant people felt confident enough to participate, and others watched how to behave and joined in.[236] In effect, Martin Luther King created a new social system for driving change in civil rights, articulating a new vision of how things could be, and leading by example. He carried others with him because he gave them a way to break the negative patterns of the past and create a different future.

We can see reframing being used to deal with current issues, too. Take the example of the ecological footprint versus the ecological handprint.[237] The ecological or carbon footprint frames the relationship between people and nature negatively. It sets up the idea of humans trampling on the environment, using guilt to motivate us into more sustainable actions. In contrast, the ecological handprint is a relatively new term that seeks to reframe the relationship between people and the environment by stressing that human wellbeing and environmental wellbeing are interconnected.

The ecological handprint sees positive social justice movements and positive environmental movements as helping one another flourish. It is possible to uplift humanity as we lower our footprint and as we lower out impact on the environment we can create better communities. For example, a campaign to introduce solar cookers in rural China has resulted in less pressure on the scarce resource of firewood while simultaneously freeing up the village women who traditionally collect the fuel to spend time on other activities, such as caring for the elderly, childrearing and education.[238]

Professionals whose job it is to change other people's behavior are beginning to explore the power of positive reframing. Traditionally, many campaigns that try to improve systems have tended to tell people what not to do rather than what they could do. They have framed things negatively. These campaigns, against smoking, drinking, gambling and so on, are anti behaviors rather than pro activities and try to motivate us by fear. Simply scaring us into reacting to threats, however, limits our commitment, imagination and collaboration.[239]

That's why so much research is now going into incentivizing behavioral change. Economists, for example, are looking at how financial rewards encourage people to meet weight loss targets.[240] The UK government is exploring how incentives might encourage people to adopt greener energy habits.[241] In Canada, a company has set up a loyalty program that rewards people for healthy behaviors by providing them with discounted products.[242] Canadians can join the site for free, log their healthy activities and collect points that they can then spend. People, perhaps unsurprisingly, respond better when there is a reward promised rather than a punishment threatened. It is more effective to create systems that operate on this basis at the outset, but if we can't build a new system we can often reframe existing problems and solutions more positively.

We can do more than just resist negative systems through questioning of the status quo and reframing, however. We can also act systems intelligently by contributing to positive experiences within effective systems or even create new systems. It is easy to admire Ken Carter and Rosa Parks' actions, but, let's face it, many of us will not choose to take on major public battles with large and powerful systems – particularly when we are likely to become the object of animosity as a result of our actions as Carter and Parks did. However, it does not matter if a system is huge or tiny, if it is our nation or our family. All of us can make a difference in the everyday systems we live in quietly but assuredly. What matters is that we respond effectively, making beneficial choices for ourselves, others and the systems we share, and an effective response is enhanced by preparation.

Prepare and Act

When a footballer does an amazing scissor kick with his back to the goal and places the ball in the net it looks like luck. But luck is often the name we give to preparation and opportunity colliding. Another footballer, less experienced and less dedicated may not make the same shot because he or she doesn't have the same level of familiarity with the boundaries of the field, the position of the goalposts, the trajectory of the ball, and the limits of his or her skills. He or she is less lucky because he or she is less prepared in that system.

Similarly, it could seem that the civil rights movement was lucky to end up with the unassuming Rosa Parks as its icon. But, in fact, the activists were prepared. They were waiting for the right person and the right opportunity to come together so they could act with maximum impact. Rosa Parks was prepared, too. She might have initially acted spontaneously as an individual, but her actions and their consequences took place in the context of a number of social systems. Parks was an active member of the NAACP, an organization of like-minded people who felt that laws in the US were inequitable. She belonged to a specific system that supported her views and actions. She also identified and drew strength from the broad cultural and familial systems she was embedded in, saying after the event "When I made that decision I knew that I had the strength of my ancestors with me."[243]

In other words, our ability to take effective actions in systems is enhanced if we are familiar with a system, supported within that system, and alert to the

opportunities for intervention that present themselves. But, given the dynamic and changing nature of systems, being prepared can be challenging. We cannot make plans, assume paths of action, or bank on particular outcomes with certainty. Consequently, adapting our perception, our thoughts, our attitude and behavior to the system at hand in the moment is systems intelligent behavior. There are a number of ways, however, that we can improve the chances of our responsiveness to situations being effective.

Attending to Microbehaviors

Remember the Kingsolver family's quest to eat local food for a year? As they researched the industrial food chain's impact on the environment they found out that most food items in a typical meal in the US have traveled at least fifteen hundred miles from their point of origin to plate. The Kingsolvers calculated that if every US family ate just one meal a week sourced locally oil consumption would be reduced by one point one million barrels of oil a week.[244] "Not everybody can walk away from the industrial food pipeline altogether, but all of us can take a few steps, and the benefits are immediate," pointed out Barbara Kingsolver.[245] In other words, small actions can have big effects.

Despite the possibilities that tiny changes in behavior have for systems, it is rare that we reflect on the impact of microbehaviors when we consider why something doesn't work. It is far more tempting to look for big picture explanations. So when our company's latest deal isn't the success it was forecast to be we say the economy is bad, the time was not right, or changing technology has affected things. Errors and downsides are explained away with the macro. But maybe the deal didn't go so well because of something small and simple. Maybe the negotiating team used too much advocacy and too little inquiry. Maybe someone felt slighted. Maybe key people were hungry and so distracted. We tend to underestimate the impact of the micro.

The medical community has found this out via a decade of research on the use of checklists. In 2001, a critical care specialist and his research team decided to investigate the usefulness of checklists for intensive care teams in hospitals. Choosing just one task – the insertion of a central line – they asked nurses to report when doctors missed a step in this very routine procedure. Shockingly, over a month, more than one step was skipped in over a third of cases. To enforce the checklist, the researchers enlisted the nurses, with the support of the hospital administration, to remind doctors to follow the steps. The result was a dramatic decrease in the rate of infection and huge financial savings for the hospital.[246]

Despite the outstanding results achieved by using a checklist in the research, health professionals were initially reluctant to adopt the practice. It seemed so simple it was practically insulting. Doctors are highly trained, experienced professionals who deal with complicated and complex activities on a daily basis. Checklists were just a stupid piece of paper telling them to do things they already knew to do. But, it turns out, that checklists act as a kind of "cognitive net."[247] They prevent us from making mental mistakes, of memory, attention and thoroughness. They force us to take actions instead of allowing us to fall into non-action. Developing and adopting checklists, a special project of surgeon Atul

Gawande, has had an amazing impact on the outcomes of surgical procedures around the world.

The interesting point about checklists is that they seem as if they are forcing us to adopt norms of behavior, and in some ways they are. But they also encourage discipline, teamwork and preparation in complex situations where small actions or non-actions can have devastating effects. They force those following them to attend to their microbehaviors rather than relegate them to a type two automatic process. This is crucial because most people are not very good at seeing the small things that can make a big difference. We are primed for the big picture because attending to all the little details can be overwhelming, which is not to say that we should overlook the big picture.

Having a Vision

Traditionally, companies entice people to spend money on their products, leading their firm to prosper while helping to expand the economy, albeit likely with some negative impact on the environment. It's a business model that has worked for many years. However, outdoor company Patagonia positions itself a little differently to its competitors. Their mission statement of "*Build the best product, cause no unnecessary harm, use business to inspire and implement solutions to the environmental crisis*" prioritizes environmental sustainability over economic profit. The company has articulated a vision of how they want to operate and created a system that services that vision.

Often, positive actions within systems start with vision. Vision is something that causes us to act in the present how we would act if the future that we imagine were already here. In other words, it's about having a dream of a future that may bear little resemblance to the present, and then behaving as if that future was a reality. Vision needs to be an active force not just a bunch of words. As management expert Peter Senge puts it, "It's not what the vision is, it's what the vision does."[248] With aspirational intentions and imagination we can take ourselves and others beyond the status quo. In a company context the senior executives might focus on *creating* the business rather than *running* the business. In a school setting, a teacher might envision the kind of pupils they want to *leave* the class at graduation, rather than focus on the kind of pupil that *walks in* at the beginning of the year. Vision is about creating a future, not managing the present.

Patagonia, for example, has developed the Common Thread Initiative. Visit their website http://www.patagonia.com/us/common-threads and you will be actively discouraged from buying too much of their product. Instead, under the mantra of "reduce", they advise how to make your Patagonia gear last longer and urge you not to buy what you don't actually need. In addition, they also encourage repairing, recycling and reusing. And Patagonia does more than moralize at its customers; it practices what it preaches. For instance, the company both offers a repair service and accepts old clothing back for recycling. It also has several initiatives promoting reuse. People can donate their old Patagonia clothes to charity or sell them on the company website or via a partnership with EBay. Furthermore, the company donates factory seconds to environmental activists in the field and unsold ranges to people who lose their belongings in disasters.

The Common Thread Initiative tries to inspire its customers to act more Systems Intelligently with respect to the environment, but the company also carefully considers its suppliers. Aiming to be a socially and environmentally responsible company it has partnered with other organizations that care about people and the earth. For example, it promotes fair labor practices and safe working conditions throughout its supply chain and sources its resources from likeminded organizations. In short, Patagonia is attending to the network of connections it has with others and seeing how they collectively contribute to the larger environment. Patagonia as a company has been able to see itself as a system embedded in many other systems. It seems to understand its own impact on the environment and how the collective actions of its customers and suppliers contribute to that.[249] And its practices all stem from a vision.

The beauty of vision is that it pulls us in the direction we want to be going. Daily life typically consists of a series of conscious and unconscious reactions to what goes on in the systems we live in. We respond in the moment with little thought as to how our actions contribute to a bigger picture. Intelligent action in systems is more often characterized by a proactive rather than reactive approach. It is possible not just to prevent a system from spiraling downward by taking actions that promote positive outcomes but also to push a system upwards.

Connecting with Others

A vision is all the more powerful if it is shared. In the process of creating a shared vision of what the future might be, we often have insights about what is possible that we might never have had alone.[250] That's why an effective way to respond to issues within systems is to collaborate for change rather than try to impose or spread it alone. As Peter Senge and his co-authors argue in their discussion of how to tip organizations into sustainable business practices, dealing with systems is a team sport, and the more people who work together on issues the quicker ideas and actions will spread.[251]

True collaboration needs more than good intentions and lip service, though. It needs preparation as we make the effort to build relationships. Tony Hsieh of Zappos, for example, emphasizes the value of creating genuine relationships over the more fashionable networking. Networking values transactions. It is about making connections based on what people can do for one another. Entering a relationship, on the other hand, is about being interested in the people you meet. Hsieh encourages people to see the value in friendship for friendship's sake rather than business networks. In his experience, relationships that are nurtured over two to three years often end up providing surprising, unintended benefits, but that's not what should motivate connecting with people.[252]

Instead, we should be motivated by the realization that in systems we are inescapably connected to others. This stands in marked contrast to seeing ourselves as separate from others and pursuing our own agenda.[253] The former is about betterment of the system by and for everybody, the latter about imposing our ideas of betterment on others. Even simple interventions can have astonishing effects. A study of a manufacturing plant in the US, for example, found that by allowing employees on the assembly line to make decisions about their uniform and their shift roster the organization increased productivity dramatically.[254] People want to feel that they are contributing to the shape of a system – it gives them a sense of autonomy and control in their lives. Systems benefit from both a diversity of ideas and collaborative efforts towards change.

Effective responsiveness via collaboration requires particular skills, such as the ability to convene, facilitate building networks, see through others' eyes, and forge genuinely shared aspirations.[255] Open hearts and minds have to go hand-in-hand with a determination to see and understand systems and work together across arbitrary boundaries.[256] Working with others to create a shared vision means abandoning ego-driven behavior and giving in to the process. People need to come together in inquiry mode not advocacy, or as executive coach Robert Hargrove puts it, it's about bringing ingredients and cooking together, not bringing a pre-cooked dish.[257] In that way, people can input into the systems that matter to them and engage in the change process.

Both new and existing connections facilitate our ability to respond effectively in a system. It is extremely helpful, for example, if we can find a sponsor in the system with more power than us to help us change the system.[258] In effect, Rosa Parks found herself sponsored by the network of connections she was embedded in. But even in everyday systems we can make smart choices about who to engage with. In our extended family, for example, there may be a much-loved person who has the respect of almost everyone else, a "connector." If we want to change the way the wider family treats an individual member, a strategic whisper in that person's ear may have far more influence than if we approach everyone individually ourselves.

Connectors in social systems are those people who provide central links to many others.[259] They are the social glue of a group. As such, they have incredible power to be able to transmit messages and behaviors through a system. [260] Connectors are sociable people who cultivate relationships. They do not have to be best friends with everyone; they just have a wide social circle. Research on social networks tells us there is actually more influence in having many weak ties with people than just a few strong ones because more people are exposed to what is being spread.[261]

Connectors also often straddle boundaries. While most of us are picky about our friends, preferring to choose people who are most like us to develop relationships with, connectors enjoy getting to know people from many walks of life. In organizations, for example, we can have much more influence if we get on with the accountants, the factory hands and the receptionists than if we are only friendly with our own immediate colleagues. Rosa Parks, for example, was likely a connector. When she was arrested in Montgomery, Alabama, the reaction of her close friends and the amazing number of weak ties she had in the in the community, thanks to her involvement in numerous clubs and service organizations, created a movement with strength.[262]

You may have already recognized yourself as a connector or not. If you are, it is much easier for you to effect changes in systems than it is for the rest of us. Even if we are not a connector, however, we can still benefit from the power of connectors by, well, connecting with them. By seeing who the connectors are in a system that we want to change, and allying with them, we can increase the chances of our ideas spreading throughout the system and hopefully creating a tipping point. If we can win the connector in our workplace over to our new resource-saving, environmentally-friendly innovative practice, then the chances of it being taken up across the organization or work group are dramatically increased. Or if we can convince our well-connected local government representative that our idea is beneficial for the community we may create impetus to change. The nature of the messenger is critical to creating a tipping point, or, in systems terms, leverage.[263]

Leverage

In the 1960s, the American legal system enshrined segregation laws against African Americans on the basis of their status being "separate but equal." The resultant racial discrimination in such public facilities as schools, restaurants, swimming pools, and public transportation systematized economic, educational, and social disadvantages for non-whites. Any one of those facilities could have been the site for a protest. But choosing a bus boycott in particular to make a stand against segregation was an inspired and Systems Intelligent choice because it used the power of leverage.

African Americans made up seventy-five per cent of bus users in Montgomery, so boycotting that mode of transport had an enormous impact on the economics of the bus system, run by whites. In addition, the bus system was a powerful symbol of racial inequality for African Americans. The visual reminder of systemic racism that public transport gave to African Americans made transportation a volatile site for race relations. Rosa Parks herself recalled buses taking white children to elementary school while black kids had to walk to their school. "I'd see the bus pass every day," she said. "But to me, that was a way of life; we had no choice but to accept what was the custom. The bus was among the first ways I realized there was a black world and a white world." Boycotting buses was an action that had maximum impact on communities on both side of the civil rights debate.

Paul O'Neill's tenure as CEO of aluminum company Alcoa also nicely illustrates the power of leverage, of attending to something apparently minor and indirectly improving the big picture. Coming in as the new head of an enormous and previously very successful company, O'Neill was seen as the man who would stop the downhill slide that had begun in the 1980s. Stakeholders at Alcoa, including staff and investors, expected O'Neill to focus on higher profits and lower costs. After all, the company was in the money making game. Instead, he focused on workplace safety, to the initial disgust of the stakeholders.

Despite Alcoa being in a dangerous industry – the production of aluminum – O'Neill decided to set the company a target of zero injuries. This was a dramatic shift from being an organization that expected some injuries, if not fatalities, to its workers, to being a company that prioritized injury prevention. O'Neill saw the health and safety record as a leverage point. He understood that by being forced to attend to safety, the organization would also be forced to challenge its current beliefs about best practice in manufacturing, communication, quality control and so on.[264] Challenging the assumptions in just one area, one leverage point, of the organization ended up changing the whole system.

A colleague of ours travels often and is a connoisseur of fine food. When he goes to small, local restaurants, particularly in foreign countries, he considers himself to be taking a gamble on the quality of the meal. He has found that building a relationship with the staff provides a leverage point that increases his chances of having a successful dining experience. Instead of immediately ordering from the menu like most customers, he chats to the wait staff about themselves. In other words, he offers a new input into the restaurant system. When they are at ease, he asks them if he might talk to the chef, explaining his interest in food. Usually, the wait staff is happy to oblige and go to the kitchen in search of the chef. Invariably a bemused chef makes his or her way to the table. Our friend engages the chef in conversation, asking how long they have been cooking, their culinary influences and so on. Eventually, he asks the chef "What is your favorite dish to cook?" The chef replies. Our friend whispers to him or her, "Let's forget about the menu…why don't you cook me what you love to make." The chef, flattered at the attention and pleased to be given free reign more often than not provides our friend with a special dish.

No matter where we are in a system, and no matter what type of system it is, we can have an impact on its patterns. All we need to do is find a point of leverage. In the town of Montgomery, buses were a leverage point. In Alcoa, tightening health and safety turned out to be a leverage point. In a small restaurant, making the staff and chef feel valued is a leverage point. All these examples illustrate the power of pressure in the right place can have on our capacity to influence a system.

In essence, leverage is about minimum input for maximum output. Because of the connected nature of systems, simple acts can create a snowball effect where the small change we introduce feeds on itself, building into a pattern of self-reinforcing growth that over time becomes substantial.[265] As journalist Malcolm Gladwell summarized in his popular book *The Tipping Point*, "with the slightest push…in just the right place" things that seem immovable, unchangeable can be tipped.[266] Seeking out leverage points – the elements, moments, and people where change will have the most impact on the system as a whole – is one of the most Systems Intelligent actions we can take.

The Butterfly Effect

A few years ago the phrase "butterfly effect" entered the general lexicon. In popular usage, the catch phrase came to illustrate that small events could have large consequences. People began to talk about how a butterfly flapping its wings in the Amazon could cause a tornado in Texas. The science behind the anecdote shows that the behavior of some large, complex systems (like the weather) is very hard to predict because the system can be such that a tiny change in one area can have a strong impact over time and distance. Social systems can experience the same phenomenon. Yet, most of us underestimate the power of leverage. We tend to visualize instigating change as difficult, especially in the face of large systems. We feel like change comes in small hard-won steps, one after the other. We don't always realize that one small action in the right place at the right time can have more impact than many other actions combined.[267]

It sometimes seems impossible, for example, to imagine how the actions of one person might change an entire entrenched system of government. Mahatma Gandhi managed it, though, and he drew on the power of leverage along the way. Gandhi waged a long campaign against the British occupation of India, but there were clear tipping points in the process. One of these was when he marched from Sabarmati Ashram to the coast near the village of Dandi so he could produce his own salt and thus avoid the British taxes on the essential condiment. During his twenty-three day, two-hundred-and-forty mile walk, many other Indians joined him along the way and the resulting publicity brought India's fight for independence to the world stage.

Gandhi's choice to focus on the salt tax as the focus of protest was met with incredulity amongst India's independence supporters at the time, but demonstrates his systems awareness and wisdom. By choosing the salt tax, Gandhi focused on an item of daily use that resonated with all Indians, no matter what their class or religion. Rather than protest against abstract issues like poor political laws, he galvanized the people around a tangible product. The tax on salt hurt the poorest people the most and represented almost ten percent of tax revenue for the British. Salt became a powerful symbol of the oppression of Indians by the Raj and the salt march demonstrated how effective civil disobedience could be as a technique for battling social and political injustice.[268]

In fact, the salt march is a fantastic example of effective responsiveness in general and the power of leverage in particular. Gandhi purposefully looked at where he could have the most impact in a huge and oppressive system. He chose a seemingly minor law around which to bring together a disparate group of members of the system who might otherwise not have much in common. He understood that the system he was trying to change was large and complex so he knew that the small intervention he would make in 1930 might not pay off until many years later, and indeed it was 1947 before India won independence. Despite this, he was determined to take action, and willing to sacrifice his own comfort (he was arrested for his actions) for the greater good of himself, others and the governance of India. Gandhi found a leverage point that ultimately contributed to the downfall of colonial rule.

Recognizing Leverage Points

Our ability to find useful leverage points can be instinctive but it is also enhanced by our systems awareness. When we understand that systems can provide leverage points, we increase the likelihood that our intervention will be effective. Of course, there is no single rule that tells us where, when and how to best intervene in a system. Nor are there rules that we can learn by rote because every system is different, and every system is always changing. Nevertheless, we can still look for opportunities that can be leveraged.

In 2012, a group of environmental activists from many walks of life hopped on a biodiesel bus and took the fight to prevent climate change to university campuses around America.[269] By early 2013, students on two hundred and fifty six college campuses had joined them. Their aim was to force universities to stop investing in fossil fuel related businesses. The group's argument – if it's wrong to wreck the climate then it is wrong to profit from the act of wrecking it.

College endowment funds in the US are worth billions of dollars, some estimates saying four hundred billion dollars in just the top five hundred funds. That's a lot of money, and plenty of it is being invested in dirty energy to maximize profits to the universities. Unsurprisingly, most universities are not embracing the call for change. Harvard, for example, has said it will not consider divesting from companies connected to fossil fuels, despite seventy-two percent of its student body voting for divestment.

But, the students intend to be persistent. They have organized. They have researched. They have joined a network of organizations fighting for the same cause. They have the visible economic and environmental impact of climate change on their side. And they have looked for and found a point of leverage.

Divestment of stocks related to fossil fuels is not a very sexy or media friendly topic, but calling for colleges to not invest in dirty fuel companies talks the language that fossil fuel companies understand – money. If pension funds and religious organizations investments join the crusade, as they have been invited to, that will hurt. When a country's top educational establishments stop supporting your business because they understand it to be ethically wrong, the publicity generated makes shareholders uncomfortable and nervous. Not only does divestment affect the dirty energy companies, though. It also has the potential to spur the development of clean energy. All those funds need to be invested somewhere, and if fossil fuels are off the table on moral grounds then sustainable organizations present a far more attractive alternative.

The students are starting the fights on campuses around the country, but the overall goal is to bring change to government policy. Where universities collectively lead, governments usually follow. Already they have had successes. Three colleges quickly dismissed fossil fuel related stocks from their portfolios. The unintended consequence? One of the schools, Unity College in Maine, reported an increase in donations and a surge in enrolment inquires after announcing its decision to invest in environmentally friendly companies.

The issues around sustainability involve many complex and sometimes competing systems – natural, technological, political and social. Yet with the right attitude, collaboration across arbitrary systems boundaries and an understanding of how systems work, many leverage points can be found and exploited for the betterment of systems.[270] Effective responses can be found even for complex problems.

In some ways, dealing with large, complex systems is actually an advantage as there are often more leverage points to be found than in smaller, simpler systems. In smaller systems, like a family, it is sometimes too easy to intervene at only a superficial level. We might, for example, ask that our spouse spend less money if our finances are looking troubled, or tell our kids to study harder if their grades slip. But these adjustments don't really get to the heart of the system. They don't address why the problems are occurring in the first place, so are unlikely to change the system in the long run.

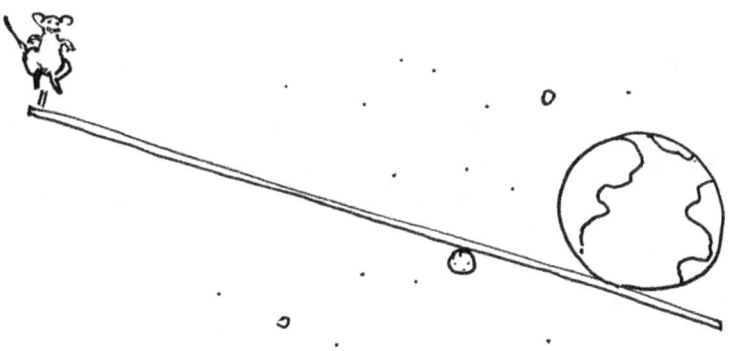

To intervene effectively in a system it is important to make sure we have (and share) all the appropriate information. Just as we can't judge when to refill the oil in our car unless we are alert to its feedback mechanisms, we can't judge what is helpful for a social system unless we are attuned to what is going on in that system. So it is important to find out why we are fraught financially and why our child is struggling in school by collecting the relevant information.

Once we learn about the system, we can consider whether an effective response might be to change the rules of the system. Rules relate to incentives, punishments and constraints, including a system's scope and boundaries.[271] The rules of a system set people's behavior, so changing the rules can change that behavior. Changing how income is distributed in bank accounts, for example, may change a couple's spending behavior, as would cutting up credit cards or setting up a budget. Likewise, creating new expectations around time spend on study, or how much time we spend helping our children, or offering incentives for positive outcomes may change the way our offspring approach schoolwork. The ability to change the rules in a system is a powerful tool.

We can also harness the power of numbers to increase our ability to gain leverage in a system. Harnessing collective power is particularly effective if we are trying to bring about change in a very large social system where we have little formal power. For example, the 1955 boycott of buses in Montgomery, Alabama enlisted the collective power of the black community to instigate structural change of the segregation system. Likewise, the It Gets Better movement began as a YouTube message uploaded by two people and turned into a worldwide phenomenon. In effect, these movements, and others like them, are collective systems interventions.

Leverage through numbers can take the form of evolution (a natural progression) or revolution (an abrupt change). Both extremely powerful types of change are driven by collective action. People buy into the change. New systems emerge to replace old, tired ones, and the better they fit with their environment or context, the more likely they will be successful.[272] So, for example, the rise in the number of older, fitter adults brought about by the wealthy aging baby boomer population is driving an evolution in the way developed nations house their older people. Retirement homes are changing from single room, spartan accommodations to communal villages with lifestyle amenities. Similarly, greater awareness of the finite nature of natural resources like oil and an emphasis on healthy living (coupled with rising costs associated with fuel and healthcare), has seen many cities develop networks of bike paths so people can take a healthier, cheaper, and greener means of transport.

The chances of effective actions are also great in systems where many small connecting networks work together. Organizations like Fair Trade, for example, have become powerful in shaping global markets for the likes of coffee and bananas because they have been able to draw together various individuals and networks including church groups, student organizations and trade groups. They have shown the person on the street that their individual actions make a difference by showing them the systemic connections they the coffee-drinker or the banana-eater have with a grower on the other side of the world. Fair Trade labeling allows the everyday consumer to make a choice about the kind of trading system he or she wants to support. Fair Trade has created a new market outside the normal market and encouraged people to collaborate on an alternative system of exchange.

Collaborative systems skills are as yet underappreciated in daily life but this is where real leverage can come from.

The advent of social media and other communication technology has made leverage through connection easier than ever. When snow and a subsequent backlog of planes meant a flight sat on the tarmac in Detroit for seven hours in 1992, passengers were understandably angry. Despite their complaints and threats of lawsuits, however, the incident fizzled out without any major impact to the airline. The passengers' experience had no lasting impact on the individual airline or the industry as a whole. Fast forward fourteen years and a similar case had significantly different outcomes. Passengers who were kept on an aircraft for eight hours took to the internet after their ordeal. In response to a short media article, one passenger posted a long account of the event online and invited fellow passengers to get in touch with her. They did, and soon they had formed an action group, prepared an online petition and were in demand in the media. Their proposed bill of passengers' rights made it to Congress and was adopted voluntarily by at least one airline.[273] Industry change was driven by the emergence of a new system thanks to collective action.

Part of the art of finding leverage within a system is to recognize the right time to make an intervention so that the effects will be rapidly felt and have immediate positive impact. Being able to feel the state of a system is also crucial to identifying leverage points. What is the prevailing atmosphere of our family, our workplace or our relationship? What feedback is the system providing us with and how are we adjusting our behavior based on that feedback? Noticing and adjusting to simple things like other people's stress levels will help us to adapt our own inputs into a system for maximum effect.

Crazy Wisdom

Because we know the outcome of Rosa Park's action so well, it is easy to take her story for granted. With the benefits of hindsight we can ascribe purpose and intent to her decision to refuse to change seats. But it was only after the event that history traced the success of the civil rights movement to one woman's choice, on one bus ride, on one December evening. We pinpoint an isolated action that set off a chain reaction culminating in the civil rights movement overturning segregation laws. Yet, when Rosa Parks got on the bus that day she didn't know what was going to happen. When she chose not to shift seats, she didn't know exactly what the consequences would be. She took a chance, but a chance based on preparation and action that resisted a negative system and came to exploit a leverage point.

Every day, we have the potential, the possibility, the prospect of acting and changing systems in ways that trigger beneficial, exciting consequences. Understanding that helps us to unleash our Systems Intelligence. It gives us the motivation to act. It shows us we have the power to change systems that crush some of their members and to maintain systems that work well. By recognizing and exploiting leverage points, making a stand against negativity, and being prepared to contribute positively to the systems around us we can be agents for transformation and sustainability.

Executive coach Robert Hargrove calls the kind of action needed to push people out of their comfort zones into new behaviors "crazy wisdom" – the ability to be shocking, colorful, dramatic, and wise as one awakens others to new possibilities.[274] Patagonia's persuading customers to buy less of its product is crazy wisdom. Mahatma Gandhi's march to the sea to avoid the British salt tax is crazy wisdom. Coach Carter's decision to lock a winning team out of their gymnasium is crazy wisdom. Their actions positively contributed towards making better systems that nurture the human spirit while investing in a common cause.[275] They found effective responses to the situations at hand because they considered the system at hand and acted intelligently within it. We can do the same. We have far more impact than we usually realize on the systems around us and can take responsibility for how the systems we experience function. We just need to be attentive to situations and our own influence on them so we can respond effectively.

Effective Responsiveness: What Can I Do Today?

Challenge the negative
Be the new monkey. Question the status quo and the assumptions behind things.
Learn to recognize oppressive, ineffective and negative systems.

Take responsibility for being the instigator of change. Don't apportion blame.
Defy the norms of a system that is corrupt or ineffective.

Reframe issues for others to help them see things in new ways and buy into system change.

Prepare and act
Inspire others with your positive vision of how a system could be. Act as if your vision were a reality. Encourage others to follow your lead.

Build shared vision with others.
Look for collaborators and connectors to help with improving systems.

Try enacting "crazy wisdom" to push people to see things differently.
Use the transformative power of microbehaviors.

Leverage
Consider whether your intended actions will deliver the greatest impact for the least effort. Will your efforts have a butterfly effect?

Look for small or large structural changes that will improve a system. For example, what rule or policy changes might alter people's behavior?

Ally yourself with connectors within systems.

Use all the tools available, like social media, to find leverage points.

Pat attention to feedback from others as you act.

Aim to look beyond obvious, superficial interventions. Try to see and think about life in systems at a deeper level.

Look for ways you can enrich a system by adding new elements or introducing new inputs and actions.

Wise Action

Experience is not what happens to you; it's what you do with what happens to you. ~Aldous Huxley[276]

For many years, the United States' National Park Service has tried to figure out how to protect the natural resource of the forest under its care. Its high level objective is to have forests that are full of healthy trees. Up until the 1960s, the service set the goal of eliminating forest fires. The task and its benefits seemed straightforward; after all, forest fires are clearly destructive to the health of trees. The organization felt preventing forest fires was an ethical and ecologically sound strategy to protect the environment in its care.

But the National Park Service had not fully attuned itself to the ecosystem it was designated to protect. It had not yet realized that fires are actually essential to the overall health of the forest. Assuming that because fires are hazardous to humans they would be similarly undesirable for forests, its members failed to think about the larger systems at work.

In fact, wildfires serve important functions in the forest ecosystem. [277] Various species of trees and animals have adapted to take advantage of the natural occurrence of fires. The clearing of combustible material from the forest floor sets off a series of ecological responses by returning nutrients to soils, encouraging growth of older fire-resistant trees, and promoting the establishment of seedlings.

Establishing a zero-tolerance policy for forest fires in an effort to promote healthy forests unintentionally causes a number of other problems. Large amounts of accumulated debris on the forest floors (thanks to a lack of regular burn offs) means that when fires do catch, they burn hotter and more dangerously. Particular species of tree rely on fire to crack open their seeds – without the fires, these trees do not reproduce. Other trees over-flourish when there is no periodic burning, resulting in densely packed foliage, again leading to hotter and harder-to-control burns, burns more likely to threaten housing and human life. It has taken trial and error and much research for the National Park Service to understand these aspects of the complex forest ecosystem.

Nowadays there is little disagreement that fire is an essential agent of change in forest ecosystems. The current argument is over which type of fires are better – natural wildfires or prescribed burns. Some argue that nature should be left to take its own course, but the potential for such fires to endanger human life and property makes this impractical in many regions. Others prefer controlled burns that allow safer management of risk. However, environmentalists have argued that controlled burns contribute to a decline in water and air quality, and negatively affect wildlife.

The issue of climate change has muddied the waters around forest management even further. Climate change has meant that fire seasons are now longer and more intense, the fires burning bigger and hotter than ever before. Those fires – controlled or natural – and their smoke further exacerbate global warming, creating a vicious circle of concern to climate activists. In parallel, forest conservationists point to fire's necessity for healthy ecosystems, but also want to avoid the response to climate change being deforestation to prevent fires.[278] The public, confused about what to make of the conflicting relationship between fires, forest and climate, worries primarily about human and property safety.

There is no easy and obvious solution for what the National Park Service should do.[279] People who place different emphasis on different parts of the ecosystem favor different approaches. New issues emerge over time. Problems and solutions are only revealed as a result of experimentation, adaptation and discovery. Furthermore, experts on forests emphasize that successful fire policy requires sensitivity to context at the local, regional level.[280] A blanket policy will not work when forest ecosystems are diverse and dynamic, requiring different responses at different times. Each local branch of the National Park Service needs to attune to the part of the system it sees at the same time as managing the overall goals of the organization.

The functioning of complex systems – like forests – is difficult to capture and can seem overwhelming. So many relationships and ongoing changes have to be taken into account it is easy to be paralyzed into non-action. Occasionally, the smartest action is not to respond, particularly if our response is likely to add to a spiral of unintended and perhaps negative consequences. But, typically, acting with systems intelligence means doing something. The challenge is to know what to do, to figure out the wise action.

But what is wise action? Neuroscience equates wisdom with an increased capacity "to recognize patterns and anticipate situations, to predict a likely future, and to act appropriately" [281] – abilities that were missing from the initial naïve embrace of forest fire prevention. We often see the better course of action with the benefit of hindsight rather than foresight. Retrospectively, acting wisely can seem like it should have been easy and obvious. The challenge is for us to make wise choices in the moment, when it is tempting to not think in systems terms, to be impatient for results, or to let our emotions get the better of us. We can do that by drawing on our ability to be insightful about systems, focused on a distant time horizon, and emotionally composed.

Insightful Action in Systems

You may remember that systems perception and attunement, discussed back in chapters one and two, called attention to the systems in our lives. They reminded us to sense hidden systems, multiple, overlapping systems and the big picture as well as what is right in front of us. Wise action comes from our ability to use what we sense about the systems around us to inform the choices we make. Two approaches that often lead to insightful action in systems are taking into account indirect pathways and embracing adaptability.

Indirect Pathways

Eradicating forest fires seemed like a sensible approach to maintaining healthy trees, but the wiser action turned out to be to allow natural burn cycles to occur. Thanks to the indirect pathways within systems the seemingly obvious response is not always the best response. Systems rarely operate in linear ways. We can end up spending too much time looking for direct causal links and easily identifiable chain reactions that are simply not there to be found. It can be far more effective to step back and focus on the bigger picture, searching for unobvious connections and indirect routes. Thinking carefully about how the overall system works, increases the chance of acting wisely within it.

Take the problem of the increasingly unequal distribution of wealth in the US. Much discussion around this topic focuses on corporate salaries, unemployment and taxes. After all, unequal wealth is about money; or is it? Journalist Nicholas Kristof took a different tack when he proposed the expansion of early childhood education to reduce the inequality of wealth distribution in the US.[282] Rather than bickering over increases in taxes and caps on bonuses and the general discourse around the then-headlining Occupy Wall Street movement, Kristof argued that the country need to talk about education. He claimed that the biggest source of structural inequality is that many young people are never given the skills to participate fully in society. Well before they start kindergarten, there are significant gaps between children of the rich and children of the poor, and it is a gap that widens as they move through the school system.

Showing a good grasp of the system, Kristof pointed out that funding early childhood education was not about developing the students' academic ability so they could earn more money, but more about the indirect payoffs. Many education initiatives amongst the underprivileged only result in fleetingly better test results. Because the intellectual outcomes are not guaranteed, funding special programs will not necessarily lead to the production of high-achieving students who go on to become high-earners. Instead, it is other benefits of such programs that are far reaching and help to close the income gap. Children involved in intervention programs end up less likely to repeat grades, in better health, and more likely to attend school more often and, consequently, graduate. They may not become high paid lawyers or doctors, but they have a far better chance of being steadily employed. Tellingly, many countries in northern Europe – countries that don't have the same levels of inequality as the US – have implemented policies to address universal access to early childhood education for many years.

Given that, it is not surprising to find a similar example of the benefits of understanding indirect paths in systems – the concept of baby boxes – comes from a Nordic country. In Finland, the government gives every expectant mother a box of useful and diverse items for motherhood: clothing for baby, nappies, a teething toy, consumables like nappy cream, a picture book, and even condoms. The tradition began by helping out low-income families in the 1930s, but was extended to all Finns regardless of income in 1949 and continues today. The mother can choose to accept cash instead of the baby box, but ninety five percent opt for the box – not just because it is worth more overall but also because it represents a rite of passage.[283]

Why does the Finnish government pay for this service? Because they recognize the indirect benefits that it brings to the country as a whole. To receive the gift, women are required to visit a doctor, ensuring they have medical attention during their pregnancy. Besides the tangible benefits of the contents, the baby box is a powerful symbol to Finns that says all children are equal and all are valuable. It's a gift that is given freely with the intention that the immediate recipient benefits directly and that Finnish society will benefit over the long term. Finland currently has one of the lowest infant mortality rates in the world and also reports having some of the happiest mothers. The baby box is a great example of a wise action within a system.

Prospecting

Improving early childhood education and helping new mothers are obvious cases of wise action in large social systems, but because there are connections and pathways within systems, seemingly sensible actions can sometimes have surprising consequences. Some are positive. The wrecks of ships sunk in shallow waters, many as a result of war, have had the unexpected benefit of promoting the growth of coral reefs rich in marine life that are scientifically and recreationally valuable. Some are quite counterintuitive. For example, high financial bonuses, instead of motivating workers to do their jobs better as you might think can cause employees to underperform because of anxiety.[284] Some are negative. When environmentalists initially encouraged the use of palm oil to decrease pollution caused by the consumption of fossil fuels, they did not anticipate that its production would lead to even more carbon dioxide to be released into the atmosphere. The felling and burning of rainforests to make way for palm oil plantations ended up worsening the problem they were trying to address. To develop our ability to act wisely we shouldn't assume the obvious and intended will happen. Instead, we can remind ourselves of the likelihood of unintended consequences and the sometimes-counterintuitive effects of behavior in systems, and act in ways that take that into account.

That's not always easy. Much of what happens in systems lies outside our field of vision. We tend to forget that we can only see a partial picture of the system. Just because we don't hear our manager praising us doesn't mean she doesn't do it when we aren't around. Or just because we don't see our children acting compassionately in the playground doesn't mean they aren't. It is not always possible to see all the people in a system at the same time and we certainly never see ourselves and the intentions we are conveying to others. Because we always work with partial information, we don't always realize what happens as a result of our behavior. The consequences of our actions might be felt beyond our experience.

We also struggle to escape the effects of *presentism*, which psychologist Daniel Gilbert defines as "the tendency for current experience to influence one's views of the past and the future."[285] It can be difficult for us to imagine that a system might look different next week, or next year, and that makes it hard for us to accurately imagine the consequences of our actions.

However, our minds have the ability to evaluate many possible futures, and revise those evaluations as things happen. In daily life we are constantly imagining possible acts and outcomes and evaluating options before deciding what we do. (Shall I tell my mother this? If I do, she might do that. If I don't perhaps such and such will happen....) This capacity is called prospecting.[286] When we prospect with a systems perceptive, we are more likely to act wisely because we have mentally simulated outcomes and considered the "what-ifs" of our actions. Prospecting is liberating because it reminds us that we actually choose behaviors within systems and so influence the future that comes about as a result.

Our behavior in systems also becomes more intelligent through active experimentation rather than passive experience. By being prepared to try new things we may find the indirect route. We may well be disappointed occasionally but we will also learn. Learning though experimentation is key to adapting to change. It means we can constantly revise our expectations and adjust our actions. In other words, we can use a feedforward/feedback model,[287] where we first imagine, then act, then revise our imaginings based on feedback and so on. The more we anticipate the effects of our actions on the future the more intelligently we can act within systems.

We can also enhance our wisdom by being willing to listen to others' advice. One of the typical features of systems is that their dynamics are determined by feedback. It is the people who are connected to us who reflect our behavior in action. The reactions they have to our behavior create a feedback loop that lets us know how we are doing. To understand the implications of our actions for others, it is helpful to ask them directly how they feel. Remember, our own view of the system, not to mention our own view of ourselves, is one-sided. We only see the system and ourselves from our limited point of view. Others will see the system and us differently and may provide telling insights into how we come across and ways we can improve our participation in the systems we are acting in. Accepting feedback magnanimously shows a willingness to be flexible and adaptable in our way of thinking about and interacting with the world.

Adaptation

It is tempting to think of systems intelligence as simply figuring out the system, providing an input or intervention and then achieving the desired outcome. In many ways, that's what we do on a daily basis. A kiss on our daughter's head gets us a smile; a birthday dinner at a special restaurant pleases our partner. Except, we, others, and the system are always evolving. Social systems are not fixed entities. Companies, sports teams, activist groups and community organizations come and go, emerging from the connections between people and dissipating when those connections are broken. They may be long-lasting or temporary. They also fluctuate over the course of their lifetime, ebbing and flowing according to the dynamic connections that emerge within them.

Consequently, we need to adjust all the time. We need to perceive and attune to the system as it is now, today, not to what it was last year, or last week or even yesterday. What works now won't always work. That kiss that our daughter looks forward to now may soon annoy her, and our partner may come to resent our lack of creativity in birthday plans. We often unthinkingly act in ways that suit the systems we expect to be present, working on automatic pilot and use the same strategies over and over again. These strategies likely were effective for us in the past, and may be effective for us in the future, but because they become so ingrained they prevent us from seeing alternative possibilities.[288]

Sticking unquestioningly to what we usually do and are comfortable with doesn't work effectively when conditions fluctuate constantly and challenges extend over long time horizons. To adapt, we need to question our old ways of thinking and operating within systems, especially when they are not working well. Because new contexts, new systems, are always emerging, we benefit from altering our thoughts and behavior to match the environment we find ourselves in. Adaptability is about learning in small steps, through error, self-monitoring and being willing to change course as things emerge.[289] Understanding that is what leads to wise action in systems.

Unfortunately, we tend not to celebrate the characteristics of adaptability and flexibility, particularly in leaders. Instead, now and historically, we favor those who act confidently, without hesitation or re-evaluation of their decisions. Confident certainty attracts the positive attention of media, business leaders, and politicians.[290] Those who hedge their bets are far less popular. We tend to make heroes out of those who attack problems directly and reactively rather than those who use indirect methods and long-term thinking, partly because the results of these take time to manifest

Yet, if we understand systems, we understand that our knowledge about the dynamics of them is imperfect and emerges as we do things, not before. Franklin D. Roosevelt is one leader who openly acknowledged this. Roosevelt described his management of the difficulties he faced during his presidency, including the Great Depression, as "bold, persistent experimentation." He constantly changed and adapted his approach, favoring trying things and admitting failure and trying something else if they didn't work out. Roosevelt understood his authority was limited by the complexity of the environment, the unpredictable reactions of others, and the open-ended nature of the problems the country faced.[291] Understanding that complex, unfolding and unpredictable problems require incremental, adaptive, creative solutions is part of wise action.

Carrying Skills Between Systems

Adaptability is also crucial to wise action because of the presence of multiple systems in our life. We all engage with numerous systems, often simultaneously. We are members of our family, we join sports teams, we volunteer in community organizations, we go to work. Unsurprisingly, we tune in better to the systems we are most comfortable with. We may detect the subtlest of mood changes in our spouse, for example, but be oblivious to how our manager is feeling. We may understand the dynamics of our own small workgroup in the office, but not pay much attention to how another team in our organization gets along. It is easier to act wisely in the systems we know well and are most attuned to.

Even though we have tremendous intelligence in the particular systems within which we are immersed regularly, we may struggle to adapt to other contexts. Our assertive decision making, for example, may be useful in our role as an emergency worker but not so effective in a new romantic relationship. Yet, we

can fall into the trap of assuming that all systems' contexts are like the particular contexts that we are most familiar with. Consequently, if being outgoing and talkative has worked well for us in one setting, we might assume that others will always respond well to those attributes in us, and push that style even when it doesn't really work.

They key is to approach life in systems with particular higher-level orientations – such as positive engagement or spirited discovery – but to be able to draw on specific skills that are appropriate and adapted to the context. Wise action in systems is action that is appropriate to the situation. It is systems intelligent to see the need to adapt our strategies to the system at hand: what works in one context is not always appropriate for another. When we draw on this ability to adjust we can be startlingly more effective within different systems; we can be better at being better.

How do we achieve this kind of multi systems capability or unconscious adaptability? One way is to be more attuned to the systems around us before we react. Awareness about when a system changes and when multiple systems are present can help us make wiser choices. We have all had moments, sometimes quite disconcerting, when we have been conscious of multiple systems. Perhaps when you were a little child you bumped into your teacher in the supermarket. If so, you probably experienced the feelings of astonishment and strangeness that most of us have in that situation. *What is my teacher doing here? What do I say? How will she treat me?* These are all reactions to a change in systemic context. In the classroom setting, the child knows how to behave, and how their teacher will behave, but he or she is often disconcerted by the transportation of the teacher to a new context. Instinctively, they know the rules of interaction will change – that's their natural systems intelligence at work – but they are not sure just how things will go.

As adults we are far more adroit at dealing with transpositions of context. We have a well of socialized behaviors we draw from to balance our momentary loss of equilibrium. So when an old school classmate appears at a workplace meeting twenty years after we last saw them, or we bump into our neighbor during an overseas holiday, or we run into our mother while we are out with a new date, we cope. We manage to smile and chat as we attune to the unanticipated contact between two worlds. Generally, we don't consciously think about the multiple systems we encounter – we just deal with life intuitively, coping pretty well with the demands living in multiple systems places on us. At times, though, it is important to consciously balance the demands of different systems so that we can choose the best actions.

Patiently Persist

The slave trade was a lucrative one for eighteenth century Britain. By 1783, the slave trade route represented approximately eighty percent of Britain's foreign income. Goods were taken to Africa and exchanged for slaves, who were transported to the West Indies, where the empty ships were filled with plantation products to be taken back to Britain. While it benefited the economic system of Britain, however, it disturbed the social system. Not everyone in Britain was morally and ethically comfortable with making money out of human misery.

Some were willing to stand up against slavery. The Society for Effecting the Abolition of the Slave Trade had its first meeting in 1787 and William Wilberforce, politician and philanthropist, became leader of the movement.[292] The abolitionists expected a long and dirty fight as moral principles clashed against the might of money. When in 1789 Wilberforce made his first speech to the House of Commons on abolition, he didn't argue that slavery itself should be declared illegal. Instead, he focused on making the *trade* of slaves illegal. There was no way the wealthy landowners, many of whom were politicians, would agree to ending slavery. If trading slaves were illegal, however, it provided the landowners the possibility of relying on the reproduction of existing slaves to maintain their workforces.

Of course, for the abolitionists the long-term goal was to eradicate slavery altogether. They hoped that by ending the legality of trading in human flesh slavery would eventually fade away and the conditions for existing slaves would improve. In other words, the abolitionists used a systems intelligent approach. They understood how the slave system worked, how it overlapped with the economic system in Britain and how wealthy landowners would react to their attempts to change it. They saw the potential of an oblique, indirect attack on slavery. And instead of emotionally protesting they coolly plotted a path through the legal system of the day to instigate the change they were seeking.

It was to be a long battle. The unstable political climate fuelled by the French Revolution meant public support for the cause waxed and waned. Wilberforce and his supporters did not give up. Despite repeated defeats of their parliamentary bills they continued fight for abolition, remaining patient and persistent.

They eventually adjusted to the repeated defeats by making a clever change in tactics. Rather than directly campaign for the abolition of the slave trade, they looked for another angle of attack. The movement worked quietly on developing a bill that banned British subjects from aiding or participating in the slave trade where slaves were being supplied to countries that Britain was at war with. Many British ships were flying under the American flag and trading with foreign colonies so this bill effectively curbed their activities. In public, Wilberforce and the pro-abolitionists feigned disinterest in a bill that appeared to be about maritime law. Because they didn't draw attention to its effects, the Foreign Slave Trade Bill was quickly passed in 1806. As a result, the slave trade was suddenly reduced by two thirds, and a year later it became illegal for British ships to transport enslaved people.[293]

Appreciate Time and Anticipate Delays

William Wilberforce's campaign to outlaw the highly profitable slave trade took more than twenty years before its eventual success in 1807. It was to be another twenty-six years before slavery itself was made illegal. The abolitionists' prolonged fight to end the slave trade illustrates a key dimension of wise action – the willingness to have a long-term time horizon. Much of contemporary life is about instant gratification. Yet the dynamics of systems means that the effects of actions may not be perceived until some time has passed. It is systems intelligent to be steered by long-term objectives and to be willing to delay gratification for our efforts. Being persistent and patient is about letting things accumulate – over time we, and the system, can learn and improve.

Been kind to your neighbors over the years? You are likely to find they reciprocate when you need support. Ignored them? That might leave you isolated when in your time of need. Feedback is not always immediate. The longer the time lag between an action and its consequence, the harder it can be to figure out the system.[294] Actions taken in systems have both short and long term effects. We need to realize that the consequences of our actions may be delayed, and that what we are dealing with now may well be the aftermath of actions long ago. If we are to act systems intelligently we must spend time watching both the short and the long-term horizons.[295]

Interestingly, experiments show young children who understand that actions taken now can affect the future are more likely to go on to succeed in life by both academic and economics measures. In tests for self-control, researchers leave a child in a room with a tempting treat. They are told when the researcher leaves the room they can either eat it straight away or wait until the interviewer returns and receive an additional treat. Those who opt to wait, studies have found, go on to lead more successful lives than those who opt for immediate gratification.[296] These kids have figured out that rewards can be delayed in time, and so they are patient and willing to wait for that reward.

Reminding ourselves that the effects of what we do today may not reveal themselves until well into the future is a relatively simple step towards wise action. It's a phenomenon we experience in many areas of life. Studying hard at high school and college will provide significant benefits long after that study is finished. Living a healthy lifestyle might not bring immediate rewards but will advantage us as we age. Developing good savings habits in early adulthood may help us when we are starting a family or elderly. Being willing to wait for results is a skill we can cultivate.

Persist

Achieving good results over time requires perseverance as well as patience. A strategy that can help us to nurture persistence is to aim for small, successive wins. That is, instead of trying to achieve our end goal through a single step, we can scatter our efforts within a system. Changing from a couch potato to a marathon runner, for example, can only be achieved if we make small gains. We don't turn our body into an efficient running machine with one action. Nor do we typically just run a little bit further each day until we reach marathon distance. Instead, we change our diet a bit, do some more exercise, watch less TV, buy some exercise gear. We pepper our lives with gradual changes to try to build lifestyle patterns that will eventually allow us to run twenty-six miles.

The principle applies equally well to large social systems as it does to unfit bodies. Imagine your child's school is going through tough financial times. As a parent, the overall decline of a school's funding seems like an insurmountable problem for you to solve. But if you do whatever you can and persevere with that approach, you might find you can have an impact. You could offer to help in the classroom, for example, and maybe this might assist an overworked teacher. You might organize a party for the staff, to show that you and the other parents appreciate the work they do in tough times. That might make the teachers feel supported and so renew their energy in the classroom. You might enlist the community's help in providing a service, like gardening, that could save the school some money. In other words, you could find small achievable tasks that would both help the system in some way and perhaps inspire others to do the same. If a pattern of such small wins emerges, you can almost guarantee the atmosphere in the school will change.

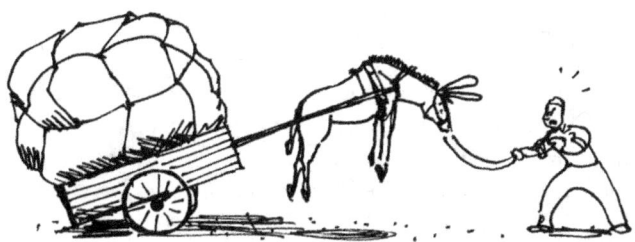

When problems are perceived as too large to fix people may be deterred from innovation. For such problems it is better to achieve a "concrete, complete, implemented outcome of moderate importance" than focus on changing the whole system at once.[297] One small win may seem insignificant, but many together build into a pattern of effective action, even if they seem to be unrelated, thanks to the indirect loops and connections within social systems. The possibility that an effort to improve the system will have massive consequences makes it important to persist with positive actions even if we can't immediately see the rewarding, cumulative impact of them.

Persistence is also enhanced by the willingness to steadfastly pursue a course of action. J. K. Rowling, author of the Harry Potter books, wrote the first book as a struggling single mother on welfare and famously was rejected by twelve publishers before Bloomsbury finally gave her a contract. The first time Sigmund Freud presented his ideas to his fellow scientists, he was booed from the stage. Walt Disney was fired for a lack of imagination, and at Sidney Poitier's first audition the casting director told him to stop wasting people's time. Perhaps the best basketball player to date, Michael Jordan, was told he did not have enough talent to succeed in the game.[298] All of these people, despite receiving negative feedback, went on to amazing success. They persevered, understanding that creating success is a process that evolves over time.

When we are trying to improve large social systems, rather than pursue individual success, we can often feel like we are chipping away at an iceberg with the proverbial toothpick. With doggedness, however, we may find allies in the system who will join us. That's what Martin Luther King and Rosa Parks did. It's what Emily Pankhurst did. It's what Nelson Mandela and Desmond Tutu did. The civil rights movement in the US, the struggle for women to gain the right to vote, the end of apartheid in South Africa – all of these positive changes in big social systems came about because of persistent action by collectives of people.

They were also accompanied by unrest and upheaval. Naturally, as with the abolitionists, when we try to change pre-existing and firmly established patterns we often meet resistance. Persistence and patience can help us to overcome that resistance, but we also need to be mindful that human systems are by their nature social entities. It is important that our idea for what a system should become is flexible because we alone are not the system. Change must be negotiated with all the members as others will be affected by our efforts. Wise action is not about controlling the change process, but about instigating it and assisting in it.

Managing Emotions

Forest fires are an emotive topic. Scientists and administrators argue passionately over how to deal with them. Opposing groups demonize and blame one another as they try to have their preferred solution accepted by the general public and into law. In the face of several large, costly fires, the debate over forest management in the US has become increasingly adversarial over the last few years.[299] The arguments are played out in policy rooms of government and, increasingly, the courts. And when we turn on our televisions during fire season we are reminded of the very real consequences of these debates. People lose their homes. Firefighters lose their lives.

When the policy makers for the Forest Service, government representatives and environmental activists are arguing their respective positions on fire management they likely forget the bond that unites them. In their own way, each group is trying to make the world a better place. But it is all too easy to lose sight of the common goals we share when we are passionately advocating a particular means to achieve that goal. We are so overcome by our own emotional connection to a particular perspective that we do not attend to the emotions of others.

Yet, it is our empathic connection – our capacity to empathize, to recognize and feel someone else's pain or joy – that provides the glue that keeps people working together.[300] The concept of emotional intelligence (EI) has significantly contributed to our understanding of humanity in terms of empathetic connection.[301] To be high in EI we need several skills. First, we need to be aware of our emotions. Second, we need to manage the emotions we experience – keeping our emotions in check is a crucial aspect of our well-being as excessive emotions undermine our stability. Next, we can use emotions to motivate ourselves. Finally, we can recognize emotions in others and handle relationships well.[302] While we cannot avoid feelings emerging, we can learn to deal with them rather than being overwhelmed by them. When we live more intelligently with our emotions, they help rather than hinder us in life.

Systems intelligence adds another layer of abilities to EI because it involves us understanding our emotional lives as connected to the structures within which they occur. Systems generate emotions in us. Steven Pinker, in *The Better Angels of our Nature,* argues social systems play a role in fostering empathy. The interconnectivity of the modern world and strong, democratic governments, he claims, have contributed to exposing us to and making us more empathetic with different cultures and a wider variety of people. This in turn has reduced human violence over recent history. Jeremy Rifkin, in *The Empathic Civilization,* similarly makes a compelling case for human evolution pushing us to become more empathetic and emotionally connected to ensure the survival of our species and our habitat.

But systems not only generate emotions in us, we also generate emotions in systems. We do not live alone. Our emotions come about because of our experiences in the world and our experiences in the world inevitably occur in systems. It is not enough for us to simply focus on our own emotional states or two-person psychology. We can do much better if we understand our emotions in context. If we attune to ourselves, others *and* the systems we share, then we can start acting wisely in human relationships and organizations. Managing emotions is effectively a full-time job as everyone is always feeling something. The key is to harness the emotions we are feeling and use them to enhance our experiences of systems.

Abraham Lincoln's wise actions after he won the US presidency demonstrate the powerful effect managing emotions well can have in systems. Anticipating the animosity and polarization that would fester if he excluded those who disagreed with him from political power, Lincoln famously invited his main rivals into his cabinet.[303] Lincoln acted unexpectedly to create a more effective system. He is remembered for his extraordinary ability to befriend those who opposed him, smooth potential conflicts, share credit for success and accept responsibility for failure, and learn from his mistakes. In other words, he acted with the understanding that the best strategy for going forward in a divisive system (politics) was to foster empathetic relationships, to manage people's emotions, and to focus on what was best for the future while doing so.

Coping with Challenging Emotions in Systems

Life in systems is not always easy. Things don't always go our way. Sometimes we are in a grumpy mood; sometimes we lose our temper; sometimes it feels as if the system is working against us. Negativity is part of the dynamism of life. Being systems intelligent is not about eliminating negative emotions, but about not allowing those emotions to interfere with our judgment. Basically, it means that if we have negative experiences we don't fall apart. We keep our cool. We can deal with them, perhaps even use them to our advantage. Even during negative experiences, we can look for ways to use the systemic setting effectively to bring about constructive changes.

Managing emotions is particularly crucial because change in systems is rarely a smooth process. Energy and tension are dimensions of life, especially if we are working at improving systems. It is possible to harness negative emotions that we experience so that they work for us, not against us. Feeling anger towards our boss because she has just refused our request for time off may be appropriate for a short time. If our immediate feelings turn to thoughts of revenge or become prolonged outrage, however, then our anger has become inappropriate.[304] A systems intelligent response would be to move from anger towards our employer's decision to some systems-sensitive perspective taking.

•What information about the workplace might our boss be privy to that we are not?
•What pressures might there be on her?
•Could someone else have asked for time off at the same time?

Attempting to put what has angered us in context within the wider system helps to channel the negative emotion to a more neutral focus and keep it under control.

What works for anger can also work for other challenging emotions like worry and sadness. People find it very hard to shake negative moods because they often lack the skills for changing their thought processes. Many psychologists recommend that people attempting to overcome being mired in negativity draw on the skills of attunement and mindfulness discussed earlier. The first step in treating a tendency to worry, for example, is to teach a person self-awareness so they recognise, and can interrupt, the patterns that signal a spiral into anxiety. This is coupled with relaxation techniques designed to slow the body's involuntary physical response to worry. Finally, people are encouraged to be mindful of their thought patterns so they can be critical of the assumptions their brains rush to make.[305] In effect, psychologists prompt their clients to treat their bodies and minds as an integrated system.

The same techniques that help our body as a system also work in social systems. Most of us regularly underestimate the influence of systems on our individual thoughts, feelings and actions and on the thoughts, feelings and actions of those we interact with. We tend to see individuals as discrete beings, in charge of manufacturing their own behavior. Yet, the effect of living in systems on our emotions is pretty obvious when we think about it. Imagine you are trying to write an email on your computer and the screen keeps freezing on you. You get angry. In the comfort of your own home, you might react with a few choice expletives or even fling something across the room in frustration. But what if the same thing happens at work? Chances are at work you will manage your anger differently. You'll be mindful of who is around, the expectations of your workplace, how you want people to perceive you, and you will adjust your response accordingly. If not, you'll likely suffer some consequences. Managing emotions is a systems phenomenon that we handle every day. Once we are aware of that, we can work to do it even better, especially in the face of difficulties.

We can, for instance, achieve a change in our emotions by changing the nature of the system. To take a macro example, Finland has emerged as a leader in global mediation. Part of the country's success in mediating thorny international disputes lays in its recognition of how systems and emotions impact one another. A remote, relatively sparsely populated country blessed with an abundance of beautiful lakes and forests, Finland offers disputing parties a system-altering location for talks. Groups and individuals in conflict can be removed from the tensions of their own environments to a neutral, natural and private space, far away from the prying eyes of the media and interested stakeholders. Something as simple as changing the setting in which the disputing parties meet can have a profound effect on the dynamics of their interaction. [306] That's because they have no established patterns of interaction for this new setting; the change in context helps to shake up their existing destructive patterns and allow something new to emerge. On the micro level, choosing to discuss a contentious issue with our spouse in the city gardens may have a similar effect.

Emotions, both negative and positive, are contagious so it is not uncommon for them to spread through systems. A family or workplace or sports team, for example, might develop a shared sense of anxiety, or disappointment, or fear. A systems intelligent intervention under these circumstances is to invite the group together to reflect on their emotions, to attune to the feeling of the system. Once people realise they are feeding off one another's emotions and creating spiral of negativity that makes the whole system negative they are better equipped to change the dynamics. They can work collectively to create a more positive atmosphere, particularly if there is systems intelligent leadership from within the group.

Consequently, wise action also involves supporting others and their emotional experiences in the system through our actions and interactions. We might ask ourselves

- In what way can I help?
- How can I encourage this person?
- How can I validate them and their skills?
- How can I change the system to bring about positive outcomes for them?
- What insights about the system can I offer?
- What connections can I make that would help them?[307]

When we translate these reflective questions into actions we embrace the possibility of uplifting the system by fostering constructive relationships and cultivating positive emotions. When Nelson Mandela befriended his prison guards and treated them with dignity and respect to model a new way for blacks and whites to interact in South Africa, for example, he attended to the emotions of the people in the system. Dan Savage did the same when he started the It Gets Better project, as did Coach Carter, Desmond Tutu and the activists who supported Rosa Parks.

Acting Wisely

Systems idiocy is all around us. People act reactively without insight or reflection. They want immediate results. They give up too soon. They are overcome by emotions. The consequences of unwise behavior in systems may be as globally devastating as an armed conflict or as personally painful as a failed relationship. Whether on a large or small scale, systems idiocy does not benefit ourselves, others or the systems we share. We would do much better to focus on acting wisely.

When we consciously adopt a systems view of the world we acknowledge that many aspects of life are difficult to understand. We move beyond seeing everything as being about individuals who can control and command the social, ecological and physical environment and come to understand that the outcome of our actions depends not just on what we do, but on how others interpret what we do and the context in which we do things. Part of being systems intelligent is acting as if we can make happen whatever it is we want to make happen, knowing that we cannot and yet being willing to work with whatever does happen.[308]

Furthermore, if we understand systems, we understand that our knowledge about the connections we have with others is imperfect and emerges as we do things, not before. There are always more options available to us than we think. With wisdom, we will choose appropriate actions, even if we have to patiently persist, manage our emotions and adapt along the way – as William Wilberforce and the abolitionists did many years ago.

Wise action, then, calls for us to be thoughtful in our engagement with systems. It is important to be aware that our well-intended actions may have what at first seem negative outcomes, only to become and remain positive over time. It is important to understand that small, repeated efforts can yield results. It is

important to know that good things take time. Wisdom might be associated with age, but we do better on measures of wisdom the more attentive we are to things outside of ourselves – that is, the more oriented we are to the systems around us. We can't accelerate our rate of maturity, but we can learn to be attuned to what's going on in and around us and how we react to it.

Wise Action: What Can I Do Today?

Adapt

Remind yourself that social systems are always dynamic. Make decisions and take actions that reflect this understanding.

Experiment with your actions until you find what works. Take the time to reflect on the consequences of your behavior.

Anticipate that there will be unintended consequences to what you do.

Prospect. Imagine alternative futures and choose your actions wisely based on what might happen.

Listen to advice from others.

When interacting with a group of people, make an effort to see the multiple systems in the room and adapt your inputs to suit the situation.

Patiently Persist

Don't be put off by perceived failure – try a new approach or allow more time for changes to emerge.

When thinking of a system you'd like to change, try also to think of the parts of the system that are outside your field of vision.

Make an effort not to expect instant gratification. Be prepared to wait for results.

Look for small victories. Make changes where you can throughout the system.

Negotiate change.

Consider when might be a good time to intervene and over what time frame it is realistic to see the results of your actions.

Manage emotions

Be mindful of your emotions.

Adapt your reactions appropriately to the environment at hand.

Learn to feel comfortable with tension. Understand it is part of change.

Attune to the emotions of others.

Support others as they try to manage their own emotions.

Remember to be alert to the emotional systems that underlie the more obvious connections between people. Triggering a more positive emotion might bring about change in the visible system.

If the system repeatedly generates negative emotions, look for ways to change the system.

Positive Attitude

"Feel. Imagine. Do. Share." ~ Design for Change[309]

When Kiran Bir Sethi's young son came home from school one day with a red line drawn through his homework, Sethi was annoyed. The boy's teacher had used red ink to let the child know that his essay did not conform to what was expected of him. But her son didn't understand what was wrong with his essay and the teacher had not bothered to explain to him. Crossing our his efforts with red pen seemed to Sethi a method likely to crush her son's spirit rather than inspire him. She felt the incident was symptomatic of India's educational approach. Instead of teaching children to conform to preexisting structures, to fear making a wrong decision and to feel helpless in the education system Sethi thought school should be a place that gives children confidence in their competence. And so she founded Riverside School.[310]

With a curriculum designed to empower children to be active in shaping their own lives, Riverside's philosophy is built around two words: "I can." Sethi eloquently explains how she arrived at this approach.

> "Look at a child from birth to two years old; they go from crawling to standing in those two years. The kid does not believe that this is an impossible feat; he or she just does it. In those two years, a parent gives them constant motivation, 'Come! Come! You can! You can!' The moment a child starts talking and moving, a parent starts saying to them, 'Don't go! Stop! Sit down! Keep quiet! It is ridiculous!"[311]

Adults, she believes, unwittingly end up stifling the natural curiosity, creativity and confidence that children have. And, in the process, they also curb a child's natural System Intelligence.

There is an alternative. Humans are social animals and our attitudes and emotions are both systemic and contagious. We "infect" people with them. For Sethi, it is clear that if teachers are bored, listless and uninspired then the children in their care will mirror these traits. In contrast, if a teacher is passionate and energized then the child is likely to catch the same attitude. The infectiousness of the positive "I can" outlook can be exploited to encourage children to not accept the world at face value but set out to change the aspects they don't like.

Riverside School is located in Ahmedabad, India, but Sethi's ideas have radiated much farther since its beginnings in 2001. In 2009, she conceptualized and promoted India's largest design contest for schools. The competition had more than one hundred thousand students working to address some of India's most challenging difficulties. Since then, the Design for Change contest has gone global. It's focus on child-driven solutions has led to Taiwanese children designing umbrella holders for their mothers' shopping carts, Swedish children turning an untidy clump of cables into something beautiful, and Mexican children building a civic square. [312] Design for Change is about infecting children and their communities with optimism and positivity and the belief they can make a difference.

Positivity is powerful. Consider the difference a compliment makes to us – we stand taller, smile, do things differently. It visibly lifts us. Even tiny changes such as in how someone says our name or how people greet us can create uplift. Positivity sets the overall tone for our life in systems. If the other dimensions of systems intelligence have been like the ingredients for a recipe, positivity can be considered the cooking process that binds those ingredients together and transforms them into a dish.

One of the most obvious systems that our attitude has an impact on is our own body. The placebo effect provides one of the earliest and most well-documented demonstrations of how mental outlook is connected with wellbeing. Up to two thirds of patients given sugar pills instead of real medication will show marked physiological and emotional improvement simply because they believe they are being administered an effective treatment.[313] Since the first experiments on the placebo effect in the 1950s, the connection between wellbeing and belief has been consistently explored, as has the effect of positivity on our health. We now know that positive emotions do things like help reduce the stress on our cardiovascular systems and contribute

to longevity.[314] The power of positive thinking can even help our bodies to heal following surgery.[315]

A positive attitude benefits aspects of not only physical health, but also psychological performance. What researchers call dispositional optimism – our expectation that good things will happen – generates everything from fewer feelings of loneliness to greater tolerance for pain.[316] Positivity, it turns out, is also a key component of creativity. Both sustained happiness and fleeting moments of delight help us do better at solving insight puzzles, for example. In addition, when we are in a good mood we are generally more relaxed, and when we are relaxed our brain also relaxes and so becomes open to making connections that we can't make when we are concentrating. That's why so many of us have our brilliant ideas in the shower, when we are just waking up in the morning or when we are daydreaming.[317] The power of a positive mood is that it allows us to get a better sense of how things hang together – something that is crucial for seeing, feeling and acting in the systems around us.

Given that a positive attitude brings physical and psychological benefits, knowing how to be more positive becomes essential for living with systems intelligence. Few would disagree with the idea that being in a good mood is better than being in a bad mood. Yet, many of us tend to think we have little control over how we feel. We are steeped in the idea that optimism and pessimism are largely unchangeable personality traits. We assume that even our fleeting moods are dictated by circumstances beyond our control, be they situations in life, other people, or the genes our parents gave us. The good news is that while some aspects of outlook are inherent, we can also balance our natural temperament with learned experience. We can deliberately cultivate a positive attitude.

Positive Psychology

All of the scientific proof that points to the benefits of having a positive attitude is changing the focus of research activity in fields that study human social systems. Relatively young research movements are advocating an uplifting approach to understanding lived experience. Appreciative inquiry, a method of organizational development, for example, does this by looking at what is going right in organizations instead of focusing on fixing problems. Researchers look to find what is working well in organizational systems and then build on that by collaborating with the members of the systems being studied.[318] Similarly, whereas traditional systems thinking applied to organizations has typically been about describing and controlling, today researchers are becoming interested in imagining and working towards positive futures.[319]

The same shift is occurring in psychology. Increasingly, academics are shifting focus from cure to prevention, illness to wellness, and problem solving to creative innovation. Psychologists have traditionally been interested in abnormal behavior, correcting deviations, and identifying problems. Nowadays, more and more contemporary psychologists are interested in positive psychology, which focuses on learning how to develop the resources to enhance our lives rather than on what creates problems. The positive psychology movement questions and challenges psychology's traditional emphasis on studying human problems, including personality disorders, antisocial behavior and mental illness – all the negative aspects of our minds. Instead, its proponents argue, society would be better served if researchers could understand more about positive emotions, happiness, and mental wellbeing.

Being Positive

Amongst other things, positive psychology has challenged our old views about optimism, pessimism and happiness. The pessimist and the optimist are two archetypes that we are all familiar with, and that culturally we tend to make fun of. We mock optimists for seeing the world as they wish it were rather than how it really is. We mock pessimists for always expecting the worst. Yet most of us would prefer the company of the optimist over the pessimist. That's because a positive outlook does not just affect the individual who has that outlook, it also affects the people around them and the systems they engage with.

Historically, psychology has treated pessimism and optimism as fixed character traits with people placed somewhere on the continuum between one or the other. However, it turns out we are all capable of being positive. Researchers are finding that rather than being a fixed personality trait, we can learn to adopt the mindset we need.[320] Strategic optimism, not to be confused with over confidence, may better equip us to deal with life, to trust that things will work out and not be brought down by problems.

The differences between being negative and positive are particularly evident when it comes to dealing with setbacks. The person with a negative attitude is inclined to think that the situations that frustrate them are permanent, pervasive and personal.[321] When habitual pessimists are not offered a position after a job interview they tend to think that they will never pass the interview stage, that nobody will ever offer them a job, and that there is clearly something deficient about them. In contrast, a person with a positive attitude sees a negative situation as a temporary problem, particular to the situation, and likely a result of circumstances or other people. Their response to the lack of a job offer is more likely to be that they think that they will have better luck next time, they probably weren't the right fit for that particular organization, or that maybe the winning candidate was exceptional.

Unsurprisingly, research shows that persistent pessimists underachieve compared to optimists of similar talents, and are more likely to become depressed, have worse physical health and more troubled personal relationships than optimists.[322] Positive people are more likely to be successful in everything from sports to health to business. When insurer Metropolitan Life tested job applicants for optimism, for example, they found that those who scored highest on the scale outsold others in their first year by twenty-seven percent.[323] Other businesses have experienced similar results and now make optimism-training part of staff development.[324]

Positivity is multi-faceted. While we tend to equate it with extroverted qualities like joy, laughter, verve, it can also be quieter, manifesting as curiosity, anticipation, and contentment. In some ways its opposites are sensory deprivation, numbness, deadening, boredom, apathy, and disengagement rather than negativity. Positivity can either be non-active in the sense of mindfulness, presentism, and harmony with the here and now or it can be active engagement. Either way it is characterized by a sense of hope and uplift.

Hope, or the trust that things will work out in the end, is crucial to our wellbeing. Harvard economist Esther Duflo, for example, has revealed that hope plays an important role in alleviating poverty. An absence of hope it seems, keeps people focused on merely surviving. Without hope, the poor do not have the mindset to work on aspirations and dreams because they are focused on how to get through each day. Even small amounts of support, just enough to create some anticipation that things could change, leads to thriving.[325] People change to a future orientation and act differently because they have something to motivate them. But we can help others on a much more personal scale, too, by cultivating optimism in them. We can remind our spouse of their past accomplishments, we can involve our children in activities that induce flow, and we can acknowledge trustworthy behavior amongst our colleagues.

Being positive is obviously more beneficial than being negative for life in systems. Systems are active and dynamic and with an optimistic attitude we can use those features to create or seek out points where positive change can be made. A person with a positive attitude also copes better with situations that change over time and understands difficulties can be the result of sets of circumstances and structures rather than individuals. In contrast, if we have a negative outlook we are more likely to be frustrated by systems, take undesirable events personally, and mistakenly assume outcomes are permanent. It is just as well that it is possible for us to train ourselves to be more positive and less negative, even if we do have a natural tendency towards being gloomy. [326] A positive attitude multiplies our portfolio of possible actions allowing people to push to the limits of their capabilities.

Broadening and Building

A positive attitude also helps develop psychological strength and resilience, as the broaden and build -theory of positive psychology proposes. One of the biggest revelations of this research has been the finding that positive emotions have a huge impact on our overall wellbeing as individuals, and, by extension, the systems we live in. Positive psychologist Barbara Fredrickson has shown that positive emotions have a major evolutionary purpose. They simultaneously broaden our momentary mindset and build our intellectual, physical and emotional resources.

When we are feeling positive we see more and we are more curious and adventurous. Feelings like happiness, joy, amusement and so on encourage us to try new thoughts and actions, leading to personal growth and development. This is the broaden aspect of the theory. The build component comes from the fact that over time our willingness to try new things means we have built up a wide repertoire of different skills. We develop states of mind and modes of behavior that prepare us for hard times to come. Even though the positive emotions themselves may not last long, we benefit from them well after they have passed. When we experience positive emotions it is a sign that in that moment we are thriving and flourishing, but those emotions will also help us to keep thriving and flourishing in the future by increasing our resilience.[327]

How do we go about cultivating positive emotions? Research points to the need to build four types of resources. Our *intellectual* resources can be built by developing problem solving techniques and making the effort to learn new information. It is more difficult to be positive if we are intellectually stagnant. Our *physical* resources are built through engaging in physical activity. Through this we can develop better coordination, a strong body and a fit heart. We also need to build *psychological* resources by developing resilience, goals, a strong sense of identity and an optimistic outlook. Finally, our *social* resources can be cultivated by maintaining the relationships we have and developing new bonds with others. Think about something as simple as a casual basketball game. The players might consider themselves to just be having fun, but in the process they are also working on their physical, social, and intellectual resources as they run around, interact, and think strategy.

When we are filled with positive emotions, experiments conducted by Fredrickson and others show, we demonstrate increased imaginative ability, greater inventiveness, and a stronger ability to focus on the "big picture." In other words, improved individual optimism and positivity help us to better see systems and adapt within them. During a good mood we are better at thinking flexibly and with complexity and thus find it easier to find solutions to all kinds of problems. We also are more expansive and upbeat in our planning and decision-making when we are in a happy state of mind.[328] The broaden and build -theory shows we strengthen ourselves as a system by accumulating beneficial experiences.

Building our own resilience through experiencing positive emotion not only benefits us as individuals, but also benefits the systems we live in and others participating in those systems. Consider how in times of trouble we turn to people we know to be emotionally strong and capable. Consider, too, the effects emotionally resilient people can have on group dynamics, lifting everyone's spirits to overcome difficulties the group might experience. Such people have important roles in social systems. The Dalai Lama provides an excellent illustration of the power of positivity in action. Despite the plight of the Tibetan people that he represents and the reverence he generates in those who meet him, he remains infectiously upbeat, delighting in interaction with others and giggling like a child as he spreads his message of altruism and tolerance.[329] His warmth and humor make the impact of his message more powerful, draw people to him and give hope to his fellow Tibetans.

Balancing Negativity and Positivity

An important factor in being able to broaden and build our resources lies in achieving the right balance of emotions in our lives. In essence, if we generally maintain a happy and optimistic outlook then we build up reserves of wellness that help us to cope better than the pessimistic person when bad things do happen. The ideal ratio of positive to negative emotions according to positive psychology research is three to one.[330] If we experience three times as many positive feelings as we do negative, then we can absorb the negative experiences because we have built up a sufficient store of resilience.

Take, for example, the system of marriage. Well-respected marriage researcher John Gottman has found that the ratio of positivity to negativity during arguments explains the likely success of a marriage. Couples who have more positivity seem to develop a buffer system so that when damaging things happen they can dismiss them as an aberration ("He's in a bad mood today" or "She's tired"). Those who set a pattern of negativity in their interactions are far more likely to have their relationship end in divorce. That's because if there's a history of negativity we are more likely to draw lasting conclusions about the other person that affect how we think about them ("He's so selfish" or "She such a complainer").[331] A positive attitude benefits the system of marriage as well as the individuals. That means they think about not just reacting to one another as individuals but on building up positivity for "us" – the couple as a whole.

Positivity can be built by various means. One of these is to share good experiences, and encourage others do the same. This may seem a little counterintuitive – after all common sense tells us that it is helpful to have social support when things go wrong for us, not when they go well. Yet, when people share their joyous experiences with one another after a happy event they derive a number

of benefits. First, telling others about their experience adds to the positive effects of the experience itself because they get the chance to relive the happy emotions they experienced at the time. In addition, the process of telling the story commits this experience more firmly to memory. When the listener recognizes and validates the good news, this strengthens their relationship and lifts the self-esteem of the teller.[332] Thus the simple act of encouraging others to share their successes can enhance the wellbeing of relationships within a system.

Non-profit organization Positive Coaching Alliance has built its practice on the idea of having more positivity than negativity in children's sport. Disheartened by an increase in poor sportsmanship, a focus on winning at all costs, and player aggressiveness in youth sport, founder Jim Thompson put together a program aimed at making participation in sport a positive experience. He realised the coaches, as leaders, had a huge impact on the attitude of children in their teams. So the group focuses on training coaches to understand that being "relentlessly positive" leads to success on the scoreboard. The goal is for the coach to create an athletic environment that children can enjoy and that enhances their self-development. One concept that the Alliance uses is the "emotional tank" – the idea that children can only take so much criticism. They train coaches to increase the ration of praise to criticism to build a well of positivity, just as renowned basketball coach and Alliance supporter Phil Jackson did with his teams and just as positive psychology research advocates.[333]

Balancing positivity and negativity takes conscious effort on our part. Humans suffer from what psychologists call negativity bias, a tendency to emphasize the negative. [334] In most situations we focus on and give more dominance to negative experiences (such as when one setback seems to ruin an otherwise successful day).

One negative person can easily bring a team down, but it is much harder for one positive person to uplift a team. The impact of negativity is far stronger because we are much more sensitive to it.

In addition, we often experience a kind of asymmetry of information – we are hyper alert to being on the receiving end of negativity but often unaware when we are bringing about negative feelings for others. Imagine your boss says to you "good job, but…" The loudest part of the sentence is the "but" and all you focus on is the criticism that follows. Yet, if you say "good job, but…" to your spouse

after they have made an effort to cook a nice meal, you probably think you are praising them and offering helpful advice. You likely forget that they may hear only criticism. It can be easy to see how everyone else is behaving but forget to reflect on the contributions of our own actions.

Reflection-in-action is a great skill we can use to overcome both our tendency to be negative and react poorly to negativity. By reflecting-in-action we can catch ourselves in the process of generating negativity and then compensate. If we hear ourselves criticizing our spouse, or friend, or colleague, for example, we can then make an effort to find positive things to say to them to balance out criticism. Of course, the praise should not be forced or manufactured. Nor does it have to occur within quick succession of the criticism. The important thing is that overall positive feedback outweighs negative feedback in systemic relationships.

Though we can work at being less critical of others, it is unlikely we will go through life without receiving criticism. In social systems, we often experience disappointments, setbacks, and criticism. Many of us take these things personally. With a positive attitude and reflection-in-action we can turn negative feedback into a spur to improvement. Reminding ourselves that criticism is a useful form of feedback we can learn from and that there are structures at work that affect both our and others' behavior are helpful. We can avoid placing blame and being accusatory because we understand that there is a bigger picture that we may not be able to see shaping the other person's behavior. Facing criticism positively allows us to maintain a bright and constructive approach, and avoid seeing ourselves as a victim and blaming others and circumstances.

Engineers spend a lot of time turning things into numbers, even intangible and therefore apparently unquantifiable things like risk. We rarely analyze our emotions or attitude in the same way. Imagine if you had to rank yourself on a grumpiness index every day. Or if someone else was measuring you with a kindness-o-meter. How would you rate? Measuring our attitude in systems would almost certainly be an eye opening experience. Many of us would probably be surprised at how easily we default to a non-positive attitude. We tend to be defensive in daily life, protecting ourselves from bad things before they even happen; we anticipate negativity. We also pay much more attention and give much more weight to negative interactions and events. That comes at the cost of losing focus on the possibility of uplift. With enhanced reflective practices we can pay closer attention to the attitude we adopt and project.

Happiness

In 1999, two young mountaineers became trapped by a storm on a ledge in the French Alps. By the time rescuers arrived, one man had perished and the other had suffered severe frostbite. Survivor Jamie Andrews lost not only his friend but also both hands and both feet to the ordeal.

Andrews could easily have succumbed to despair. Instead, after an initial stage of grief and self-pity, he chose to focus on recovery. He learned how to care for himself. He returned to work. He married. He had a child. And perhaps most remarkably, he began to climb mountains again, often raising money for charity in the process. Asked about his astonishing story, Andrews comments on his "good luck" and "all the good things that happen" in his life.[335]

Jamie Andrews took a negative experience and turned it into a positive event that motivated his life. George Kohlrieser, who recounts Jamie's story in his book on leadership, attributes Jamie's success in the face of adversity to having a "secure base." Secure bases, he explains, are the people, goals, or things with which we strongly bond. They provide us with comfort, strength and energy and enable us to turn negative experiences into positive ones. For Jamie his secure bases were his fiancée, his mother, his medical team and the friend he lost. Having those positive relationships, having supportive systems in place, enabled Jamie to find happiness again.

Most, if not all, people want to be happy. But we often couch our pursuit of happiness in the language of goal achievement. If we could just have that much more money, or own that house, or find our soul mate, or lose weight then we would be happy. The problem is, the things we think will make us happy often don't. Even if we achieve the goals we set, we usually find that happiness remains elusive, or at best is only temporary as it was for Tony Hsieh when he made his fortune.

Over the last few decades, human happiness has been studied more than ever before. Psychologist Martin Seligman, to take the work of one expert, has found that being more attentive to our thoughts can foster happiness. To promote happiness about our past, we can deliberately cultivate gratitude and forgiveness as these help us to feel more positive. To cultivate happiness about the future we can learn how to hope and how to talk ourselves out of pessimistic thoughts. In the present, our focus should be on savoring pleasurable experiences, avoiding repeated indulgences that dull our appreciation, and being more mindful. [336] Pursuing happiness, according to Seligman's formula, means focusing on thinking about our thinking, calling to mind the reflective dimension of systems intelligence and the benefits of positive engagement and spirited discovery, for example.

Cultivating the mindsets that bring sustained happiness does more than make us happy as individuals. It also benefits the systems we live in. Emotions travel through systems and a positive attitude helps us to uplift those around us and consequently the systems we collectively make up. There is evidence of this from research like fittingly-titled SMILE study conducted in Australian nursing homes. Over a three-year period, staff members in nursing homes were trained in fostering playful relationships with the four hundred dementia-suffering residents. Games, jokes and songs were introduced into the homes with the result that residents seemed more content, and twenty percent were less agitated in their behaviors. While twenty percent might not sound like an overwhelming success, that's about the same percentage of dementia patients who normally respond to antipsychotic medication. In other words, positive interactions had as much of an effect as prescribed drugs. Unsurprisingly given the nature of systems, there was an unintended consequence to the research project: the staff also benefitted from the experiment. They reported feeling invigorated and felt their jobs were enhanced by being part of a meaningful programme.[337]

The relationship between a positive attitude and positive systems is a two way street. On the one hand, individuals with positive attitudes help create positive systems. On the other, positive systems help create a positive attitude in individuals. It is important we attend to both our own attitude, through broadening and building for example, but also that we understand how the system influences us just as we influence it. In times of adversity, for example, we need secure bases to help lift our mood. But we are more likely to have those bases if we have contributed positively to the system in better times. Other members of the systems we participate in are more likely to be drawn to support us in tough times if we have made deposits in the positivity bank.

The Greater Good

Systems intelligence at its heart is about acting in ways that seek to achieve positive outcomes for oneself, others and the systems that we share. The US National Park Service struggled to do this initially. The Truth and Reconciliation in South Africa, led by Desmond Tutu, did a much better job of balancing individual and system needs. Rosa Parks acted in a way that was meant help her community. Rachel Carson aimed to help the environment through her actions, as did the Kingsolver family. Dan Savage acted to support LGBT youth. Tony Hsieh tried to create a positive organization. They all expanded their "horizon of caring," as Donella Meadows so eloquently puts it, living in a world that is about us, not me.[338]

Acting for the greater good benefits everyone, including the altruistic person. For example, when we give someone a gift we generally expect to make them happy. We probably don't expect that giving gifts will make us live longer. Yet, a team of health researchers has found that an unexpected side effect of giving social support is good for our health and helps us live longer.[339] Note that it is giving, not receiving, that is key. It turns out that instrumentally helping others enhances our wellbeing.

The benefits of such behavior are well illustrated by the book *Give or Take*. Author and psychologist Adam Grant shows how giving is important for success in many walks of life. Hard work, talent and luck take us so far, but the kinds of connections we have with others matter, too. In systems intelligence terms, the relationships in the system matters as much as the individual. Most people, it turns out, either take from others, match what they do, or give. In many system settings, like business and politics, it would make sense to assume that takers do well. But, surprisingly, those who give freely without expectation of return tend to do better across many measures of success.

Why? Acting for the greater good serves as a counterforce to holding back in systems. Typically, particularly in organizational settings, argues Grant,[340] we tend to become matchers focusing on fairness rather than givers. As a result, we can become trapped in behaviors that are accepted as standard but are a pretty lousy standard. Not smiling, not being enthusiastic, not offering help – all these are pretty normal in some contexts. We become so busy matching each other's holding back that we miss the opportunity for uplift. The alternative is to abandon our imaginary ledger and freely give rather than expect an exchange or attempt to match what others are doing or not doing.

In the collaborative settings and global economy we have now, being a giver is more systems intelligent than being a taker. Social networking, for example, has enhanced our opportunities for pro-social behavior. Social media sites help create many loose connections for givers to capitalize on. Dan Savage's success with the It Gets Better project is testament to that. In fact, the availability of this new system of connection means is makes more sense in today's environment to be a giver than in the past. We never know when or how we may meet someone again in future, but it is clearly better to have them remember us as kind rather than selfish. That is not to say we approach giving from a calculating perspective. Quite the opposite. It is impossible to calculate the benefits of being a giver in systems because you do so without any expectation of direct reward. The helping in return may come with delays, if it comes at all. A giver is a

person who generates good outcomes in the invisible systems of human connection, deliberately in the sense they are purposely generous, but not deliberately in the sense of with any illusion of control.

At first, it can seem challenging to act for the greater good. We tend to attach to strongly to our personal history and patterns of interaction. As a result we worry that we will look manipulative and others will regard our newly generous actions with suspicion. Perhaps these fears will realize themselves, but we need to commit to the behavior for the good of the whole anyway. Our first tries may not succeed but any rebuff shouldn't set us back. Like a star footballer we have to expect a few misses before we regularly make the goal.

In essence, Kiran Bir Sethi's educational philosophy is about teaching children to think of the greater good. To her, it is clear that all kids believe they can change the world into a better place, and Sethi believes it is the job of adults to empower them to facilitate that change. The problem is most adults, dulled by their own experiences in life, flatten the natural self-belief and entrepreneurial qualities out of their children. The result? A perpetuation of a mindset that accepts the world as it is found, a missed opportunity to experience pro-social behavior and the dampening of children's natural positive energy. By providing the opportunity for children to experience an alternative outlook, Sethi argues, we can cultivate their confidence and optimism.

Four simple words – feel, imagine, do, share – empower the pupils at Riverside School and other children around the world that have embraced Sethi's Design for Change philosophy. Children are encouraged to feel anything that bothers them. In other words, they are encouraged to attend to their environment and notice what is not working as well as it could be. Then, they unleash the power of their imaginations as together they figure out ways to address whatever problem they have identified. Finally, with the support of the school community they enact the solutions they have imagined and tell others about what they have done via social media. In the process, they both experience and spread a positive attitude.

The Power of a Positive Attitude

You will have noticed as you read the stories of the people used to illustrate the dimensions of systems intelligence in this book that they all contributed positively to the systems around them. They sought to change systems for the better. Yet, it is possible to be systems literate without being motivated by the desire to uplift others. Bernie Madoff, the financier who pulled off the largest fraud in US history, knew how to work a system. No doubt he successfully engaged with his clients, made wise (from his perspective) decisions that kept his scheme afloat for the long term, and reflected on the best ways of maintaining his fraud. Madoff, and others like him, however, lack a sense of positivity. While such people are skilled in many dimensions of systems intelligence their behavior damages others as they seek to use their understanding of particular social systems for self-aggrandizement and exploitation. Intelligent behavior in systems is underpinned by a desire for oneself, others and the system itself to benefit. It is imbued with optimism, positivity and the search for uplift.

When we are truly optimistic about life we inspire people and the systems around us. A positive attitude underpins the other factors that make up systems intelligence. How can we attune to others if our view of the world is colored by pessimism? How can we embrace spirited discovery if we feel negatively about life? How can we positively engage with others if our own spirit is depressed?

Think back to the real life stories reflecting systems intelligence in action and illustrating each of it dimensions. Rachel Carson showed she had the ability to see systems when she explored the impact of pesticides on the environment. But Silent Spring was not a depressing book that foretold of doom. Instead it was a challenging warning that assured its readers it was not too late to prevent lasting damage. It offered a vision of a better future and sought to have people act to create that vision by using a systemic perspective.

Archbishop Desmond Tutu's experiences under apartheid and the horrific accounts of crime he had to listen to as chair of the Truth and Reconciliation Commission could have turned him into a bitter and pessimistic man. But it didn't. Instead, he retained his sense of humor, cultivated positivity in his interactions with others, and tried to inspire his country to become a better version of itself. Similarly, Barbara Kingsolver's account of her family's efforts to live without the industrial food chain could have been framed negatively. She could have focused on all the dire consequences of processed food, but instead she stressed the joys and adventures of trying to feed a family without supermarkets.

If anyone was going to be pessimistic about the world, you'd think it would have been Dan Savage, Bullied himself as a child and then witness to the horrific effects of bullying on LGBT teens, he could have been forgiven for withdrawing from society at large. But he didn't. Instead he trusted that enough people cared about the experiences of young people exploring their sexuality to create something positive out of something negative.

Tony Hsieh, on the other hand, had lived the American dream. A multi-millionaire at a young age he'd expected to be lastingly happy as a result of his achievements. Only he wasn't. He needed to get to know himself at a deeper level to find out what really brought him joy, and once he'd done that, he decided he wanted to help others increase their capacity for happiness too. So he created a company that put happiness at its heart.

Rosa Parks was more focused on justice than happiness, but without optimism, without belief in the human ability to change oppressive systems into systems where all could flourish she likely would not have fought the battle she did. Nor would the money others who joined her have participated if they weren't optimistic about success. William Wilberforce and the abolitionists had to struggle for many years to achieve the destruction of the system of slavery, yet they never gave up. Positivity is the oxygen that fuels the fire of systems intelligence.

Positive Attitude: What Can I Do Today?

Optimism
Monitor your mood – cultivate happiness by being aware of your thinking processes.

Find balance – make sure you invest in positive behavior and communication in your relationships. For example, give sincere compliments to people more frequently.

Inspire optimism in others by encouraging their efforts rather than dampening them.

If something negative happens, mindfully consider a strategy to deal with it. Don't just react in the heat of the moment.

Develop resilience by accumulating positive experiences.

Happiness
Express gratitude for the good things that happen today.

Savor any pleasurable experiences you have.

Think positively about something that will happen tomorrow.

The greater good
Give freely, with no expectation of reward.

Abandon the "ledger mentality" and cultivate generous actions.

Encourage and praise system-enhancing actions in others.

Conclusion

"We are what we repeatedly do. Excellence, then, is not an act, but a habit." ~
Aristotle[341]

A Fresh Perspective

Some decades ago, renowned scholar Gregory Bateson suggested that most of the problems in the world are caused by a mismatch between how we think the world works and how it really works.[342] Bateson felt that we needed to transform our thinking away from a fragmented, silo approach to a systems perspective so we could act with the bigger picture in mind. It's time to answer Bateson's call by perceiving ourselves as whole people who dwell within other wholes and are interconnected on many levels.

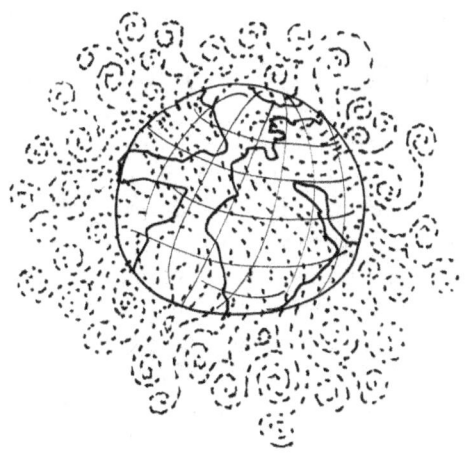

We live in a world characterized by interdependencies, be they social, technological, economic or environmental. Social networking contributes to a change of government. Video clips go viral creating shared international phenomena. Markets and banks crash, and the effects cascade around the globe. A drought in one country pushes up the price of food around the world. The array of interconnections between ourselves, others, and organizing structures – the sheer scale and scope of our current interconnectivity through social systems – can be both exciting and overwhelming.

People collectively needs to act more systems intelligently to best deal with the both the challenges and the opportunities these interconnections bring. The systems that link us together provide an opportunity for contagious betterment. When individuals flourish, the groups they belong to flourish. When groups flourish, individuals flourish. The key is finding an approach to life that uses interconnectivity to create positive uplift rather than collective diminishment. Acting systems intelligently unlocks such an approach.

Given that we interact with systems daily, it makes sense that we do our best to understand how they work and enhance our experience of them. Our natural systems intelligence develops when we are able to recognize the systems present but usually unnoticed in our everyday experience. [343] We can benefit from considering what systems we are engaged with, what they look like, how they behave, and how they influence how we behave. Just as importantly, we can consider our own impact on and contribution to the systems in our life. Understanding how we both perpetuate and create systems, and how we all see the same systems from our own unique perspectives, helps us to make systems intelligent choices. Nurturing our innate systems intelligence brings the hope, promise and potential that not only do we live well with systems, we can live better, and we can become better at being better.

A New Habit

That is not to say that helping our systems intelligence to flourish will be either easy or instant. For most of us, it has been our habit to lose sight of the systems around us, to take them for granted. We have fallen into the trap of assuming only our perception of a system is correct, of imagining a system is permanent, or failing to adapt to change. It has been too easy to forget the emotional dimension of life as we are carried away with our logic, or to impose one system's rules on another. We too often work on automatic pilot and use the same strategies over and over again. These strategies perhaps were effective for us in the past, and may be effective for us in the future, but because they become so ingrained they prevent us from seeing alternative possibilities.[344] To act intelligently, we need to question our old ways of thinking and operating within systems, especially when they are not working well.

But once our attention is drawn to the systems at hand and we begin to understand the influence of context on everyone's behavior our eyes open to new possibilities. Armed with fresh thought processes, attitudes and skills, we can work towards nurturing and creating constructive systems. Practicing behaviors and attitudes that enrich our experience of systems can enhance our wellbeing. We can build our systems intelligence through a commitment to deliberate, repeated choices about our attitudes and our actions. By choosing to act in new ways that are relatively simple, enjoyable and uplifting, yet sufficiently challenging that we achieve personal growth, we will be motivated to use them often.

We can make it a habit to look for the systems around us, and acknowledge the visible and invisible connections we have with others. We can habitually explore alternative viewpoints, expect systems to change, and anticipate that we need to change with them. Taking into account people's emotions and attuning can become natural for us. It is possible to think about how we are engaging and try new strategies when things don't work out. We can consciously move from emotional reaction to constructive action. We can recognize the influence of the social structures around us on our own and others' behavior. We can resist negative and ineffective systems and imagine how things might be different. We are capable of looking for opportunities to improve the systems around us, spotting leverage points, and managing our own limitations. When we repeatedly do these things we will have made it a habit to act with systems intelligence.

When we act systems intelligently we have a better chance of creating healthy social systems that develop people's respect, individuality, and potential while creating community and possibilities. Healthy systems balance the paradoxes inherent in systems life. They allow members to flourish individually and express their uniqueness, even while they integrate as team players. They welcome variety and difference but create a sense of commonality. They preserve and protect effective traditions but explore and adapt to the new and unfamiliar. These kinds of systems inspire us to ask what can this system do that's never been done before? What can it do better? In flourishing systems, members feel a sense of purpose and want to contribute to them because involvement gives them satisfaction.[345]

The Benefits of Acting Systems Intelligently

As you read about the eight dimensions that make up systems intelligence you will have identified your own strengths and weaknesses. We are all naturally stronger in some aspects than others. The introvert, for example, is likely to be naturally more reflective than the extrovert. But just because we have preferences for behaving in certain ways does not mean that we cannot learn to act differently. Improving in just one dimension that may not come naturally to us can give us enormous leverage. It helps us to strengthen ourselves. It gives us more options so we have a portfolio of actions available to us that we can select from in any given context.

The concept of systems intelligence allows us to look at our skills in a different way. We all have the skills that are described in this book. We can all be positive; we can all be patient, we can all reflect on our beliefs. But we don't usually connect these skills to one another and we don't usually connect these skills to the context we find ourselves in. Imagine your behavioral choices in life are a set of musical instruments. Sometimes you choose the flute; sometimes you choose the violin. Each makes a pleasant sound when played well. Now imagine you have a whole woodwind or a whole string section at your disposal. A set of instruments that work harmoniously together. This is how to envisage the various skill clusters of each dimension of systems intelligence. When we combine the related skills together we achieve a richer effect that when we draw on one skill alone.

Now go one step further. Let's combine the woodwind and the string and the other sections of an orchestra together for a particular piece of music. At times the string section will dominate, but at other times other sections will come to the fore. The overall effect though is an integrated and beautiful piece of music. In the same way, when we as individuals have all the dimensions of systems intelligence to draw on we are more likely to create an exponentially more positive outcome than when we draw on a single skill.

216

Recognizing how skills work together in systems gives us more options to choose from. Understanding systems intelligence gives ways to adapt our behavior according to the context. It helps make us better-rounded individuals, able to use our talents in concert with and with regard to the situation. It also broadens our outlook. We each see what we think is the context at any given time, but the problem is others see things slightly differently. So what we believe are the right actions are not always well received by others. Developing our systems intelligence competencies allows us to see beyond our internal prism. We learn not to take for granted that our perspective on the world is the only perspective – we can begin to reflect on alternative viewpoints. At the same time, the concept of systems intelligence makes the context accessible. Instead of being overwhelmed by the big picture we can find ways to have influence that may just involve tiny changes in what we do or how we think. Familiarity and fluency with the eight factors of Systems Intelligence gives us the chance to exert more influence over our lives.

Leading with Systems Intelligence

But it is not just our own lives that we can make better. Systems intelligence is emerging as a prerequisite for the effective leadership of today's systems. As the world becomes increasingly connected, increasingly complex, and increasingly dynamic, it needs people who can balance the big picture with local connections, rationality with intuition, the future with the present, the cognitive and the emotional, the intended and the unintended. When dealing with complex problems like climate change, economic upheaval and social conflicts, where many systems collide, we need leaders who can act intelligently in systems. We need people who can inspire others to develop their own systems intelligence and initiate and create systems intelligent organizations.

For many years now, academics and practitioners have produced a significant amount of literature on leadership. Researchers have studied what it takes to be a good leader, how people persuade others to follow them, and the impact of formally appointed leaders on their organizations. A popular approach to the study of leadership has been to focus on the traits, characteristics and behavior of leaders. As a result, numerous lists have been generated that describe the psychological attributes of a leader. These lists have been used to create "how to" guides that leaders can supposedly follow to lead well. [346] Becoming an effective leader according to this model appears to depend on an individual's personality and their ability to learn particular behaviors.

Leading with systems intelligence has a different emphasis. Our individual traits and characteristics are just a starting point. Instead of seeing people as a fixed collection of predictable traits, systems intelligence draws on a growth mindset, seeing people, and the systems they live in, as dynamic, capable of growth, and able to transform.[347] We have the power to choose who and how we are being in the world by making decisions about our behavior. Everyone can transform systems through their behavior, regardless of their personality or their place in the hierarchy, because they are connected to others.

Systems intelligent leadership draws on our capacity to inspire others to strive for a better life in systems. Being able to help others flourish in systems does not need to emerge from formal positions of power. Instead, as systems expert Barry Oshry succinctly puts it, transformative power in systems comes from "the *belief* that one can make a difference, a *deep understanding* of systems processes, and the *courage* to act."[348] By offering an inspiring vision, communicating in an effective way, and demonstrating systems-commensurate behaviors we can lead by facilitating others to nurture their systems intelligence.

How does this work in practice? A good place to start is to initiate a conversation that asks three key questions.

- What does the current system generate (for me, others and the system itself)?
- To what extent is that we want?
- How do we want the system to mold us as human beings?

The answers will shape everyone's contribution to any given system.[349] Consequently, a systems intelligent leader pays attention to all aspects of a system, including the emotional level, the context, the material features, and the people. He or she adapts and explores, and intervenes for change, even if just at the micro-level. To lead with systems intelligence is to orient ourselves towards uplift and elevation.[350] When our goal is to make the system and everyone's experience of the system the best that it can be in all its dimensions then our actions will carry us in that direction.

The Challenge

Systems intelligence is not just an idea. It is action-oriented. The challenge is to turn our understanding of systems into action. Typically, we underestimate the impact we can have on the greater good. Yet, history is littered with examples of individuals who have changed the world and its systems. The stories of Rosa Parks, Mahatma Gandhi and Nelson Mandela and all the others mentioned in this book illustrate the effectiveness of systems intelligence. Together with other examples, the stories show that it is possible that deliberate and sustained systems intelligent behavior can make a huge difference to large social systems. But the beauty of systems is that we don't have to set out to change all elements in the complex world. Even small changes in our everyday lives can make a big difference to the quality of our life and that of others.

We can all make those changes. We can orient ourselves to a longer time frame, but also dwell in the present. We can begin to look for the bigger picture even while we focus on the local connections we can influence. We can reflect on our behavior, our emotions and our thinking processes. We can find the moments and situations when we can change the script and be creative, open-minded and courageous. We can attend to the systemic context at the conscious level. We can choose to broaden our typically narrow perspectives, to look for and attune to others and the systems we share.

There's famous quote from Victor Hugo often paraphrased as there is nothing so powerful as an idea whose time has come.[351] Systems intelligence is an idea whose time has come. When people offer new ideas, we have the choice to become detractors, bystanders, or proponents. This book has hopefully convinced you of the value of seeing the world through a systems lens and looking for the opportunity to behave systems intelligently. Take up its challenge and become a proponent of cultivating your capacity to flourish and to enrich the systems you belong to. Be better, better.

Notes

[1] *Emotional Intelligence* by Goleman introduced the concept to the general audience, but the original researchers on Emotional Intelligence were Peter Salovey and John Mayer who had already written several academic papers on the concept in the early 1990s.

[2] Meadows, "Dancing With Systems".

[3] See MIT-based Peter Senge's bestseller, *The Fifth Discipline: The Art and Practice of the Learning Organization.*

[4] Almost all environmental researchers take a systems perspective, but not all also include human thinking as part of the environmental system. For interesting work in that area see Meadows' *Thinking in Systems: A Primer* and Senge and colleagues' *The Necessary Revolution: How Individuals and Organizations are Working Together to Create a Sustainable World.*

[5] See Sternberg *Beyond IQ: A Triarchic Theory of Human Intelligence* and *Successful Intelligence. How Practical and Creative Intelligence Determine Success in Life.*

[6] Gardner, *Frames of Mind: The Theory of Multiple Intelligences.*

[7] *Emotional Intelligence* and *Social Intelligence: The New Science of Human Relationships,* both popularized by Daniel Goleman, for example, assist us to manage and navigate the world of human feelings.

[8] The Systems Intelligence research team at Aalto University in Helsinki, Finland, has established that systems intelligence consists of eight dimensions.

[9] Research designed to develop the self-evaluation tool for Systems Intelligence has confirmed that these factors can be identified in psychometric tests.

[10] Carson, *Silent Spring.*

[11] The biographical information on Carson comes from various sources, including www.rachelcarson.org, http://en.wikipedia.org/wiki/Rachel_Carson and Koehn's article "From Calm Leadership, Lasting Change".

[12] For various academic perspectives on systems, see the works of Charles Churchman, Michael Jackson, Peter Senge, Donella Meadows and John Sterman.

[13] Children between the ages of twelve and eighteen learn locally about environmental topics like biodiversity, climate change, water and forests using the same materials, and then share their results on the web. But they also do practical things. ENO's tree planting program, for example, aims to have schoolchildren across the globe plant 100 million trees by 2017. See https://sites.google.com/a/enoprogramme.org/enotreeday/home

[14] http://www.surfrider.org/

[15] Environmental education in recent years, however, has adopted a systems perspective and children in many countries are now taught about how their actions affect the environment in systemic ways.

[16] Harig, "For Enie Els, the Eyes Have It".

[17] http://en.wikipedia.org/wiki/Rachel_Carson

[18] Kay, *Obliquity*, p. 9.

[19] http://www.leadershipnow.com/visionquotes.html

[20] Carson, *Silent Spring*, p. 133. The fire ant case was just one of many that led Carson to conclude that pesticides would be better termed "biocides" because their effects were rarely limited to the pests they targeted.

[21] Information on the organization can be found at http://www.doctorswithoutborders.org/aboutus/.

[22] Senge et al., *The Necessary Revolution*, p. 169.

[23] The original research on organ rates was carried out by Eric Johnson and Daniel Goldstein (published in 2004 in the article "Defaults and Donation Decisions") but Dan Ariely brought their findings to public attention when he spoke about them at a TED conference. See http://www.ted.com/talks/dan_ariely_asks_are_we_in_control_of_our_own_decisions.html.

[24] To illustrate, of the Fortune 500 companies in 1955, only around 14% still made the list in 2011. Others had ceased trading, merged, gone bankrupt or not made the list. See the article "Fortune 500 Extinction" in *CSInvesting*.

[25] Details on the cane toad can be found at http://australianmuseum.net.au/Cane-Toad.

[26] Some critics blame *Silent Spring* for the ban on DDT production and subsequent rise in deaths from malaria (see comments in Finkel's article "Malria: Stopping a Global Killer"), though Carson's emphasis was on its indiscriminate spraying as an agricultural pesticide.

[27] Senge, *The Fifth Discipline: The Art and Practice of the Learning Organization*.

[28] See Donella Meadows' article "Dancing with Systems" and http://www.presidency.ucsb.edu/ws/index.php?pid=7923.

[29] See Bateson's *Steps to an Ecology of Mind: Collected Essays In Anthropology, Psychiatry, Evolution, And Epistemology*. Bateson's daughter Nora has produced a film summarizing his many years of work called *An Ecology of Mind*. For information about the film see http://www.anecologyofmind.com/.

[30] http://www.goodreads.com/author/quotes/5943.Desmond_Tutu

[31] Information on Archbishop Tutu comes from his website http://www.tutu.org/home/, his book *No Future Without Forgiveness* and the biography *Tutu: Authorized* written by Sparks and Tutu.

[32] http://www.dadalos.org/int/vorbilder/vorbilder/tutu/bedeutung.htm

[33] This is a story that Tutu tells. See the article "Archbishop Tutu in His Own Words" in *BBC News*.

[34] In an experiment, Stern asked mothers to purposefully act "out of tune" with their babies, for example by speaking in an unexpected tone or ignoring them. When the mother "tuned out" of the shared vitality affect created in interaction with her baby, the child would stop playing and turn to look at the mother. See Stern, *The Interpersonal World of the Infant: A View from Psychoanalysis and Developmental Psychology*.

[35] Rifkin, *The Empathic Civilization: The Race to Global Consciousness in a World in Crisis*.

[36] Sweeney, "Learning to Connect the Dots: Developing Children's Systems Literacy".

[37] In Jeremy Rifkin's book *The Empathic Civilization: The Race to Global Consciousness in a World in Crisis*, he explains how our capacity empathy is a crucial part of our lives as humans. Evidence from orphanages in the 1950s, for example, points to emotional deprivation in infants resulting in physical weakness and reduced IQ.

[38] See Baron-Cohen's *Mindblindness: An Essay on Autism and Theory of Mind* and the work of British anthropologist Robin Dunbar, *How Many Friends Does One Person Need? Dunbar's Number and Other Evolutionary Quirks*.

[39] See Baron-Cohen, *Mindblindness: An Essay on Autism and Theory of Mind* and Gladwell's *The Tipping Point: How Little Things Can Make a Big Difference*.

[40] See Howard Gardner's thoughts in "Thinking About Thinking" and in *Five Minds for the Future*, Robert Kegan's *The Evolving Self: **Problem and Process in Human Development*** and *In Over Our Heads: The Mental Demands of Modern Life*, and Daniel Kahneman's *Thinking, Fast and Slow* to name but a few. The collection of essays edited by John Brockman, *This Will Make You Smarter: New Scientific Concepts to Improve your Thinking*, also contains a number of contributions on metacognition.

[41] Sparks and Tutu, *Tutu: Authorized*, p. 88.

[42] See the article "Did the Hudson Plane Crash Pilot's Glider Experience Help Him Land Flight 1549?" in *Popular Mechanics*.

[43] http://en.wikipedia.org/wiki/Chesley_Sullenberger

[44] Oshry, *Leading Systems: Lessons from the Power Lab*, p. 8.

[45] Strauch, *Secrets of the Grown-Up Brain: The Surprising Talents of the Middle-aged Mind*

[46] Gigerenzer's book *Gut Feelings: The Intelligence of the Unconscious* outlines the fallacy of this approach over listening to our gut.

[47] See http://en.wikipedia.org/wiki/Homo_economicus.

[48] Ariely, *The Upside of Irrationality: The Unexpected Benefits of Defying Logic at Work and at Home*, p. 9.

[49] Ariely, *The Upside of Irrationality: The Unexpected Benefits of Defying Logic at Work and at Home*, p. 47.

50 The works of the neuroscientist Antonio Damasio explore the relationship between our cognition and our feelings. For a summary of some recent research, see David Brooks' article "The Young and the Neuro" in the *New York Times*.

51 Jeremy Rifkin discusses this in *The Empathic Civilization: The Race to Global Consciousness in a World in Crisis* as does Dan Ariely in *The Upside of Irrationality: The Unexpected Benefits of Defying Logic at Work and at Home*.

52 Ariely, *The Upside of Irrationality: The Unexpected Benefits of Defying Logic at Work and at Home*

53 Kahneman, *Thinking, Fast and Slow*.

54 Gerd Gigerenzer explores these in his book *Gut Feelings: The Intelligence of the Unconscious*.

55 Saarinen and Hämäläinen, "The Originality of Systems Intelligence."

56 Goleman, *Social Intelligence: The New Science of Human Relationships*.

57 Keltner, "The Compassionate Species".

58 Gladwell, *The Tipping Point: How Little Things Can Make a Big Difference*, p. 83-85.

59 Sparks and Tutu, *Tutu: Authorized*, p. 248.

60 Karen Hayes, an independent filmmaker, recounts the story of the Rwanda dinner in Sparks and Tutu's book *Tutu: Authorized*, p. 295.

61 Bishop et al., "Mindfulness: A Proposed Operational Definition", p. 230; 232.

62 Sparks and Tutu, *Tutu: Authorized*, p. 233.

63 Bishop et al., "Mindfulness: A Proposed Operational Definition".

64 Langer, "Minding Matters: The Consequences of Mindlessness-Mindfulness".

65 We already know that mindfulness brings benefits. Research on creativity, for example, shows bright ideas are linked to people's ability to notice themselves daydreaming – creative people both let their minds wander and pay attention to what they are thinking about.

66 See, for example, Martin Seligman's *Authentic Happiness: Using the New Positive Psychology to Realize Your Potential for Lasting Fulfillment*, Charles Duhigg's *The Power of Habit: Why We Do What We Do in Life and Business* and Daniel Kahneman's *Thinking, Fast and Slow* respectively.

67 Some high sports and performing stars have become famous for the oddity of their pre-performance rituals. Michael Jordan, the famous basketball player, apparently always wore his North Carolina college shorts under his Chicago Bulls uniform and world tennis superstar Rafael Nadal lines his water bottles up so that the labels face the baseline he is playing from. Chris Martin, lead singer of Coldplay includes brushing his teeth as part of his pre-concert rituals. Robert Plant, nowadays, apparently likes a cup of tea and to iron his clothes before performing. Though these examples are slightly humorous, what Jordan, Nadal, Martin and Plant do is all about tuning in to the right headspace. The rituals they perform are about synchronizing their mental focus, their emotional state, and their physical presence. It is about having some part of the system fixed and within their control, right before they are about to enter a state of dynamic emergence where anything might happen.

68 Csikszentmihalyi, *Flow: The Psychology of Optimal Experience.*

69 For a good summary of attribution theory, see Fiske and Taylor's *Social Cognition.*

70 Zimbardo, *The Lucifer Effect: Understanding How Good people Turn Evil,* p. 212.

71 Pronin, "How We See Ourselves and How We See Others".

72 http://beforeitsnews.com/spirit/2012/11/why-we-are-all-essentially-good-by-archbishop-desmond-tutu-2448854.html

73 Tutu, *No Future Without Forgiveness.*

74 Anecdote adapted from www.businessballs.com. The television show was made by the Open University in the UK.

75 See Fredrickson's article "Your Phone vs. Your Heart" summarizing her research.

76 Restak, *The Naked Brain: How the Emerging Neurosociety is Changing How We Live, Work, and Love,* p. 3.

77 Brooks, "The Young and the Neuro".

78 Goleman, *The Brain and Emotional Intelligence: New Insights,* p. 54.

79 Restak, *The Naked Brain: How the Emerging Neurosociety is Changing How We Live, Work, and Love.*

80 Details of Ekman's work can be found at http://www.paulekman.com/.

81 In fact, a lack of empathy is considered to be part of what is referred to as "the dark triad" of personality traits – narcissism, Machiavellianism, and psychopathy as Goleman dicusses in *Social Intelligence: The New Science of Human Relationships.*

82 **Gigerenzer, *Gut feelings: The intelligence of the unconscious.***

83 Gilbert, *Stumbling on Happiness.*

84
http://www.brainyquote.com/quotes/authors/d/desmond_tutu.html#DM H2GsoyIYbI2TzZ.99

85 Sparks and Tutu, *Tutu: Authorized,* p. 256.

86 See the discussion around *Ubuntu* in Sparks' and Tutu's book *Tutu: Authorized,* pp. 254-257.

87 See Hobson, *The Cradle of Thought: Exploring the Origins of Thinking* and Beebe and Lachmann, *Infant Research and Adult Treatment: Co- constructing Interactions.*

88 Baron-Cohen, *Mindblindness: An Essay on Autism and Theory of Mind.*

89 Saarinen, "Kindness to Babies and Other Radical Ideas", p. 156.

90 The sources for Rosenthal's study are Rhem, "Pygmalion in the Classroom"; Rosenthal and Jacobsen, *Pygmalion in the Classroom: Teacher Expectation and Pupil's Intellectual Development* and Watkins and Mohr, *Appreciative Inquiry: Changes at the Speed of Imagination.*

91 In the meantime, Rosenthal argues that one major lesson can be taken from his decades of research: "…what I think this research shows is that there's a moral obligation for a teacher: if the teacher knows that certain students can't learn, that teacher should get out of that classroom." See Christopher and Yeomans' book *Psychology for Teaching Assistants.*

92 Tutu, *No Future Without Forgiveness,* pp. 10-36.

93 Tutu, *No Future Without Forgiveness,* p. 85.

94 Tutu, *No Future Without Forgiveness*, p. 84-90.

95 http://www.dadalos.org/int/vorbilder/vorbilder/tutu/bedeutung.htm

96 http://sites.uci.edu/chpleaders/tag/desmond-tutu/

97 See Endlsey "Theoretical Underpinnings of Situation Awareness: A Critical Review" and "Situation Awareness in Aviation Systems."

98 Endsley, "Theoretical Underpinnings of Situation Awareness: A Critical Review", p. 6.

99 Kay, *Obliquity*, p. 100

100 See Baron-Cohen, *Mindblindness: An Essay on Autism and Theory of Mind* and http://en.wikipedia.org/wiki/Mind-blindness.

101 Tutu, *No Future Without Forgiveness*.

102 Kingsolver et al., *Animal, Vegetable, Miracle: Our Year of Seasonal Eating*, p. 23.

103 Barbara Kingsolver shares her family's change of lifestyle in *Animal, Vegetable, Miracle: Our Year of Seasonal Eating*, the book she co-wrote with her husband Steven L. Hopp and elder daughter Camille Kingsolver.

104 The authors provide sources for their facts at the end of *Animal, Vegetable, Minercale: Our Year of Seasonal Eating*.

105 Stanovich, "Distinguishing the Reflective, Algorithm and Autonomous Minds: Is It Time for a Tri-process Theory?"

106 Further information about mindsight can be found at http://drdansiegel.com/home/.

107 http://drdansiegel.com/about/mindsight/

108 http://drdansiegel.com/resources/healthy_mind_platter/

109 Duhigg, *The Power of Habit: We Do What We Do in Life and Business*.

110 Wilson, *Strangers to Ourselves: Discovering the Adaptive Unconscious*.

111 Gilbert, *Stumbling on Happiness*, p. 63.

112 Kahneman, *Thinking, Fast and Slow*.

113 Stanovich sees our mindware as primarily consisting of our reflective capabilities. See Stanovich, *The Robot's Rebellion: Finding Meaning in the Age of Darwin*, p. 79.

114 See Stanovich, *What Intelligence Tests Miss: The Psychology of Rational Thought* and *Rationality and the Reflective Mind*.

115 Senge, *The Fifth Discipline: The Art and Practice of the Learning Organization*, p. 174. Senge discusses the impact of mental models on life in organizations.

116 Senge et al., *The Necessary Revolution: How Individuals and Organizations are Working Together to Create a Sustainable World*.

117 Senge, *The Fifth Discipline: The Art and Practice of the Learning Organization*, p. 176.

118 Senge, *The Fifth Discipline: The Art and Practice of the Learning Organization*, ch 10.

119 Kerwin, "None Too Solid: Medical Ignorance" in *Knowledge: Creation, Diffusion, Utilization*.

120 Here we have drawn on the ideas Robert Hargrove presents in *Masterful Coaching*, p. 183. Hargrove himself was inspired by organizational scholar Chris Argyris.

121 The ladder of inference was proposed by Chris Argyris in his book *Overcoming Organizational Defenses: Facilitating Organizational Learning*. Discussion of the ladder of inference can also be found in in Senge's *The Fifth Discipline: The Art*

and Practice of the Learning Organization, Senge et al.'s *The Necessary Revolution: How Individuals and Organizations are Working Together to Create a Sustainable World,* p. 256 and Hargrove's *Masterful Coaching,* p. 39.

[122] Based on Argyris' model.

[123] Kingsolver et al., *Animal, Vegetable, Miracle: Our Year of Seasonal Eating,* pp.18-19.

[124] http://www.emotionalcompetency.com/distortions.htm

[125] For more on how our mind works, see Wilson and Dunn's article "Self-knowledge: Its Limits, Value, and Potential for Improvement".

[126] Goleman, *Vital Lies, Simple Truths: The Psychology of Self-Deception,* p. 13.

[127] To learn more about research on blaming see Bryner's article "Passing the Buck: Blaming Others is Contagious".

[128] Pronin, "How We See Ourselves and How We See Others".

[129] Kingsolver et al., *Animal, Vegetable, Miracle: Our Year of Seasonal Eating,* p. 213.

[130] Lehrer, *Imagine: How Creativity Works,* p. 128.

[131] Gilbert, *Stumbling on Happiness,* p. 97.

[132] Gilbert, *Stumbling on Happiness,* p. 94.

[133] Gilbert, *Stumbling on Happiness.*

[134] Original source is Daniel George's *A Book of Anecdotes: Illustrating Varieties of Experience in the Lives of the Illustrious and the Obscure* but also available at http://www.anecdotage.com/index.php?aid=3283.

[135] Kingsolver, *Animal, Vegetable, Miracle: Our Year of Seasonal Eating,* p. 17.

[136] For discussions on mindfulness and mindlessness see, for example, Saarinen and Lehti's "Inducing Mindfulness Through Life-Philosophical Lecturing", Saarinen and Slotte's "Philosophical Lecturing as a Philosophical Practice" and the works of Ellen Langer.

[137] See Barbara Kingsolver's response to questions about the book at http://www.kingsolver.com/faq/previous-books.html#25.

[138] Memorable quotes from Annie Hall can be found at http://www.imdb.com/title/tt0075686/quotes.

[139] See Oshry, *Seeing Systems: Unlocking the Mysteries of Organizational Life,* for further discussion of this.

[140] Kingsolver et al., *Animal, Vegetable, Miracle: Our Year of Seasonal Eating,* p. 21.

[141] Kingsolver et al., *Animal, Vegetable, Miracle: Our Year of Seasonal Eating,* p. 10.

[142] http://www.happiness-project.com/about/

[143] Billy Lucas was from rural Indiana. In 2012 the region hit the headlines again when a recording appeared on the web showing a young child singing a homophobic song in church.
"I know the Bible's right, somebody's wrong/Ain't no homos going to make it to heaven" sings the toddler to cheers and applause from the congregation. View it at http://www.dangerousminds.net/comments/child_abuse_toddler_sings_aint_no_homo_gonna_make_it_to_heaven_in_church.

[144] See the current status and history of the project at www.itgetsbetter.org.

145 The Comprehensive Soldier Fitness program, designed to reduce and prevent the adverse psychological consequences of armed service by preparing American soldiers for the experience, is largely based on the work of psychologist Martin Seligman.

146 See Reivich et al., "Master Resilience Training in the US Army" p. 29.

147 Perhaps the most well-known proponent of the need to balance advocacy and inquiry is management guru Peter Senge. His book *The Fifth Discipline: The Art and Practice of the Learning Organization* is an excellent read for those seeing how these modes play out in business organizations.

148 Some of these ideas were inspired by Cheri Baker's blog http://enlightenedmanager.com/.

149 See Folger et al., *Working Through Conflict: Strategies for Relationships, Groups, and Organizations* for more on climate and conflict management.

150 Gottman, *The Science of Trust: Emotional Attunement for Couples*, p. 14.

151 See Fisher's and Ury's book *Getting to Yes: Negotiating Agreement Without Giving In* and Roger Fisher's obituary at http://www.economist.com/node/21562880.

152 See George Kohlrieser's book *Hostage at the Table: How Leaders Can Overcome Conflict, Influence Others, and Raise Performance* for insight into the hostage negotiation process and how we might carry the same skills into everyday life.

153 See for example the technique developed by psychiatrist Tom Rusk known as ethical persuasion. An article by Rusk explaining this method can be found at http://ombudsfac.unm.edu/Article_Summaries/Ethical_Persuasion_Phase_I.pdf.

154 This quote comes from Carroll's account of his experience on his website http://www.davecarrollmusic.com/music/ubg/story/.

155 Watch the video at http://www.youtube.com/watch?v=5YGc4zOqozo.

156 See Daniel Goleman's excellent works on Emotional Intelligence, including *The Brain and Emotional Intelligence: New Insights*.

157 Goleman, *The Brain and Emotional Intelligence: New Insights*, pp. 30-32.

158 Ariely, *The Upside of Irrationality: The Unexpected Benefits of Denying Logic at Work and at Home*.

159 See Beverly Engel's book *The Power of Apology: Healing Steps to Transform All Your Relationships* and her article "The Power of Apology".

160 Engel, *The Power of Apology: Healing Steps to Transform All Your Relationships*.

161 Ariely, *The Upside of Irrationality: The Unexpected Benefits of Denying Logic at Work and at Home*, p. 152.

162 The still-powerful video is now available online at http://www.youtube.com/watch?v=t2zbbN4OL98.

163 Goleman, *Social Intelligence: The New Science of Human Relationships*, p. 52.

164 Haidt and Keyes, *Flourishing: Positive Psychology and the Life Well Lived*.

165 Jeremy Rifkin gives an account of this well-known story in *The Empathic Civilization: The Race to Global Consciousness in a World in Crisis* to illustrate empathy, but it is also a good demonstration of people's capacity to defy systemic boundaries.

[166] Gottman, *The Science of Trust: Emotional Attunement for Couples.*

[167] Seligman, *Authentic Happiness: Using the New Positive Psychology to Realize Your Potential for Lasting Fulfillment,* p. 8.

[168] See Seligman's *Authentic Happiness: Using the New Positive Psychology to Realize Your Potential for Lasting Fulfillment* and Goleman's *Emotional Intelligence.*

[169] See Axelrod's book *The Evolution of Co-operation* for theoretical explanation of co-operation.

[170] University of California - Santa Barbara, "Evolution of human generosity".

[171] Hyde herself developed a foundation and one of her followers established an international Pay it Forward Day to focus attention on the concept. See http://www.payitforwardfoundation.org/ and http://payitforwardday.com/about/about-the-day/.

[172] See, for example, http://www.randomactsofkindness.org/.

[173] The foundation's website is at http://www.randomactsofkindness.org/. In 2010, student Christopher Lo created the web-based Karma Seed service inspired by the act of kindness he experienced, giving people an opportunity to track the forward movement of their kindness as users register their kind acts. http://thekarmaseed.org/

[174] Seligman, *Authentic Happiness: Using the New Positive Psychology to Realize Your Potential for Lasting Fulfillment,* p. 43.

[175] Fredrickson, "The value of positive emotions".

[176] http://www.danpink.com/archives/2011/11/a-boss-who-says-thanks

[177] Plumb wrote:

> "I didn't get much sleep that night. I kept thinking about that man. I kept wondering what he might have looked like in a Navy uniform - a Dixie cup hat, a bib in the back and bell bottom trousers. I wondered how many times I might have passed him on board the Kitty Hawk. I wondered how many times I might have seen him and not even said "good morning", "how are you", or anything because, you see, I was a fighter pilot and he was just a sailor. How many hours did he spend on that long wooden table in the bowels of that ship weaving the shrouds and folding the silks of those chutes? I could have cared less...until one day my parachute came along and he packed it for me." See http://speaker.charlieplumb.com/about-captain/parachute-story/, from his book *I'm No Hero: A POW story as told to Glen DeWerff.*

[178] http://www.quotegarden.com/kindness.html

[179] Goleman, *The Brain and Emotional Intelligence: New Insights,* p. 55.

[180] Robert Hargrove tells the story of this company, Bally's in *Masterful Coaching,* pp. 274-275.

[181] See Google's benefits http://www.google.com/about/jobs/lifeatgoogle/benefits/ and Zappo's perks http://about.zappos.com/jobs/why-work-zappos/our-benefits, for example.

182 The information on Yunus and Grameen comes from http://www.grameen-info.org/index.php?option=com_content&task=view&id=28&Itemid=108; http://www.muhammadyunus.org/index.php/yunus-centre/about-yunus-centre and http://en.wikipedia.org/wiki/Muhammad_Yunus.

183 Parker, "Subprime Lender".

184 http://www.nobelprize.org/nobel_prizes/peace/laureates/2006/#

185 Microfinancing has come in for some criticism in recent years, but the micro finance institutions that are most criticized are often for profit. Yunus himself questions the motivations and credibility of lenders that seek to profit from the poor. See Bahree's article "A Big Slit Over Microfinance".

186 That is not to say that elevating others by importing systems from one context to another is always the answer. As philanthropist Peter Buffet, son of wealthy American investor Warren Buffet, warns, "transplanting what worked in one setting directly into another with little regard for culture, geography or societal norms" often backfires. Instead, says Buffet, we can focus on creating completely new ways of structuring systems that support humans rather than creating systems that support existing systems. Microfinancing, for example, can be seen as a way of transporting what many would say is a failed capitalistic system to poor countries rather than elevating people through the creation of a new approach to eliminating poverty. See Buffet, "The Charitable-Industrial Complex".

187 The crowdfunding model used by kickstarter (http://www.kickstarter.com), for example, is very similar in idea. Its website specifically targets funding for (traditionally poorly financed) creative projects. Individuals or groups post their project ideas and people choose to fund them or not. Unlike Kiva, this is not a loan to be repaid. The money is given freely to what the donor decides is a worthwhile cause, whether it be a movie, piece of art, or a community garden. Recipients of the money then post updates about their projects with some offering a form of reward like seeing their name in a movie's credits or providing a copy of the book or album produced.

188 http://about.zappos.com/zappos-story/in-the-beginning-let-there-be-shoes

189 A competition between two Silicon Valley radio reporters to see whether traditional or online Christmas shopping would be faster found the bricks and mortar stores won hands down. See Allen, "Chart of the Week: Online Holiday Shopping 1990-2009".

190 In 1996, Hsieh co-founded LinkExchange, which he sold to Microsoft in 1998 for US$265 million (http://worthly.com/person/tony-hsieh/).

191 Hseih, *Delivering Happiness: A Path to Profits, Passion, and Purpose*, p. 57.

192 Hseih, *Delivering Happiness: A Path to Profits, Passion, and Purpose*, p. 230.

193 Kino, "Where Art Meets Trash and Transforms Life".

194 Gockler, "Teaching for the Future: Systems Thinking and Sustainability".

195 Oshry, *Leading Systems: Lessons from the Power Lab*, pp. 8-10.

196 Gockler, J., "Teaching for the Future: Systems Thinking and Sustainability".

197 Gockler, J., "Teaching for the Future: Systems Thinking and Sustainability".

[198] Watch Fosbury's medal winning performance at
http://www.youtube.com/watch?v=rX3bCh8v1FE.

[199] Information sourced from Burnton's article "50 Stunning Olympic Moments No28: Dick Fosbury Introduces 'The Flop'" and
http://en.wikipedia.org/wiki/Dick_Fosbury.

[200] Kay, *Obliquity*.

[201] Original source is *Bartlett's Book of Anecdotes*.

[202] Hseih, *Delivering Happiness: A Path to Profits, Passion, and Purpose*, pp.25-26.

[203] Gladwell, *The Tipping Point: How Little Things Can Make a Big Difference*, pp. 253-55.

[204] Jurgen told this story to us over coffee in late 2012.

[205] Seligman et al., "Navigating Into the Future or Driven by the Past".

[206] Branson's story is told in Juhana Lampinen's blog post "Branson: Creative Thinking, Challenging the Status Quo".

[207] Strauss, "Is Supercell the Fastest-Growing Game Company Ever?"

[208] See the article "The Gamemaker's Clan" in *Blue Wings*.

[209] http://www.1000ventures.com/business_guide/crosscuttings/failure_freedom.html

[210] http://www.supercell.net/about

[211] For an interview with Hseih see Rosenbaum's article "The Happiness Culture: Zappos Isn't a Company -- It's a Mission". Tony Hsieh has also published a book called *Delivering Happiness: A Path to Profits, Passion, and Purpose*.

[212] http://money.cnn.com/magazines/fortune/best-companies/2012/snapshots/11.html

[213] Watkins and Mohr, *Appreciative Inquiry: Change at the Speed of Imagination*, p. 43.

[214] Hseih, *Delivering Happiness: A Path to Profits, Passion, and Purpose*, p. 88.

[215] Hseih, *Delivering Happiness: A Path to Profits, Passion, and Purpose*, p. 97.

[216] Hseih, *Delivering Happiness: A Path to Profits, Passion, and Purpose*.

[217] For more on Pankhurst see http://en.wikipedia.org/wiki/Emmeline_Pankhurst.

[218] Oshry, *Leading Systems: Lessons from the Power Lab*, p. 25.

[219] Meldrum, "The Guard Who Really Was Mandela's Friend".

[220] Rifkin, *The Empathic Civilization: The Race to Global Consciousness in a World in Crisis*.

[221] This phenomenon is often referred to as a self-fulfilling prophecy. For example, we might anticipate a coming public speech with nervous apprehension, imagining all the things that could go wrong. As a result, because we have played the negative tape in our minds repeatedly, we do the very things we have been trying to avoid. Read more at http://en.wikipedia.org/wiki/Self-fulfilling_prophecy.

[222] Meadows, "Dancing With the Systems".

[223] http://www.brainyquote.com/quotes/authors/r/rosa_parks.html#dKIASXKl G7izIddz.99

[224] Major sources for the story of Rosa Parks presented here are Charles Duhigg's account in *The Power of Habit: Why We Do What We Do in Life and Business* and

http://en.wikipedia.org/wiki/Rosa_Parks and
http://www.thehenryford.org/exhibits/rosaparks/story.asp.

[225] http://www.brainyquote.com/quotes/quotes/r/rosaparks404138.html#mc3d3L
2xMES447Ra.99

[226] Zimbardo, *The Lucifer Effect: Understanding How Good people Turn Evil*, p. 211.

[227] This story is popular with management consultants who use it to demonstrate
the unthinking behavior that takes place in organizations. This version was
adapted from Vermeulen's blog post "The Monkey Story".

[228] Zimbardo, *The Lucifer Effect: Understanding How Good people Turn Evil*, p. 226.

[229] See Zimbardo's website http://www.lucifereffect.org for more information.

[230] Fastenberg, "10 Whistleblowers Heard Around the World".

[231] Carter's principled and system-bucking actions attracted media interest and he
won national acclaim for his stand. In 2005, the story of Richmond High's
basketball team was released as the inspirational movie Coach Carter. For
more on Coach Carter's story see
http://en.wikipedia.org/wiki/Coach_Carter and http://coachcarter.com/.
Carter continues to try to make a difference.

[232] Merron, "How Real Is the Reel 'Coach Carter'?"

[233] Story adapted from www.businessballs.com.

[234] Story adapted from www.businessballs.com.

[235] Baucells and Sarin, *Engineering Happiness: A New Approach for Building a Joyful Life*,
p. 156.

[236] Charles Duhigg provides an excellent analysis of King's reshaping of the civil
rights movement in *The Power of Habit: Why We Do What We Do in Life and
Business*, pp. 241-243, which we draw from here.

[237] http://ecologicalhandprints.org/

[238] The impact of solar cookers can be seen in many communities around the world
on the following website http://www.solarcookers.org/index.html.

[239] Senge et al., *The Necessary Revolution: How Individuals and Organizations are Working
Together to Create a Sustainable World*, pp. 292-293.

[240] http://www.human.cornell.edu/outreach/upload/CHE_PAM_EconomicsofOb
esity.pdf

[241] Behavioral Insights Team, *Behavioral Change and Energy Use*.

[242] https://www.bestliferewarded.com/about-us.aspx

[243] http://www.thehenryford.org/exhibits/rosaparks/story.asp

[244] Kingsolver, *Animal, Vegetable, Miracle: Our Year of Seasonal Eating*, p. 5.

[245] http://www.kingsolver.com/faq/previous-books.html#25

[246] Gawande, *The Checklist Manifesto: How to Get Things Right*,
pp. 37-39.

[247] Gadawe, *The Checklist Manifesto, How to Get Things Right*, p. 48.

[248] Senge, "What the Vision Does". See also Senge et al., *The Necessary Revolution:
How Individuals and Organizations are Working Together to Create a Sustainable
World*, p. 324.

[249] How can Patagonia hope to grow as a company when it is actively telling people
to buy less clothing? Patagonia prides itself on making quality, long-lasting

clothes – for a high price. Its target market may well be less sensitive to price increases than other sectors. Ironically, their responsible message may also attract many new customers, leading them to sell more clothes. We don't need to view this cynically, however, because the more people that buy into Patagonia's sustainable message the more people there will be who will reduce, repair, recycle and reuse. The company is also creating alternative revenue paths by selling upstream as well as down stream. In other words, rather than just selling to individual customers it can also resell old clothing back to its suppliers for recycling. Their ground-breaking strategy is more likely to succeed than it might be for other organizations because it is a family-owned company and so there is none of the pressure from shareholders that public companies feel. It can be profitable even while producing a high-quality product with a clear conscience. See E. Lowitt's blog post "Patagonia's "Buy Less" Campaign May Lead to More Revenue".

[250] Senge et al., *The Necessary Revolution: How Individuals and Organizations are Working Together to Create a Sustainable World*, pp. 217; 224-225; 302.

[251] Senge et al., *The Necessary Revolution: How Individuals and Organizations are Working Together to Create a Sustainable World*.

[252] Hseih, *Delivering Happiness: A Path to Profits, Passion, and Purpose*, pp. 81-82.

[253] Hargrove, *Masterful Coaching*, p. 183.

[254] Duhigg, *The Power of Habit: Why We Do What We Do in Life and Business* p. 151.

[255] Senge et al., *The Necessary Revolution: How Individuals and Organizations are Working Together to Create a Sustainable World*, p. 225-226.

[256] Senge et al., *The Necessary Revolution: How Individuals and Organizations are Working Together to Create a Sustainable World*, p. 275.

[257] See his metaphor in *Masterful Coaching*, p. 154.

[258] Hargrove, *Masterful Coaching*, pp. 229-230.

[259] See Malcolm Gladwell's *The Tipping Point: Little Things Can Make a Big Difference* for his analysis of personality types.

[260] A relatively easy test works out whether a person is a connector or not. From a random list of 250 surnames taken from a phonebook, Gladwell allocated a point if the person knew (in a fairly loose sense of the word) somebody of that name. He found from his informal survey that college students tended to know people with around 20 names on the list, while middle-aged respondents averaged closer to 40, not a surprising result given the disparity in life experience and years to make acquaintances. The interesting result that his test showed, however, was that in both groups, the highest scorers knew over 90 people from the list of surnames. These individuals with at least twice the number of social acquaintances than average were the connectors. See *The Tipping Point: Little Things Can Make a Big Difference*.

[261] Granovetter, "The Strength of Weak Ties".

[262] Duhigg, *The Power of Habit: Why We Do What We Do in Life and Business*, p. 119-220.

[263] Gladwell, *The Tipping Point: How Little Things Can Make a Big Difference*, p. 91.

264 Duhigg tells O'Neill's story in *The Power of Habit: Why We Do What We Do in Life and Business,* pp. 99; 106-107. Senge et al. also use Alcoa as an example of a how a clear vision shapes an organization in *The Necessary Revolution: How Individuals and Organizations are Working Together to Create a Sustainable World,* pp. 324-325.

265 Senge et al., *The Necessary Revolution: How Individuals and Organizations are Working Together to Create a Sustainable World,* p. 204.

266 Gladwell, *The Tipping Point: How Little Things Can Make a Big Difference,* p. 259.

267 Dizikes, "The Meaning of the Butterfly: Why Pop Culture Loves the 'Butterfly Effect' and Gets it Totally Wrong".

268 See http://en.wikipedia.org/wiki/Salt_march and Fischer's book *The Life of Mahatma Gandhi.*

269 See Bill McKibben's article "The Case for Fossil-Fuel Divestment" in *Rolling Stone* for a participant's account of the trip and its impact. Other sources include http://www.endowmentethics.org/ffdivestment and http://gofossilfree.org/

270 Senge et al., *The Necessary Revolution: How Individuals and Organizations are Working Together to Create a Sustainable World,* p. 99-100.

271 Meadows, "Places to Intervene in a System (In Increasing Order of Effectiveness)".

272 Meadows, "Places to Intervene in a System (In Increasing Order of Effectiveness)".

273 The story of the two flights can be found in detail in Clay Shirky's book *Here Comes Everybody: The Power of Organizing Without Organizations,* pp. 175-182.

274 Hargrove, *Masterful Coaching,* p. 19.

275 Hargrove discusses similar ideas when he reflects on stewardship in his conclusion to *Masterful Coaching.*

276 http://www.brainyquote.com/quotes/topics/topic_wisdom.html#BGHctMXA ADfFuLQQ.99

277 See the article "Wild Fires: Dry, Hot, and Windy" in *National Geographic.*

278 Resource Media, "Messaging Forest Protection in an Era of Global Warming".

279 See economist John Kay's book, *Obliquity,* for discussion of forest fires and complexity, p. 53.

280 Berry, *Forest Policy Up in Smoke: Fire Suppression in the United States.*

281 Strauch, *Secrets of the Grown-Up Brain: The Surprising Talents of the Middle-aged Mind,* p. 46.

282 Kristof, "Occupy the Classroom".

283 The *BBC News Magazine* ran a story on baby boxes. See Lee, "Why Finnish Babies Sleep in Cardboard Boxes".

284 Ariely, *The Upside of Irrationality: The Unexpected Benefits of Defying Logic at Work and at Home.*

285 Gilbert, *Stumbling on Happiness,* p. 121.

286 Seligman et al., "Navigating into the future or driven by the past".

287 Seligman et al., "Navigating into the future or driven by the past".

288 See Robert Hargrove's *Masterful Coaching*, p. 34, for a similar perspective. For us, Hargrove's approach is somewhat simplistic as he presumes that an individual can entirely determine his or her own behavior. We argue that to we need to see our behavior in the context of systems so that we can make better decisions about the kinds of changes we can and should make.

289 Meadows, "Dancing with Systems".

290 Kay, *Obliquity*.

291 Kay, *Obliquity*, pp. 128-129.

292 The movie *Amazing Grace* tells the story of William Wilberforce's campaign to end the slave trade.

293 http://en.wikipedia.org/wiki/William_Wilberforce

294 Meadows, "Places to Intervene in a System (In Increasing Order of Effectiveness)".

295 Meadows, "Dancing wtih Systems"

296 See the story from Lehrer's article "Don't! The Secret of Self-Control".

297 Weick, "Small Wins: Redefining the Scale of Social Problems".

298 Some inspirational stories can be found at http://www.des.emory.edu/mfp/efficacynotgiveup.html.

299 See Dr J. Vaughn's conference paper at http://forestfire.nau.edu/pdf_files/SHOW_ME_THE_DATA!.pdf.

300 Rifkin, *The Empathic Civilization: The Race to Global Consciousness in a World in Crisis*.

301 See Daniel Goleman's book seminal book *Emotional Intelligence* for a good introduction to the concept. There are many other books and academic papers available, too.

302 Goleman, *Emotional Intelligence*, pp. 42-44; 56.

303 Adam Grant gives an interesting analysis of Lincoln's decision in *Give and Take: A Revolutionary Approach to Success*.

304 Goleman, *Emotional Intelligence*, p. 59.

305 Goleman, *Emotional Intelligence and the Brain: New Insights*.

306 Piiparinen and Brummer, *Global Networks of Mediation: Prospects and Avenues for Finland as a Peacemaker*, p. 122.

307 Adapted from Rosengren's article "The Many Benefits of Helping Others Succeed".

308 Oshry, *Seeing Systems: Unlocking the Mysteries of Organizational Life*, p. 81.

309 http://www.dfcworld.com/icanmodel.html

310 Cabarello, "A Conversation with Educator & Riverside School Founder, Kiran Bir Sethi".

311 Cabarello, "A Conversation with Educator & Riverside School Founder, Kiran Bir Sethi".

312 http://www.dfcworld.com/

313 Watkins and Mohr, *Appreciative Inquiry: Appreciative Inquiry: Change at the Speed of Imagination*.

314 Danner et al., "Positive Emotions in Early Life and Longevity: Findings from the Nun Study".

315 Villarica, "How the Power of Positive Thinking Won Scientific Credibility".

316 Villarica, "How the Power of Positive Thinking Won Scientific Credibility".

317 Lehrer, *Imagine: How Creativity Works*, p. 32.

318 Watkins and Mohr, *Appreciative Inquiry: Change at the Speed of Imagination*.

319 See Senge et al., *The Necessary Revolution: How Individuals and Organizations are Working Together to Create a Sustainable World* as an example of the shift in systems thinking.

320 See Paul's article "The Uses and Abuses of Optimism and Pessimism". Strategically, pessimism can be useful to us because it helps us to temper our emotional reactions when things go badly for us and helps us in planning for worst-case scenarios. It can offer us protection against disappointment and loss.

321 Seligman, *Authentic Happiness: Using the New Positive Psychology to Realize Your Potential for Lasting Fulfillment*, p. 24.

322 Seligman, *Authentic Happiness: Using the New Positive Psychology to Realize Your Potential for Lasting Fulfillment*.

323 Brusman, "Optimism – Resilience in the Face of Adversity".

324 See, for example, http://www.australianbusinesstraining.com.au/optimism.html.

325 See the article "Hope Springs a Trap" in *The Economist*.

326 Goleman, *Emotional Intelligence*.

327 See Fredrickson's works including "The Value of Positive Emotions" and *Positivity: Groundbreaking Research Reveals How to Embrace the Hidden Strength of Positive Emotions, Overcome Negativity, and Thrive*, and visit her website at http://www.unc.edu/peplab/people.html#blf.

328 Goleman, *Emotional Intelligence*, pp. 85-86.

329 An example of the impact of the Dalai Lama's demeanor can be found at Ward's article "Dalai Lama's Giggle Wins Over Liverpool".

330 See Barbara Fredrickson's website at http://www.positivityratio.com/.

331 Gottman has published numerous academic articles on marriage, relationships and parenting and has written the book *The Science of Trust: Emotional Attunement for Couples*. Malcolm Gladwell discusses Gottman's work in the first chapter of *Blink: The Power of Thinking Without Thinking*.

332 Gable et al., "What Do You Do When Things Go Right? Supportive Responses to Positive Event Disclosures"

333 Bornstein, "The Power of Positive Coaching".

334 Rozin and Royzman, "Negativity Bias, Negativity Dominance, and Contagion".

335 Kohlrieser, *Hostage at the Table: How Leaders Can Overcome Conflict, Influence Others, and Raise Performance*, p. 67.

336 *Authentic Happiness: Using the New Positive Psychology to Realize Your Potential for Lasting Fulfillment* is Seligman's book dedicated to helping people understand and improve their happiness.

337 See article "Laughter – Good Medicine for Dementia Patients" at *Fox News*.

338 Meadows, "Dancing with Systems".

339 Brown et al., "Providing Social Support May Be More Beneficial Than Receiving It: Results From a Prospective Study of Mortality".

[340] Most of us act as givers in intimate systems like friendships and marriage, but in the workplace more matchers emerge, says Grant in *Give and Take: A Revolutionary Approach to Success*.

[341] http://www.brainyquote.com/quotes/keywords/habit.html#bxpg60JyQgJsSGf3.99

[342] See Bateson's *Steps to an Ecology of Mind: Collected Essays In Anthropology, Psychiatry, Evolution, And Epistemology*. Bateson's daughter Nora has produced a film summarizing his many years of work called *An Ecology of Mind*. For information about the film see http://www.anecologyofmind.com/.

[343] Senge et al. directly refer to our "natural systems intelligence" in *The Necessary Revolution: How Individuals and Organizations are Working Together to Create a Sustainable World*, p. 189.

[344] Hargrove makes a similar point in *Masterful Coaching*, p. 34, but does not really consider the impact of the existing systems on people's behavior. For us, Hargrove's approach is somewhat simplistic as he presumes that an individual can entirely determine his or her own behavior. We argue that to we need to see our behavior in the context of systems so that we can make better decisions about the kinds of changes we can and should make.

[345] Oshry, *Seeing Systems: Unlocking the Mysteries of Organizational Life*, pp. 205-206; 216.

[346] Hargrove, *Masterful Coaching*.

[347] Dweck, *Mindset: The New Psychology of Success*.

[348] Oshry, *Leading Systems: Lessons from the Power Lab*, p. 8.

[349] Take a small business, for example. Organizational members could think about what their current patterns of interaction generate – for them individually, for others and for the business as a whole. A small business might generate products, services, advertising and profits. But it might also generate loyalty, respect and enthusiasm, or, resentment, indifference and anger. The staff could reflect on whether their relationships are what they would prefer. Then they can negotiate the type of system they would like to have and make a commitment to work towards that. These three simple questions are just as effective at opening collaborative efforts in other systems like families, romantic relationships and community groups.

[350] See Esa Saarinen's "The Paphos Seminar. Elevated Reflections on Life as Good Work," for example.

[351] The original quote by Hugo is *"There is one thing stronger than all the armies in the world, and that is an idea whose time has come."* (http://www.goodreads.com/quotes/333543-there-is-one-thing-stronger-than-all-the-armies-in)

Bibliography

Allen, K. P. (2009, November 18). Chart of the Week: Online Holiday Shopping 1990-2009. Practical Ecommerce. Retrieved from http://www.practicalecommerce.com/articles/1373-Chart-of-the-Week-Online-Holiday-Shopping-1999-2009

Archbishop Tutu in His Own Words. (2010, July 22). BBC News. Retrieved from http://www.bbc.co.uk/news/world-africa-10734471

Argyris , C. (1990). Overcoming Organizational Defenses: Facilitating Organizational Learning. Boston, MA: Allyn and Bacon.

Ariely, D. (2010). The Upside of Irrationality: The Unexpected Benefits of Defying Logic at Work and at Home. New York, NY: Harper.

Axelrod, R. (1990). The Evolution of Co-operation. London, Great Britain: Penguin Books.

Bahree, M. (2010, October 1). A Big Slit Over Microfinance. Forbes. Retrieved from http://www.forbes.com/global/2010/1011/companies-akula-yunus-iskenderian-clinton-global-big-split.html

Baron-Cohen, S. (1997). Mindblindness: An Essay on Autism and Theory of Mind. Cambridge, MA: MIT Press.

Bateson, G. (2000). Steps To An Ecology Of Mind: Collected Essays In Anthropology, Psychiatry, Evolution, And Epistemology. Chicago, IL: University of Chicago Press.

Batson, C. D. (1987). Prosocial Motivation: Is it Ever Truly Altruistic?. Advances in Experimental Social Psychology, 20: 65-122.

Baucells, M., & Sarin, R. (2012). Engineering Happiness: A New Approach for Building a Joyful Life. Berkeley, CA: University of California Press.

Beebe, B., & Lachmann, F. M. (2005). Infant Research and Adult Treatment: Co-constructing Interactions. Hillsdale, NJ: The Analytic Press.

Behavioral Insights Team (2011). Behavioral Change and Energy Use. London, Great Britain: Cabinet office. Retrieved from https://www.gov.uk/government/uploads/system/uploads/attachment_data/file/48123/2135-behaviour-change-and-energy-use.pdf

Berry, A. (2007). Forest Policy Up in Smoke: Fire Suppression in the United States. Durham, NC: PERC.

Bishop, S. R., Lau, M., Shapiro, S., Carlson, L., Anderson, N. D., Carmody, J., ... & Devins, G. (2004). Mindfulness: A Proposed Operational Definition. Clinical Psychology: Science and Practice, 11(3), 230-241.

Bornstein, D. (2011, October 20). The Power of Positive Coaching. The New York Times. Retrieved from http://opinionator.blogs.nytimes.com/2011/10/20/the-power-of-positive-coaching/?gwh=EDD11E354639F6C8DABF6CE3FA8FF002&gwt=pay&assetType=opinion

Brockman, J. (Ed.). (2012). This Will Make You Smarter: New Scientific Concepts to Improve your Thinking. New York, NY: Harper Perennial.

Brooks, D. (2009, October 12). The Young and the Neuro. The New York Times. Retrieved from http://www.nytimes.com/2009/10/13/opinion/13brooks.html

Brown, S. L., Nesse, R. M., Vinokur, A. D., & Smith, D. M. (2003). Providing Social Support May Be More Beneficial Than Receiving It: Results From a Prospective Study of Mortality. Psychological Science, 14(4), 320-327.

Brusman, M. (n.d.) Optimism – Resilience in the Face of Adversity. Retrieved from http://www.evancarmichael.com/Leadership/2038/Optimism--Resilience-in-the-Face-of-Adversity.html

Brymer, J. (2010, January 19). Passing the Buck: Blaming Others is Contagious. NBC News. Retrieved from http://www.nbcnews.com/id/34940422/ns/health-behavior/t/passing-buck-blaming-others-contagious/#.U_yG_MV_uri

Buffet, B. (2013, July 26). The Charitable-Industrial Complex. The New York Times. Retrieved from http://www.nytimes.com/2013/07/27/opinion/the-charitable-industrial-complex.html?_r=0

Burnton, S. (2012, Tuesday 8). 50 Stunning Olympic Moments No28: Dick Fosbury Introduces 'The Flop'. The Guardian. Retrieved from http://www.theguardian.com/sport/blog/2012/may/08/50-stunning-olympic-moments-dick-fosbury

Cabarello, L. (2011, November). A Conversation with Educator & Riverside School Founder, Kiran Bir Sethi. Catalyst. Retrieved from http://catalystreview.net/2011/11/a-conversation-with-educator-riverside-school-founder-kiran-bir-sethi/

Carson, R. (1962). Silent Spring. Boston, MA: Houghton Mifflin Company.

Christopher, A., & Yeomans, J. (2005). Psychology for Teaching Assistants. Staffordshire, Great Britain: Trentham Books.

Churchman, C. W. (1968). The Systems Approach. New York, NY: Delacorte Press.

Csikszentmihalyi, M. (1990). Flow: The Psychology of Optimal Experience. New York, NY: Harper & Row.

Damasio, A. (2003). Looking for Spinoza: Joy, Sorrow and the Feeling Brain. Orlando, FL: Harcourt, Inc.

Danner, D. D., Snowdon, D. A., & Friesen, W. V. (2001). Positive Emotions in Early Life and Longevity: Findings from the Nun Study. Journal of Personality and Social Psychology, 80(5), 804-813.

Did the Hudson Plane Crash Pilot's Glider Experience Help Him Land Flight 1549? (2009, October 1). Popular Mechanics. Retrieved from http://www.popularmechanics.com/science/4299754

Dizikes, P. (2008, June 8,). The Meaning of the Butterfly: Why Pop Culture Loves the

'Butterfly Effect' and Gets it Totally Wrong. Boston Globe. Retrieved from http://www.boston.com/bostonglobe/ideas/articles/2008/06/08/the_meaning_of_the_butterfly/?page=full

Duhigg, C. (2012). The Power of Habit: Why We Do What We Do in Life and Business. New York, NY: Random House.

Dunbar, R. (2010). How Many Friends Does One Person Need? Dunbar's Number and Other Evolutionary Quirks. London, Great Britain: Faber & Faber.

Dweck, C. S. (2006). Mindset: The New Psychology of Success. New York: Random House.

Endsley, M. R. (1999). Situation Awareness in Aviation Systems. In D. J. Garland, M. R. Endsley and V. D. Hopkins (Eds.), Handbook of Aviation Human Factors (pp. 257-276). Mahwah, NJ: Lawrence Erlbaum Associates.

Endsley, M. R. (2000). Theoretical Underpinnings of Situation Awareness: A Critical Review. In M. R. Endsley and D. J. Garland (Eds.), Situation Awareness Analysis and Measurement (pp. 1-24). Mahwah, NJ: Lawrence Erlbaum Associates.

Engel, B. (2001). The Power of Apology: Healing Steps to Transform All Your Relationships. New York, NY: John Wiley & Sons, Inc.

Engel, B. (2002, August 2). The Power of Apology. Psychology Today. Retrieved from http://www.psychologytoday.com/print/23400

Fadiman, C., & Bernard, A. (2000). Bartlett's Book of Anecdotes. New York, NY: Little, Brown and Company.

Fastenberg, D. (2011, May 30). 10 Whistleblowers Heard Around the World. Aol Jobs. Retrieved from http://jobs.aol.com/articles/2011/05/30/10-whistleblowers-heard-around-the-world/

Finkel, M. (2007, July). Malaria: Stopping a Global Killer. National Geographic. Retrieved from http://ngm.nationalgeographic.com/2007/07/malaria/finkel-text

Fischer, L. (1997). The Life of Mahatma Gandhi. London, Great Britain: HarperCollins.

Fisher, R., & Ury, W. L. (1981). Getting to Yes: Negotiating Agreement Without Giving In. New York, NY: Penguin.

Fiske, S. T., & Taylor, S. E. (1991). Social Cognition (2nd ed.). New York, NY: McGraw-Hill.

Folger, J. P., Poole, M. S., & Stutman, R. K. (2005). Working Through Conflict: Strategies for Relationships, Groups, and Organizations (5th ed.). New York, NY; Boston, MA; San Francisco, CA: Addison Wesley Longman Inc.

Fortune 500 Extinction. (2012, January 6). CSInvesting. Retrieved from http://csinvesting.org/2012/01/06/fortune-500-extinction/

Fredrickson, B. L. (2003). The Value of Positive Emotions. American Scientist, 91(4), 330-335.

Fredrickson, B. L., & Losada, M. F. (2005) Positive Affect and the Complex Dynamics of Human Flourishing. American Psychologist, 60(7), 678-686.

Fredrickson, B. L. (2009). Positivity: Groundbreaking Research Reveals How to Embrace the Hidden Strength of Positive Emotions, Overcome Negativity, and Thrive. Oxford, Great Britain: Oneworld Publications.

Fredrickson B. L. (2013, March 23). Your Phone vs. Your Heart. The New York Times. Retrieved from http://www.nytimes.com/2013/03/24/opinion/sunday/your-phone-vs-your-heart.html?_r=0&gwh=EC07112672150929AE3DBC0B7E579E54&gwt=pay&assetType=opinion

Gable, S. L., Reis, H. T., Impett, E. A., & Asher, E. R. (2004). What Do You Do When Things Go Right? The Intrapersonal And Interpersonal Benefits of Sharing Positive Events. Journal of Personality and Social Psychology, 87(2), 228-245.

Gable, S. L., Gonzaga, G. C., & Strachman, A. (2006). Will You Be There for Me When Things Go Right? Supportive Responses to Positive Event Disclosures. Journal of Personality and Social Psychology, 91(5), 904-917.

Gardner, H. (1997, October 9). Thinking About Thinking [Review of the book The Prehistory of the Mind: The Cognitive Origins of Art, Religion and Science]. The New York Review. Retrieved from
http://cogweb.ucla.edu/Abstracts/Gardner_on_Mithen.html

Gardner, H. (1993). Frames of Mind: The Theory of Multiple Intelligences (10th ed.). New York, NY: Basic Books.

Gardner, H. (2006). Five Minds for the Future. Boston, MA: Harvard Business School Press.

Gawande, A. (2010) The Checklist Manifesto: How to Get Things Right. London,Great Britain: Profile Books.

George, D. (1957). A Book of Anecdotes: Illustrating Varieties of Experience in the Lives of the Illustrious and the Obscure. London, Great Britain: Hulton Press.

Gigerenzer, G. (2007). Gut feelings: The Intelligence of the Unconscious. New York, NY: Penguin.

Gilbert, D. (2007). Stumbling on Happiness. New York, NY: Vintage.

Gladwell, M. (2005a). Blink: The Power of Thinking Without Thinking. New York, NY: Little, Brown and Company.

Gladwell. M. (2005b). The Tipping Point: How Little Things Can Make a Big Difference. London, Great Britain: Abacus.

Gockler, J. (2003). Teaching for the Future: Systems Thinking and Sustainability.Green Teacher, 70, 8-14.

Goleman, D. (1995). Emotional Intelligence. New York, NY: Bantam Books.

Goleman, D. (2005). Vital Lies, Simple Truths: The Psychology of Self-Deception. New York, NY: Simon and Schuster.

Goleman, D. (2006). Social Intelligence: The New Science of Human Relationships. New York, NY: Bantam Books.

Goleman, D. (2011). The Brain and Emotional Intelligence: New Insights. Northhampton, MA: More than Sound.

Gottman, J. M. (2011). The Science of Trust: Emotional Attunement for Couples. New York, NY: W. W. Norton & Company.

Granovetter. M. S. (1973). The Strength of Weak Ties. American Journal of Sociology, 78(6), 1360-1380.

Grant, A. (2013). Give and Take: A Revolutionary Approach to Success. New York, NY: Viking Press.

Haidt, J. D., & Keyes, C. L. M. (2003). Flourishing: Positive Psychology and the Life Well Lived. Washington D.C.: American Psychological Association Press.

Hargrove, R. (2003). Masterful Coaching. San Francisco, CA: Pfeiffer.

Harig, B. (2012, August 7). For Enie Els, the Eyes Have It. ESPN. Retrieved from
http://espn.go.com/golf/pgachampionship12/story/_/id/8235971/for-ernie-els-eyes-it

Heatherton, T. F., & Nichols, P. A. (1994). Personal Accounts of Successful Versus Failed Attempts at Life Change. Personality and Social Psychology Bulletin, 20(6), 664-675.

Hobson, P. (2002). The Cradle of Thought: Exploring the Origins of Thinking. London, Great Britain: Pan Macmillan.

Hope Springs a Trap. (2012, May 12). The Economist. Retrieved from http://www.economist.com/node/21554506

Hseih, T. (2010). Delivering Happiness: A Path to Profits, Passion, and Purpose. New York, NY: Business Plus.

Hämäläinen, R. P., & Saarinen, E. (Eds.) (2004). Systems Intelligence - Discovering a Hidden Competence in Human Action and Organizational Life. Systems Analysis Laboratory, Research Reports, A88. Espoo: Helsinki University of Technology. Retrieved from http://systemsintelligence.aalto.fi/SI2004.html

Hämäläinen, R. P., & Saarinen, E. (2006a). Systems Intelligence: A Key Competence in Human Action and Organizational Life. Reflections: The SoL Journal, 7(4), 17-28.

Hämäläinen, R. P., & Saarinen, E. (2006b). Systems Intelligence: A Key Competence for Organizational Life. Reflections: The SoL Journal 7(4), 191–201.

Hämäläinen, R. P., & Saarinen, E. (Eds). (2007). Systems Intelligence in Leadership and Everyday Life. Espoo: Systems Analysis Laboratory, Helsinki University of Technology. Retrieved from http://systemsintelligence.aalto.fi/SI2007.html

Hämäläinen, R. P., & Saarinen, E. (Eds.). (2008a). Systems Intelligence: A New Lens on Human Engagement and Action. Espoo: Systems Analysis Laboratory, Helsinki University of Technology. Retrieved from http://systemsintelligence.aalto.fi/SI2008.html

Hämäläinen, R. P., & Saarinen, E. (2008b). Systems Intelligence—the Way Forward? A Note on Ackoff's 'Why Few Organizations Adopts Systems Thinking'. Systems Research and Behavioral Science, 25(6), 821-825.

Hämäläinen, R. P., & Saarinen, E. (Eds). (2010). Essays on Systems Intelligence, Espoo: Systems Analysis Laboratory, Aalto University School of Science Retrieved from http://systemsintelligence.aalto.fi/SI2010.html

Hämäläinen, R. P., Luoma, J., & Saarinen, E. (2011). Acting with Systems Intelligence: Integrating Complex Responsive Processes with the Systems Perspective. The Journal of the Operational Research Society, 62(1), 3-11.

Hämäläinen, R. P., Luoma, J., & Saarinen, E. (2013). On the Importance of Behavioral Operational Research: The Case of Understanding and Communicating about Dynamic Systems. European Journal of Operational Research, 228(3), 623–634.

Jackson, M. C. (2003). Systems Thinking: Creative Holism for Managers. Chichester, Great Britain: John Wiley & Sons, Ltd.

Johnson, E. J., & Goldstein, D. G. (2004). Defaults and Donation Decisions. Transplantation, 78(12), 1713–1716.

Jones, R., & Corner, J. (2007). Systems Intelligence and Its Relationship to Communication Theories. In Hämäläinen R. P., Saarinen E. (Eds.), Systems Intelligence in Leadership and Everyday Life (pp 239-249). Espoo: Systems Analysis Laboratory, Helsinki University of Technology. Retrieved from http://systemsintelligence.aalto.fi/publications/rjon07.pdf

Jones, R., Corner, J., & Hämäläinen, R. (2011). Systems Intelligence as a Lens for Managing Personal Knowledge. In Pauleen, D. & Gorman, G. (Eds.), Personal Knowledge Management: Individual, Organisational and Social Perspectives (pp. 79-98). Surrey, Great Britain: Gower.

Jones, R., & Corner, J. (2012). Stages and Dimensions of Systems Intelligence. Systems Research and Behavioral Science, 29(1), 30-45.

Jääskinen, V. (2008). Infant Research and Systems Intelligence: Some Observations. In Hämäläinen R. P., Saarinen E. (Eds.), Systems Intelligence: A New Lens on Human Engagement and Action (pp. 175 –187) Espoo: Systems Analysis Laboratory, Helsinki University of Technology. Retrieved from http://systemsintelligence.aalto.fi/publications/rjaa08.pdf

Kay, J. (2010). Obliquity. London, Great Britain: Profile Books.

Kahneman, D. (2011). Thinking, Fast and Slow. New York, NY: Farrar, Strauss, Giroux.

Kegan, R. (1982). The Evolving Self: Problem and Process in Human Development. Cambridge, MA: Harvard University Press.

Kegan, R. (1994). In Over Our Heads: The Mental Demands of Modern Life. Cambridge, MA: Harvard University Press.

Keltner, D. (2012, July 31). The Compassionate Species. Greater Good: The Science of Meaningful Life. Retrieved from http://greatergood.berkeley.edu/article/item/the_compassionate_species

Kerwin, A. (1993). None Too Solid: Medical Ignorance. Knowledge: Creation, Diffusion, Utilization, 15(2), 166-185.

Kingsolver, B., Kingsolver, C. & Hopp, S. L. (2007). Animal, Vegetable, Miracle: Our Year of Seasonal Eating. New York, NY: HarperCollins Publisher.

Kino, C. (2010, October 21). Where Art Meets Trash and Transforms Life. The New York Times. Retrieved from http://www.nytimes.com/2010/10/24/arts/design/24muniz.html?pagewanted=all&_r=1&gwh=DFDC5FE75CA114BEB54078DFB6BC7246&gwt=pay&

Koehn, N. F. (2008, October 28). From Calm Leadership, Lasting Change. The New York Times. Retrieved from http://www.nytimes.com/2012/10/28/business/rachel-carsons-lessons-50-years-after-silent-spring.html?pagewanted=all&gwh=718BA7B3B4F738822B67C6B01F76B7BD&gwt=pay&_r=0

Kohlrieser, G. (2006). Hostage at the Table: How Leaders Can Overcome Conflict, Influence Others, and Raise Performance. San Francisco, CA: Jossey-Bass.

Kristof, N. D. (2011, October 19). Occupy the Classroom. The New York Times. Retrieved from http://www.nytimes.com/2011/10/20/opinion/occupy-the-classroom.html?module=Search&mabReward=relbias%3Ar%2C%7B%222%22%3A%22RI%3A16%22%7D&_r=0

Lampinen, J. (n.d.) Richard Branson: Creative Thinking, Challenging the Status Quo [Blogpost]. Retrieved from http://www.rework365.com/richard-branson-creative-thinking-challenging-the-status-quo/

Langer, E. J., & Piper, A. I. (1987). The Prevention of Mindlessness. Journal of Personality and Social Psychology, 53(2), 280–287.

Langer, E. J., Perlmuter, L., Chanowitz, B., & Rubin, R. (1988). Two New Applications of Mindlessness Theory: Alcoholism and Aging. Journal of Aging Studies, 2(3), 289-299.

Langer, E. J. (1989a). Minding Matters: the Consequences of Mindlessness-Mindfulness. In L. Berkowitz (Ed.), Advances in Experimental Social Psychology (Vol. 22, pp.137-173. New York, NY: Academic Press.

Langer, E. J. (1989b). Mindfulness. Reading, MA: Addison-Wesley.

Langer, E. J. (1992). Matters of Mind: Mindfulness/Mindlessness in Perspective. Consciousness and Cognition, 1(3), 289-305.

Langer, E., Pirson, M., & Delizonna, L. (2010). The Mindlessness of Social Comparisons. Psychology of Aesthetics, Creativity and the Arts, 4(2), 68-74.

Laughter – Good Medicine for Dementia Patients. (2011, September 29). Fox News. Retrieved from http://www.foxnews.com/health/2011/09/29/laughter-good-medicine-for-dementia-patients/#ixzz1lka4MwwZ

Lee, H. (2013, June 4). Why Finnish Babies Sleep in Cardboard Boxes. BBC News Magazine. Retrieved from http://www.bbc.com/news/magazine-22751415

Lehrer, J. (2009, May 18). Don't! The Secret of Self-Control. The New Yorker. Retrieved from http://www.newyorker.com/magazine/2009/05/18/dont-2?currentPage=all

Lehrer, J. (2012). Imagine: How Creativity Works. Edinburgh, Great Britain: Canongate.

Lowitt, E. (2011, October 3). Patagonia's "Buy Less" Campaign May Lead to More Revenue [Blog post]. Harvard Business Review. Retrieved from http://blogs.hbr.org/2011/10/patagonias-buy-less-campai/

Mayer, J. D., & Salovey, P. (1993). The Intelligence of Emotional Intelligence. Intelligence, 17(4), 433-442.

Mayer, J. D., & Salovey, P. (1995). Emotional Intelligence and the Construction and Regulation of Feelings. Applied and Preventive Psychology, 4(3), 197-208.

McKibben, B. (2013, February 22). The Case for Fossil-Fuel Divestment. Rolling Stone. Retrieved from http://www.rollingstone.com/politics/news/the-case-for-fossil-fuel-divestment-20130222

Meadows, D. H., Meadows, D. L., Randers, J., & Behrens III, W.W. (1972). The Limits to Growth. New York, NY: Universe Books.

Meadows, D. H. (2002). Dancing with Systems. The Systems Thinker, 13(2), 2-6.

Meadows, D. H. (2008). Thinking in Systems: A Primer. D. Wright (Ed.). White River Junction, VT: Chelsea Green Publishing.

Meadows, D. (n.d.). Places to Intervene in a System (In Increasing Order of Effectiveness). Retrieved from http://www.innovationlabs.com/intervention.pdf

Meldrum, A. (2007, May 20). The Guard Who Really Was Mandela's Friend. The Guardian. Retrieved from http://www.theguardian.com/world/2007/may/20/nelsonmandela

Merron, J. (2005, January 26). How Real Is the Reel 'Coach Carter'? ESPN. Retrieved from http://espn.go.com/espn/page3/story?page=merron/coachcarter_Resource Media. (2012, August 28) Messaging Forest Protection in an Era of Global

Warming. Retrieved from http://www.resource-media.org/wp-content/uploads/2012/07/Messaging-Forest-Protection-In-An-Era-of-Global-Warming-Reformatted.pdf

Oshry, B. (1996). Seeing Systems: Unlocking the Mysteries of Organizational Life. San Francisco, CA: Berrett-Koehler Publishers.

Oshry, B. (1999) Leading Systems: Lessons from the Power Lab. San Francisco, CA: Berrett-Koehler Publishers.

Parker, E. (2008, March 1). Subprime Lender. The Wall Street Journal. Retrieved from http://online.wsj.com/news/articles/SB120432950873204335?mg=reno64-wsj&url=http%3A%2F%2Fonline.wsj.com%2Farticle%2FSB120432950873204335.html

Paul, A. M. (2011, November 1). The Uses and Abuses of Optimism and Pessimism. Psychology Today. Retrieved from http://www.psychologytoday.com/articles/201110/the-uses-and-abuses-optimism-and-pessimism

Piaget, J. (1959). The Language and Thoughts of the Child. New York; NY:

Humanities Press.

Piiparinen, T., & Brummer, V. (Eds.). (2012). Global networks of mediation: Prospects and Avenues for Finland as a Peacemaker. Helsinki: The Finnish Institute of International Affairs.

Pinker, S. (2011). The Better Angels of our Nature. New York, NY: Viking Books.

Plumb, C. (1973). I'm No Hero: A POW story as told to Glen DeWerff. Independence, MO: Independence Press.

Pronin, E. (2008, May 30). How We See Ourselves and How We See Others. Science, 320(5800), 1177-1180. Retrieved from www.sciencemag.org

Reivich, K. J., Seligman, M. E. P., & McBride, S. (2011). Master Resilience Training in the US Army. American Psychologist, 66(1), 25-34.

Restak, R. (2006). The Naked Brain: How the Emerging Neurosociety is Changing How We Live, Work, and Love. New York, NY: Harmony Books.

Rhem, J. (1999). Pygmalion in the Classroom. The National Teaching and Learning Forum, 8(2), 1-4.

Rifkin, J. (2009). The Empathic Civilization: The Race to Global Consciousness in a World in Crisis. New York, NY: Tarcher.

Rosenbaum, S. (2010, June 4). The Happiness Culture: Zappos Isn't a Company -- It's a Mission. Fast Company. Retrieved from http://www.fastcompany.com/1657030/happiness-culture-zappos-isnt-company-its-mission

Rosengren, K. (2009, July 16). The Many Benefits of Helping Others Succeed. U.S. News and World Report. Retrieved from http://money.usnews.com/money/blogs/outside-voices-careers/2009/07/16/the-many-benefits-of-helping-others-realize-their-dreams

Rosenthal, R., & Jacobson, L. (1992). Pygmalion in the Classroom: Teacher Expectation and Pupils' Intellectual Development (expanded ed.). New York, NY: Irvington Publishers.

Rozin, P., and Royzman, E. B. (2001). Negativity Bias, Negativity Dominance, and Contagion. Personality and Social Psychology Review, 5(4), 296-320.

Rusk, T. & Miller, D. P. (1993). The Power of Ethical Persuasion: from Conflict to Partnership at Work and in Private Life. New York, NY: Penguin.

Saarinen, E., & Slotte, S. (2003). Philosophical Lecturing as a Philosophical Practice. Practical Philosophy, 6 (2), 7-23.

Saarinen, E. (2008a). Philosophy for Managers: Reflections of a Practitioner. In R. P. Hamalainen & E. Saarinen (Eds.), Systems Intelligence: A New Lens on Human Engagement and Action (pp. 1-27). Espoo: Systems Analysis Laboratory, Helsinki University of Technology. Retrieved from http://sal.aalto.fi/publications/pdf-files/rsaa08.pdf

Saarinen, E. (2008b). Philosophy in the 21st Century: Socratic Philosophy That Matters and Engages With People. International Academy of Philosophy, News and Views, 20.

Saarinen, E., Hämäläinen, R. P., Martela, M., & Luoma, J. (2008). Systems Intelligence Thinking as Engineering Philosophy [Extended Abstract]. Retrieved from http://sal.aalto.fi/publications/pdf-files/msaa08.pdf

Saarinen, E., & Hämäläinen, R. P. (2010). The Originality of Systems Intelligence. In R. P. Hämäläinen, and E. Saarinen (Eds), Essays on Systems Intelligence (pp. 9-26), Espoo: Systems Analysis Laboratory, Aalto University School of Science and Technology. Retrieved from http://sal.aalto.fi/publications/pdf-files/rsaa10.pdf

Saarinen, E. (2013a). Kindness to Babies and Other Radical Ideas: Rorty's Anti-Cynical Philosophy. In A. Groshner, C. Koopman, and M. Sandbothe (Eds.), Richard Rorty: From Pragmatist Philosophy to Cultural Politics (pp. 145-164). London, Great Britain: Bloomsbury.

Saarinen, E. (2013b). The Paphos Seminar. Elevated Reflections on Life as Good Work. GoodWork Project Report Series, 80. Retrieved from http://thegoodproject.org/wp-content/uploads/2012/09/80-Elevated-Reflections-Esa-Saarinen.pdf

Saarinen, E., & Lehti, T. (2014). Inducing Mindfulness Through Life-Philosophical Lecturing. In A. Ie, C. Ngnoumen & E. J. Langer (Eds.), The Wiley Blackwell Handbook of Mindfulness (pp. 1105-1131). Chichester, Great Britain: John Wiley & Sons, Ltd.

Salovey, P., & Mayer, J. D. (1989). Emotional Intelligence. Imagination, Cognition, and Personality, 9(3), 185-211.

Seligman, M. E. P. (1998). Learned Optimism. New York, NY: Pocket Books (Simon and Schuster).

Seligman, M. E. P. (2002). Authentic Happiness: Using the New Positive Psychology to Realize Your Potential for Lasting Fulfillment. New York, NY: Free Press.

Seligman, M. E., Railton, P., Baumeister, R. F., & Sripada, C. (2013). Navigating Into the Future or Driven by the Past. Perspectives on Psychological Science, 8(2), 119-141.

Senge, P. M. (1992). The Fifth Discipline: The Art and Practice of the Learning Organization. New York, NY: Doubleday.

Senge, P. M., Smith, B., Kruschwitz, N., Laur, J., & Schley, S. (2008). The Necessary Revolution: How Individuals and Organizations are Working Together to Create a Sustainable World. New York, NY: Doubleday.

Senge, P. M. (2009, November 30). What The Vision Does. Awakin.org. Retrieved from http://www.awakin.org/read/view.php?tid=669

Shirky, C. (2009). Here Comes Everybody: The Power of Organizing Without Organizations. London, Great Britain: Penguin Books.

Sparks, A., & Tutu, M. (2011). Tutu: Authorized. New York, NY: HarperOne.

Stanovich, K. E. (2005). The Robot's Rebellion: Finding Meaning in the Age of Darwin. Chicago. IL: The University of Chicago Press.

Stanovich, K. E. (2009). Distinguishing the Reflective, Algorithm and Autonomous Minds: Is It Time for a Tri-process Theory? In J. Evans & K. Frankish (Eds.), In Two Minds: Dual Processes and Beyond (pp. 55-88). Oxford, Greta Britain: Oxford University Press. Retrieved from http://keithstanovich.com/Site/Research_on_Reasoning_files/Stanovich_Two_MInds.pdf

Stanovich, K. E. (2009). What Intelligence Tests Miss: The Psychology of Rational Thought. New Haven, CT: Yale University Press.

Stanovich, K. E. (2011). Rationality and the Reflective Mind. New York, NY: Oxford University Press, Inc.

Stern, D. (1998). The Interpersonal World of the Infant: A View from Psychoanalysis and Developmental Psychology. London, Great Britain: Karnac Books.

Sternberg, R. J. (1985). Beyond IQ: A Triarchic Theory of Human Intelligence. New York, NY: Cambridge University Press.

Sternberg, R. J. (1996). Successful Intelligence. How Practical and Creative Intelligence Determine Success in Life. New York; NY: Simon & Schuster.

Sterman, J. D. (2000). Business Dynamics: Systems Thinking and Modeling for a Complex World. New York, NY: Irwin/McGraw-Hill.

Strauch, B. (2010). Secrets of the Grown-Up Brain: The Surprising Talents of the Middle-aged Mind. New York, NY: Viking.

Strauss, K. (2013, May 24). Is Supercell the Fastest-Growing Game Company Ever?. Forbes India. Retrieved from http://forbesindia.com/article/cross-border/is-supercell-the-fastestgrowing-game-company-ever/35269/1#ixzz2XNfAGgp1

Stowell, F. (2007). The Knowledge Age or the Age of Ignorance and the Decline of Freedom? Systemic Practice and Action Research, 20(5), 413-427.

Sweeney, B. L. (2012). Learning to Connect the Dots: Developing Children's Systems Literacy. Solutions 5(3), 55-62. Retrieved from http://thesolutionsjournal.org/node/1167

The Quantified Self: Counting Every Moment. (2012, March 3). The Economist. Retrieved from www.economist.com/node/21548493

The Gamemaker's Clan (2013, May). Blue Wings (p. 30). Retrieved from http://www.digipaper.fi/bluewings/110518/

Tutu, D. (1999). No Future Without Forgiveness. London, Great Britain: Rider.

University of California - Santa Barbara (2011, August 1). Evolution of human generosity. Science Daily. Retrieved from sciencedaily.com/releases/2011/07/110725162523.htm

Vermeulen, F. (2008, August 29). The Monkey Story [Blog post]. Retrieved from http://freekvermeulen.blogspot.co.nz/2008/08/monkey-story-experiment-involved-5.html

Villarica, H. (2012, April 23). How the Power of Positive Thinking Won Scientific Credibility. The Atlantic. Retrieved from http://www.theatlantic.com/health/archive/2012/04/how-the-power-of-positive-thinking-won-scientific-credibility/256223/

Watkins, J. M., & Mohr, B. J. (2001) Appreciative Inquiry: Change at the Speed of Imagination. San Francisco, CA: Jossey-Bass/Pfeiffer.

Ward, D. (2004, May 28). Dalai Lama's Giggle Wins Over Liverpool. The Guardian. Retrieved from http://www.theguardian.com/uk/2004/may/28/religion.world

Weick, K. E. (1984). Small Wins: Redefining the Scale of Social Problems. American Psychologist, 39(1), 40-49.

Wild Fires: Dry, Hot, and Windy (n.d.). National Geographic. Retrieved from http://www.sparticl.org/topic/wildfire/view/wildfires-dry-hot-and-windy/

Wilson, J. Q., & Kelling, G. L. (1982, March 1). Broken Windows: The Police and Neighborhood Safety. The Atlantic. Retrieved from http://www.theatlantic.com/magazine/archive/1982/03/broken-windows/4465/

Wilson, T. D. (2002). Strangers to Ourselves: Discovering the Adaptive Unconscious. Cambridge, MA: Harvard University Press.

Wilson, T. D., & Dunn, E. W. (2004). Self-Knowledge: Its Limits, Value, and Potential for Improvement. Annual Review of Psychology, 55, 493–518.

Zimbardo, P. G. (2007). The Lucifer Effect: Understanding How Good people Turn Evil. New York, NY: Random House.